The Tiger-Slayer, by Gustave Aimard Tr. by Sir F.C.L. Wraxall.

by Olivier Gloux

Address:
HardPress
8345 NW 66TH ST #2561
MIAMI FL 33166-2626
USA
Email: info@hardpress.net

TIGER SLA[Y]

BY GUSTAVE [AIM...]

THE
SELECT LIBRARY OF FICTION.

The best, cheapest, and most POPULAR WORKS published, well printed in clear, readable type, on good paper, and strongly bound.

Containing the writings of the most Popular Authors of the day.

TWO SHILLING VOLUMES.

When ordering, the Numbers only need be given.

SELECT LIBRARY OF FICTION.

SELECT LIBRARY OF FICTION.

HALF-A-CROWN VOLUMES,
Picture Boards; 3s. 6d. Cloth extra.

LONDON : CHAPMAN AND HALL, 193, PICCADILLY.

9-74.

THE

TIGER SLAYER.

A Tale of the Indian Desert.

BY

GUSTAVE AIMARD,

AUTHOR OF

"THE PRAIRIE FLOWER," "PEARL OF THE ANDES," "TRAIL
HUNTER," "ADVENTURERS," ETC., ETC.

LONDON:

CHARLES HENRY CLARKE, 13 PATERNOSTER ROW.

SAMUEL COWAN, STRATHMORE PRINTING WORKS, PERTH.

CONTENTS.

THE TIGER-SLAYER.

CHAPTER I.

LA FERIA DE PLATA.

FROM the earliest days of the discovery of America, its distant shores became the refuge and rendezvous of adventurers of every description, whose daring genius, stifled by the trammels of the old European civilisation, sought fresh scope for action.

Some asked from the New World liberty of conscience —the right of praying to God in their own fashion; others, breaking their sword blades to convert them into daggers, assassinated entire nations to rob their gold, and enrich themselves with their spoils; others, lastly, men of indomitable temperament, with lions' hearts contained in bodies of iron, recognising no bridle, accepting no laws, and confounding liberty with license, formed, almost unconsciously, that formidable association of the " Brethren of the Coast," which for a season made Spain tremble for her possessions, and with which Louis XII., the King-Sun, did not disdain to treat.

The descendants of these extraordinary men still exist in America; and whenever any revolutionary crisis heaves up, after a short struggle, the dregs of the

B

population, they instinctively range themselves round
the grandsons of the great adventurers, in the hope of
achieving mighty things in their turn under the leader-
ship of heroes.

At the period when we were in America chance allowed
us to witness one of the boldest enterprises ever conceived and carried out by these daring adventurers.
This *coup de main* created such excitement that for
some months it occupied the press, and aroused the
curiosity and sympathy of the whole world.

Reasons, which our readers will doubtless appreciate,
have induced us to alter the names of the persons who
played the principal parts in this strange drama, though
we adhere to the utmost exactness as regards the facts.

About ten years back the discovery of the rich Californian plains awakened suddenly the adventurous
instincts of thousands of young and intelligent men,
who, leaving country and family, rushed, full of enthusiasm, towards the new Eldorado, where the majority
only met with misery and death, after sufferings and
vexations innumerable.

The road from Europe to California is a long one.
Many persons stopped half way ; some at Valparaiso ;
others at Callao ; others, again, at Mazatlan or San Blas,
though the majority reached San Francisco.

It is not within the scope of our story to give the
details, too well known at present, of all the deceptions
by which the luckless emigrants were assailed with the
first step they took on this land, where they imagined
they needed only to stoop and pick up handsful of gold.

We must ask our readers to accompany us to
Guaymas six months after the discovery of the placers.

In a previous work we have spoken of Sonora ; but,
as the history we purpose to narrate passes entirely in

that distant province of Mexico, we must give a more detailed account of it here.

Mexico is indubitably the fairest country in the world, and every variety of climate is found there. But while its territory is immense, the population, unfortunately, instead of being in a fair ratio with it, only amounts to seven millions, of whom nearly five millions belong to the Indian or mixed races.

The Mexican Confederation comprises the federal district of Mexico, twenty-one states, and three territories or provinces, possessing no internal independent administration.

We will say nothing of the government, from the simple reason that up to the present the normal condition of that magnificent and unhappy country has ever been anarchy.

Still, Mexico appears to be a federative republic, at least nominally, although the only recognised power is the sabre.

The first of the seven states, situated on the Atlantic, is Sonora. It extends from north to south, between the Rio Gila and the Rio Mayo. It is separated on the east from the State of Chihuahua by the Sierra Verde, and on the west is bathed by the Vermilion Sea, or Sea of Cortez, as most Spanish maps still insist on calling it.

The State of Sonora is one of the richest in Mexico, owing to the numerous gold mines by which its soil is veined. Unfortunately, or fortunately, according to the point of view from which we like to regard it, Sonora is incessantly traversed by innumerable Indian tribes, against which the inhabitants wage a constant war. Thus the continual engagements with these savage hordes, the contempt of life, and the habit of shedding human blood on the slightest pretext, have given the Sonorians a haughty and decided bearing, and imprinted on them a stamp of nobility and grandeur, which separates them entirely from the other states, and causes them to be recognised at the first glance.

In spite of its great extent of territory and lengthened seaboard, Mexico possesses in reality only two ports on the Pacific—Guaymas and Acapulco. The rest are only roadsteads, in which vessels are afraid to seek shelter, especially when the impetuous *cordonazo* blows from the south-west and upheaves the Gulf of California.

We shall only speak here of Guaymas. This town, founded but a few years back on the mouth of the San José, seems destined to become, ere long, one of the chief Pacific ports. Its military position is admirable. Like all the Spanish American towns, the houses are low, whitewashed, and flat-roofed. The fort, situated on the summit of a rock, in which some cannon rust on carriages peeling away beneath the sun, is of a yellow hue, harmonising with the ochre tinge of the beach. Behind the town rise lofty, scarped mountains, their sides furrowed with ravines hollowed out by the waters of the rainy season, and their brown peaks lost in the clouds.

Unhappily, we are compelled to avow that this port, despite of its ambitious title of town, is still a miserable village, without church or hotel. We do not say there are no drinking-shops ; on the contrary, as may be imagined in a port so near San Francisco, they swarm.

The aspect of Guaymas is sorrowful ; you feel that, in spite of the efforts of Europeans and adventurers to galvanise this population, the Spanish tyranny which has weighed upon it for three centuries has plunged it into a state of moral degradation and inferiority, from which it will require years to raise it.

The day on which our story commences, at about two in the afternoon, in spite of the red-hot sun which poured its beams on the town, Guaymas, generally so quiet at that hour, when the inhabitants, overcome by the heat, are asleep indoors, presented an animated appearance, which would have surprised the stranger whom accident had taken there at the moment, and would have caused him to suppose, most assuredly, that he was about to witness one of those thousand *pronunciamentos* which annually break out in this wretched province. Still, it was nothing of the sort. The military authority, represented by General San Benito, Governor of Guaymas, was, or seemed to be, satisfied with the government. The smugglers, leperos, and hiaquis continued in a tolerably satisfactory state, without complaining too much of the powers that were. Whence, then, the extraordinary agitation that prevailed in the town? What reason was strong enough to keep this indolent population awake, and make it forget its siesta?

For three days the town had been a prey to the gold fever. The governor, yielding to the supplications of several considerable merchants, had authorised for five days a *feria de plata*, or, literally, a silver fair.

Gambling-tables, held by persons of distinction, were publicly open in the principal houses ; but the fact which gave this festival a strangeness impossible to find elsewhere was, that monté tables were displayed in every street and in the open air, on which gold tinkled, and where everybody possessed of a real had the right to risk it, without distinction of caste or colour.

In Mexico everything is done differently from other countries. The inhabitants of this country, having no reminiscences of the past which they wish to forget, no faith in the future in which they do not believe, only live for the present, and exist with that feverish energy peculiar to races which feel their end approaching.

The Mexicans have two marked tastes which govern them entirely, play and love. We say tastes, and not passions, for the Mexicans are not capable of those great emotions which conquer the will, and overthrow the human economy by developing an energetic power of action.

The groups round the monté tables were numerous and animated. Still, everything went on with an order and tranquillity which nothing troubled, although no agent of the government was walking about the streets to maintain a good intelligence and watch the gamblers.

About half way up the Calle de la Merced, one of the widest in Guaymas, and opposite a house of goodly appearance, there stood a table covered with a green baize, and piled up with gold ounces, behind which a man of about thirty, with a crafty face, was stationed, who, with a pack of cards in his hand, and a smile on his lips, invited by the most insinuating remarks the numerous spectators who surrounded him to tempt fortune.

"Come, caballeros," he said in a honeyed tone, while turning a provocative glance upon the wretched men, haughtily draped in their rags, who regarded him with extreme indifference, "I cannot always win; luck is going to turn, I am sure. Here are one hundred ounces: who will cover them?"

No one answered.

The banker, not allowing himself to be defeated, let a tinkling cascade of ounces glide through his fingers, whose tawny reflection was capable of turning the most resolute head.

" It is a nice sum, caballeros, one hundred ounces : with them the ugliest man is certain of gaining the smiles of beauty. Come, who will cover them ? "

" Bah ! " a lepero said, with a disdainful pout, " what are one hundred ounces? Had you not won my last *tlaco*, Tio Lucas, I would cover them, that I would."

" I am in despair, Senor Cucharès," the banker replied with a bow, " that luck was so much against you, and I should feel delighted if you would deign to allow me to lend you an ounce."

" You are jesting," the lepero said, drawing himself up haughtily. " Keep your gold, Tio Lucas ; I know the way to procure as much as I want, whenever I think proper ; but," he added, bowing with the most exquisite politeness, " I am not the less grateful to you for your generous offer."

And he offered the banker across the table his hand, which the latter pressed with great cordiality.

The lepero profited by the occasion to pick up with his free hand a pile of twenty ounces that was in his reach.

Tio Lucas had great difficulty in restraining himself, but he feigned not to have seen anything.

After this interchange of good offices there was a moment's silence. The spectators had seen everything that occurred, and therefore awaited with some curiosity the *dénouement* of this scene. Senor Cucharès was the first to renew the conversation.

" Oh ! " he suddenly shouted, striking his forehead, " I believe, by Nuestra Senora de la Merced, that I am losing my head."

" Why so, caballero ? " Tio Lucas asked, visibly disturbed by this exclamation.

" Caraï ! it 's very simple," the other went on. " Did I not tell you just now that you had won all my money ?"

"You certainly said so, and these caballeros heard it with me: to your last ochavo—those were your very words."

"I remember it perfectly, and it is that which makes me so mad."

"What!" the banker exclaimed with feigned astonishment, "you are mad because I won from you?"

"O no! it's not that."

"What is it, then?"

"Caramba! it is because I made a mistake, and I have some ounces still left."

"Impossible!"

"Just see, then!"

The lepero put his hand in his pocket, and, with unparalleled effrontery, displayed to the banker the gold he had just stolen from him. But the latter did not wince.

"It is incredible," he merely said.

"Eh?" the lepero interjected, fixing a flashing eye upon him.

"Yes, it is incredible that you, Senor Cucharès, should have made such a slip of memory."

"Well, as I have remembered it, all can be put right now; we can continue our game."

"Very good: one hundred ounces is the stake."

"O no! I haven't that amount."

"Nonsense! feel in your pockets again."

"It is useless; I know I haven't got it."

"That is really most annoying."

"Why?"

"Because I have vowed not to play for less."

"Then you won't cover twenty ounces?"

"I cannot; I would not cover one short of a hundred."

"H'm!" the lepero went on, knitting his brows, "is that meant for an insult, Tio Lucas?"

The banker had no time to reply; for a man of about

thirty, mounted on a magnificent black horse, had stopped for a few seconds before the table, and, while carelessly smoking his cigar, listened to the discussion between the banker and the lepero.

"Done for one hundred ounces!" he said, as he cleared a way by means of his horse's chest up to the table, on which he dropped a purse full of gold.

The two speakers suddenly raised their heads.

"Here are the cards, caballero," the banker hastened to say, glad of an incident which temporarily freed him from a dangerous opponent. Cucharès shrugged his shoulders contemptuously, and looked at the new comer.

"Oh!" he muttered to himself, "the Tigrero! Has he come for Anita? I must know that."

And he gently drew nearer the stranger, and presently stood by his side.

He was a tall man, with an olive complexion, a piercing glance, and an open and resolute face. His dress, of the greatest richness, glistened with gold and diamonds. He wore, slightly inclined over his left ear, a broad-brimmed sombrero, surrounded by a golilla of fine gold; his spencer of blue cloth, embroidered with silver, allowed a dazzling white shirt to be seen, under the collar of which passed a cravat of China crape, fastened with a diamond ring; his calzoneras, drawn up round the hips by a red silk scarf with gold-fringed ends and two rows of diamond buttons, were open at the side, and allowed his *calzon* to float beneath; he wore *botas vaqueras* of figured leather, richly embroidered, attached below the knee by a garter of silver tissue; while his *manga*, glistening with gold, hung coquettishly from his right shoulder.

His horse, with a small head, and legs fine as spindles, was splendidly accoutred: *las armas de agua* and the *zarape* fastened to the croup, and the magnificent *anquera* adorned with steel chains, completed a caparison of which we can form no idea in Europe.

Like all Mexicans of a certain class when travelling, the stranger was armed from head to foot; that is to say, in addition to the lasso fastened to the saddle, and the musket laid across the saddle-bow, he had also by his side a long sword, and a pair of pistols in his girdle, without reckoning the knife whose silver inlaid hilt could be seen peeping out of one of his boots.

Such as we have described him, this man was the perfect type of a Mexican of Sonora—ever ready for peace or war, fearing the one no more than he despised the other. After bowing politely to Tio Lucas he took the cards the latter offered him, and shuffled them while looking around him.

" Ah !" he said, casting a friendly glance to the lepero, " you 're here, gossip Cucharès ? "

" At your service, Don Martial," the other replied, lifting his hand to the ragged brim of his beaver.

The stranger smiled.

" Be good enough to cut for me while I light my pajillo."

" With pleasure," the lepero exclaimed.

El Tigrero, or Don Martial, whichever the reader may please to call him, took a gold *mechero* from his pocket, and carelessly struck a light while the lepero cut the cards.

" Senor," the latter said in a piteous voice.

" Well ? "

" You have lost."

" Good. Tio Lucas, take a hundred ounces from my purse."

" I have them, your excellency," the banker replied " Would you please to play again ? "

"Certainly, but not for such trifles. I should like to feel interested in the game."

"I will cover any stake your excellency may like to name," the banker said, whose practised eye had discovered in the stranger's purse, amid a decent number of ounces, some forty diamonds of the purest water.

"H'm! are you really ready to cover any stake I name?"

"Yes."

The stranger looked at him sharply.

"Even if I played for a thousand gold ounces?"

"I would cover double that if your excellency dares to stake it," the banker said imperturbably.

A contemptuous smile played for the second time on the horseman's haughty lips.

"I do dare it," he said.

"Two thousand ounces, then?"

"Agreed"

"Shall I cut?" Cucharès asked timidly.

"Why not?" the other answered lightly.

The lepero seized the cards with a hand trembling from emotion. There was a hum of expectation from the gamblers who surrounded the table. At this moment a window opened in the house before which Tio Lucas had established his monté table, and a charming girl leant carelessly over the balcony, looking down into the street.

The stranger turned to the balcony, and rising in his stirrups,—

"I salute the lovely Anita," he said, as he doffed his hat and bowed profoundly.

The girl blushed, bent on him an expressive glance from beneath her long velvety eyelashes, but made no reply.

"You have lost, excellency," Tio Lucas said with a joyous accent, which he could not completely conceal.

"Very good," the stranger replied, without even looking at him, so fascinated was he by the charming apparition on the balcony.

"You play no more?"

"On the contrary, I double."

"What!" exclaimed the banker, falling back a step in spite of himself at this proposition.

"No, I am wrong; I have something else to propose."

"What is it, excellency?"

"How much have you there?" he said, pointing to the table with a disdainful gesture.

"Why, at least seven thousand ounces."

"Not more? That's very little."

The spectators regarded with a stupor, mingled with terror, this extraordinary man, who played for ounces and diamonds as others did for ochavos. The girl became pale. She turned a supplicating glance to the stranger.

"Play no more," she murmured in a trembling voice.

"Thanks," he exclaimed, "thanks, senorita; your beautiful eyes will bring me fortune. I would give all the gold on the table for the suchil flower you hold in your hand, and which your lips have touched."

"Do not play, Don Martial," the girl repeated, as she retired and closed the window. But, through accident or some other reason, her hand let loose the flower. The horseman made his steed bound forward, caught it in its flight, and buried it in his bosom, after having kissed it passionately several times.

"Cucharès," he then said to the lepero, "turn up a card."

The latter obeyed. "Seis de copas!" he said.

"Voto à brios!" the stranger exclaimed, "the colour

of the heart, we shall win. Tio Lucas, I will back this card against all the gold you have on your table."

The banker turned pale and hesitated; the spectators had their eyes fixed upon him.

" Bah ! " he thought after a minute's reflection, "it is impossible for him to win. I accept, excellency," he then added aloud.

" Count the sum you have."

" That is unnecessary, senor ; there are nine thousand four hundred and fifty gold ounces."*

At the statement of this formidable amount the spectators gave vent to a mingled shout of admiration and covetousness.

" I fancied you richer," the stranger said ironically. "Well, so be it, then."

" Will you cut this time, excellency ? "

" No, I am thoroughly convinced you are going to lose, Tio Lucas, and I wish you to be quite convinced that I have won fairly. In consequence, do me the pleasure_of cutting, yourself. You will then be the artisan of your own ruin, and be unable to reproach anybody."

The spectators quivered with pleasure on seeing the chivalrous way in which the stranger behaved. At this moment the street was thronged with people whom the rumour of this remarkable stake had collected from every part of the town. A deadly silence prevailed through the crowd, so great was the interest that each felt in the *dénouement* of this grand and hitherto unexampled match. The banker wiped away the perspiration that beaded on his livid brow, and seized the first card with a trembling hand. He balanced it for a

* About £31,500. (Fact)

few seconds between finger and thumb with manifest hesitation.

"Make haste," Cucharès cried to him with a grin.

Tio Lucas mechanically let the card fall as he turned his head away.

"Seis de copas!" the lepero shouted in a hoarse voice.

The banker uttered a yell of pain.

"I have lost!" he muttered.

"I was sure of it," the horseman said, still impassible. "Cucharès," he added, "carry that table and the gold upon it to Dona Anita. I shall expect you to-night you know where."

The lepero bowed respectfully. Assisted by two sturdy fellows, he executed the order he had just received, and entered the house, while the stranger started off at a gallop; and Tio Lucas, slightly recovered from the stunning blow he had received, philosophically twisted a cigar, repeating to those who forced their consolations upon him,—

"I have lost, it is true, but against a very fair player, and for a good stake. Bah! I shall have my revenge some day."

Then, so soon as the cigarette was made, the poor cleaned-out banker lighted it and walked off very calmly. The crowd, having no further excuse for remaining, also disappeared in its turn.

CHAPTER II.

DON SYLVA DE TORRÈS.

GUAYMAS is quite a new town, built somewhat from day to day according to the fancy of the emigrants, and hence no regular lines of streets have been maintained. However, we had better mention here that, with the exception of a few houses to which that name may be fairly given, all the rest are frightful dens, built of mud, and deplorably dirty.

In the Calle de la Merced, the principal, or, to speak more truthfully, the only street in the town (for the others are only alleys), stood a one-storied house, ornamented with a balcony, and a peristyle supported by four pillars. The front was covered by a coating of lime of dazzling whiteness, and the roof was flat.

The proprietor of this house was one of the richest *mineros* in Sonora, and possessor of a dozen mines, all in work ; he also devoted himself to cattle breeding, and owned several haciendas scattered over the province, the smallest of which was equal in size to an English county.

I am certain that, if Don Sylva de Torrès had wished to liquidate his fortune, and discover what he was really worth, it would have realised several millions.

Don Sylva had come to live in Guaymas some months back, where he ordinarily only paid flying visits, and those at lengthened intervals. This time, contrary to his usual custom, he had brought his daughter Anita with him. Hence the entire population of Guaymas was a prey to the greatest curiosity, and all eyes were fixed on Don Sylva's house, so extraordinary did the conduct of the *haciendero* appear.

Shut up in his house, the doors of which only opened to a few privileged persons, Don Sylva did not seem to trouble himself the least in the world about the gossips; for he was engaged in realising certain projects, whose importance prevented him noticing what was said or thought of him.

Though the Mexicans are excessively rich, and like to do honour to their wealth, they have no idea of comfort. The utmost carelessness prevails among them.

Their luxury, if I may be allowed to employ the term, is brutal, without any discernment or real value.

These men, principally accustomed to the rude life of the American deserts, to struggle continually against the changes of a climate which is frequently deadly, and the unceasing aggressions of the Indians, who surround them on all sides, camp rather than live in the towns, fancying they have done everything when they have squandered gold and diamonds.

The Mexican houses are in evidence to prove the correctness of our opinion. With the exception of the invitable European piano, which swaggers in the corner of every drawing-room, you only see a few clumsy *butacas*, rickety tables, bad engravings hanging on the white-washed walls, and that is all.

Don Sylva's house differed in no respect from the others ; and the master's horses, on returning to their stable from the watering-place, had to cross the *salon*, all dripping as they were, and leaving manifest traces of their passage.

At the moment when we introduce the reader into Don Sylva's house, two persons, male and female, were sitting in the saloon talking, or at least exchanging a few words at long intervals.

They were Don Sylva and his daughter Anita. The crossing of the Spanish and Indian races has produced the most perfect plastic type to be found anywhere. Don Sylva, although nearly fifty years of age, did not appear to be forty. He was tall, upright, and his face, though stern, had great gentleness imprinted upon it. He wore the Mexican dress in its most rigorous exactness ; but his clothes were so rich, that few of his countrymen could have equalled it, much less surpassed it.

Anita, who reclined on a sofa, half buried in masses of silk and gauze, like a humming-bird concealed in moss, was a charming girl of eighteen at the most, whose black eyes, modestly veiled by long velvety lashes, were full of voluptuous promise, which was not gainsaid by the undulating and serpentine outlines of her exquisitely modelled body. Her slightest gestures had a grace and majesty completed by the ravishing smile of her coral lips. Her complexion, slightly gilded by the American sun, imparted to her face an expression impossible to render; and lastly, her whole person exhaled a delicious perfume of innocence and candour which attracted sympathy and inspired love.

Like all Mexican women when at home, she merely wore a light robe of embroidered muslin; her *rebozo* was thrown negligently over her shoulders, and a profusion of jasmine flowers was intertwined in her bluish-black tresses. Anita seemed deep in thought. At one moment the arch of her eyebrows was contracted by some thought that annoyed her, her bosom heaved, and her dainty foot, cased in a slipper lined with swan's down, impatiently tapped the ground.

Don Sylva also appeared to be dissatisfied. After directing a severe glance at his daughter, he rose, and, drawing near her, said,—

"You are mad, Anita; your behaviour is extravagant. A young, well-born girl ought not, in any case, to act as you have just done."

The young Mexican girl only answered by a significative pout, and an almost imperceptible shrug of her shoulders.

Her father continued,—

"Especially," he said, laying a stress on each word, "in your position as regards the Count de Lhorailles."

c

The girl started as if a serpent had stung her, and, fixing an interrogatory glance on the haciendero's immovable face, she replied,—

"I do not understand you, my father."

"You do not understand me, Anita? I cannot believe it. Have I not formally promised your hand to the count?"

"What matter, if I do not love him? Do you wish to condemn me to lifelong misery?"

"On the contrary, I regarded your happiness in this union. I have only you, Anita, to console me for the mournful loss of your beloved mother. Poor child! you are still, thank Heaven, at that happy age when the heart does not know itself, and when the words 'happiness, unhappiness,' have no meaning. You do not love the count, you say. All the better—your heart is free. When, at a later date, you have had occasion to appreciate the noble qualities of the man I give you as husband, you will then thank me for having insisted on a marriage which, to-day, causes you so much vexation."

"Stay, father," the girl said, with an air of vexation. "My heart is not free, and you are well aware of the fact."

"I know, Dona Anita de Torrès," the haciendero answered severely, "that a love unworthy of yourself and me cannot enter your heart. Through my ancestors I am a Christiano Viejo; and if a few drops of Indian blood be mingled in my veins, what I owe to the memory of my ancestors is only the more deeply engraved on my mind. The first of our family, Antonio de Sylva, lieutenant to Hernando Cortez, married, it is true, a Mexican princess of the family of Moctecuzoma, but all the other branches are Spanish."

"Are we not Mexicans then, my father?"

"Alas! my poor child, who can say who we are and

what we are?   Our unhappy country, since it shook off
the Spanish yoke, has been struggling convulsively, and
is exhausted by the incessant efforts of those ambitious
men, who in a few years will have robbed it even of
that nationality which we had so much difficulty in
achieving.   These disgraceful contests render us the
laughing-stock of other peoples, and, above all, cause
the joy of our greedy neighbours, who, with their eyes
invariably fixed upon us, are preparing to enrich themselves with our spoils, of which they have pilfered some
fragments already by robbing us of several of our rich
provinces."

"But, my father, I am a woman, and therefore
unaffected by politics.   I have nothing to do with the
gringos."

"More than you may imagine, my child.   I do not
wish that at a given day the immense property my
ancestors and myself have acquired by our toil should
become the prey of these accursed heretics.   In order
to save it, I have resolved on marrying you to the Count
de Lhorailles.   He is a Frenchman, and belongs to one
of the noblest families of that country.   Besides, he is a
handsome and brave gentleman, scarcely thirty years of
age, who combines the most precious moral qualities
with the physical qualities.   He is a member of a
powerful and respected nation, which knows how to
protect its subjects, in whatever corner of the world they
may be.   By marrying him your fortune is sheltered
from every political reverse."

"But I do not love him, father."

"Nonsense, my dear babe.   Do not talk longer of
that.   I am willing to forget the folly of which you were
guilty a few moments back, but on condition that you
forget that man, Martial."

" Never ! " she exclaimed resolutely.

" Never ! That is a long time, my daughter. You will reflect, I am convinced. Besides, who is this man ? what is his family ? Do you know ? He is called Martial el Tigrero. Voto à Dios, that is not a name ! That man saved your life by stopping your horse when it ran away. Well, is that a reason for him to fall in love with you, and you with him ? I offered him a magnificent reward, which he refused with the most supreme disdain. There is an end of it, then ; let him leave me at peace. I have, and wish for, nothing more to do with him."

" I love him, father," the young girl repeated.

" Listen, Anita. You would make me angry, if I did not put a restraint on myself. Enough on that head. Prepare to receive the Count de Lhorailles in a proper manner. I have sworn that you shall be his wife, and, Cristo ! it shall be so, if I have to drag you by force to the altar ! "

The haciendero pronounced these words with such resolution in his voice, and such a fierce accent, that the girl saw it would be better for her to appear to yield, and put a stop to a discussion which would only grow more embittered, and perhaps have grave consequences. She let her head fall, and was silent, while her father walked up and down the room with a very dissatisfied air.

The door was partly opened, and a peon thrust his head discreetly through the crevice.

" What do you want ? " Don Sylva asked as he stopped.

" Excellency," the man replied, " a caballero, followed by four others bearing a table covered with pieces of gold, requests an audience of the senorita."

The haciendero shot a glance at his daughter full of

expressiveness. Dona Anita let her head sink in confusion. Don Sylva reflected for a moment, and then his countenance cleared.

"Let him come in," he said.

The peon withdrew; but he returned in a few seconds, preceding an old acquaintance, Cucharès, still enwrapped in his ragged zarapè, and directing the four leperos who carried the table. On entering the saloon, Cucharès uncovered respectfully, courteously saluted the haciendero and his daughter, and with a sign ordered the porters to deposit the table in the centre of the apartment.

"Senorita," he said in a honeyed voice, "the Senor Don Martial, faithful to the pledge he made you, humbly supplicates you to accept his gains at montè as a feeble testimony of his devotion and admiration."

"You rascal!" Don Sylva angrily exclaimed, as he took a step toward him. "Do you know in whose presence you are?"

"In that of Dona Anita and her highly-respected parent," the scamp replied imperturbably, as he wrapped himself majestically in his tatters. "I have not, to my knowledge, failed in the respect I owe to both."

"Withdraw at once, and take with you this gold, which does not concern my daughter."

"Excuse me, excellency, I received orders to bring the gold here, and with your permission I will leave it. Don Martial would not forgive me if I acted otherwise."

"I do not know Don Martial, as it pleases you to call the man who sent you. I wish to have nothing in common with him."

"That is possible, excellency; but it is no affair of mine. You can have an explanation with him if you think proper. For my part, as my mission is accomplished, I kiss your hands."

And, after bowing once more to the two, the lepero went off majestically, followed by his four acolytes, with measured steps.

"See there," Don Sylva exclaimed violently, "see there, my daughter, to what insults your folly exposes me!"

"An insult, my father?" she replied timidly. "On the contrary, I think that Don Martial has acted like a true caballero, and that he gives me a great proof of his love. That sum is enormous."

"Ah!" Don Sylva said wrathfully, "that is the way you take it. Well, I will act as a caballero also, *voto à brios*, as you shall see. Come here, some one!"

Several peons came in.

"Open the windows!" he ordered.

The servants obeyed. The crowd was not yet dispersed, and a large number of persons was still collected round the house. The haciendero leant out, and by a wave of his hand requested silence. The crowd was instinctively silent, and drew nearer, guessing that something in which it was interested was about to happen.

"*Senores caballeros y amijos,*" the haciendero said, in a powerful voice, "a man whom I do not know has dared to offer to my daughter the money he has won at montè. Dona Anita spurns such presents, especially when they come from a person with whom she does not wish to have any connection, friendly or otherwise. She begs me to distribute this gold among you, as she will not touch it in any way: she desires thus to prove, in the presence of you all, the contempt she feels for a man who has dared to offer her such an insult."

The speech improvised by the haciendero was drowned by the frenzied applause of the leperos and other assembled beggars, whose eyes sparkled with greed. Anita felt the burning tears swelling her eyelids. In spite of all her efforts to remain undisturbed, her heart was almost broken.

Troubling himself not at all about his daughter, Don Sylva ordered his servants to cast the ounces into the street. A shower of gold then literally began falling on the wretches, who rushed with incredible ardour on this new species of manna. The Calle de la Merced offered, at that moment, the most singular sight imaginable. The gold poured and poured on; it seemed to be inexhaustible. The beggars leaped like coyotes on the precious metal, overthrowing and trampling under foot the weaker.

At the height of the shower a horseman came galloping up. Astonished, confounded by what he saw, he stopped for a moment to look around him; then he drove his spurs into his horse, and by dealing blows of his chicote liberally all round, he succeeded in clearing the dense crowd, and reached the haciendero's house, which he entered.

" Here is the count," Don Sylva said laconically to his daughter.

In fact, within a minute that gentleman entered the saloon.

" Halloh!" he said, stopping in the doorway, "what strange notion is this of yours, Don Sylva? On my soul, you are amusing yourself by throwing millions out of window, to the still greater amusement of the leperos and other rogues of the same genus!"

" Ah, 'tis you, Senor Conde," the haciendero replied calmly; " you are welcome. I shall be with you in an instant. Only these few handsful, and it will be finished."

"Don't hurry yourself," the count said with a laugh. "I confess that the fancy is original;" and, drawing near the young lady, whom he saluted with exquisite politeness, he continued,—

"Would you deign, senorita, to give me the word of this enigma, which, I confess, interests me in the highest degree?"

"Ask my father, senor," she answered with a certain dryness, which rendered conversation impossible.

The count feigned not to notice this rebuff; he bowed with a smile, and falling into a *butacca*, said coolly,—

"I will wait; I am in no hurry."

The haciendero, in telling his daughter that the husband he intended for her was a handsome man, had in no respect flattered him. Count Maxime Gaëtan de Lhorailles was a man of thirty at the most, well built and active, and slightly above the middle height. His light hair allowed him to be recognised as a son of the north: his features were fine, his glance expressive, and his hands and feet denoted race. Everything about him indicated the gentleman of an old stock; and if Don Sylva was not more deceived about the moral qualities than he had been about the physical, Count de Lhorailles was really a perfect gentleman.

At length the haciendero exhausted all the gold Cucharès had brought; he then hurled the table into the street, ordered the windows to be closed, and came back to take a seat by the side of the count, rubbing his hands.

"There," he said with a joyous air, "that's finished. Now I am quite at your service."

"First one word."

" Say it."

" Excuse me. You are aware that I am a stranger, and as such thirsting for instruction."

" I am listening to you."

" Since I have lived in Mexico I have seen many extraordinary customs. I ought to be *blasé* about novelties : still, I must confess that what I have just seen surpasses anything I have hitherto witnessed. I should like to be certain whether this is a custom of which I was hitherto ignorant."

" What are you talking about ?"

" Why, what you were doing when I arrived—that gold you were dropping like a beneficent dew on the bandits of every description collected before your house : ill weeds, between ourselves, to be thus bedewed."

Don Sylva burst into a laugh.

" No, that is not a custom of ours," he replied.

" Very good. Then, you were indulging in the regal pastime of throwing a million to the scum. Plague ! Don Sylva, a man must be as rich as yourself to allow himself such a gratification."

" Things are not as you fancy."

" Still I saw it raining ounces."

" True, but they did not belong to me."

" Better and better still. That renders the affair more complicated ; you heighten my curiosity immensely."

" I will satisfy it."

" I am all attention, for the affair is growing as interesting to me as a story in the ' Arabian Nights.' "

" H'm !" the haciendero said, tossing his head, " it interests you more than you perhaps suspect."

" How so ?"

" You shall judge."

Dona Anita was in torture ; she knew not what to do,

Seeing that her father was about to divulge all to the count, she did not feel in herself the courage to be present at such a revelation, and rose tottering.

" Gentlemen," she said in a feeble voice, " I feel indisposed : be kind enough to allow me to retire."

" Really," the count said, as he hurried toward her, and offered her his arm to support her, " you are pale, Dona Anita. Allow me to accompany you to your apartment."

" I thank you, caballero, but I am strong enough to proceed there alone, and, while duly grateful for your offer, pray permit me to decline it."

" As you please, senorita," the count replied, inwardly piqued by this refusal.

Don Sylva entertained for a moment the idea of ordering his daughter to remain ; but the poor girl turned toward him so despairing a glance that he did not feel the courage to impose on her a longer torture.

" Go, my child," he said to her.

Anita hastened to take advantage of the permission ; she left the *salon*, and sought refuge in her bedroom, where she sank into a chair, and burst into tears.

" What is the matter with Dona Anita ? " the count asked, with sympathy, so soon as she had gone.

" Vapours — headache — what do I know ? " the haciendero replied, shrugging his shoulders. " All young girls are like that. In a few minutes she will have forgotten it."

" All the better. I confess to you that I was alarmed."

" But now that we are alone, would you not like me to give you the explanation of the enigma which appeared to interest you so much ? "

" On the contrary, speak without any further delay ; for, on my part, I have several important matters to impart to you."

CHAPTER III.

THE TWO HUNTERS.

ABOUT five miles from the town is the village of San José de Guaymas, commonly known as the *Rancho*.

This miserable *pueblo* is merely composed of a square of moderate size, intersected at right angles by two streets, bordered by tumbledown cabins, which are inhabited by Hiaqui Indians (a large number of whom hire themselves out annually at Guaymas to work as porters, carpenters, masons, &c.), and all those nameless adventurers who have thronged to the shores of the Pacific since the discovery of the Californian plains.

The road from Guaymas to San José runs through a parched and sandy plain, on which only a few nopals and stunted cactuses grow, whose withered branches are covered with dust, and produce the effect of white phantoms at night.

The evening of the day on which our story commences, a horseman, wrapped to the eyes in a zarapè, was following this road, and proceeding in a gallop to the Rancho.

The sky, of a dark azure, was studded with glistening stars ; the moon, which had traversed one-third of her course, illumined the silent plain, and indefinitely prolonged the tall shadows of the trees on the naked earth.

The horseman, doubtlessly anxious to reach the end of a journey which was not without peril at this advanced hour, incessantly urged on with spur and voice his horse, which did not, however, appear to need this constantly-renewed encouragement.

He had all but crossed the uncultivated plains, and was just entering the woods which surround the

Rancho, when his horse suddenly leaped on one side, and pricked up its ears in alarm. A sharp sound announced that the horseman had cocked his pistols; and, when this precaution had been taken against all risk, he turned an inquiring glance around.

" Fear nothing, caballero ! " a frank and sympathetic voice exclaimed ; " but have the kindness to go a little farther to the right, if it makes no difference to you."

The stranger looked, and saw a man kneeling almost under his steed's feet, and holding in his hands the head of a horse, which was lying nearly across the road.

" What on earth are you doing there ? " he asked.

" You can see," the other replied sorrowfully. " I am bidding good-by to my poor companion. A man must have lived a long time in the desert to appreciate the value of such a friend as he was."

" That is true," the stranger remarked, and immediately dismounting, added, " Is he dead, then ? "

" No, not yet; but, unfortunately, he is as bad as if he were."

With these words he sighed.

The stranger bent over the animal, whose body was agitated by a nervous quivering, opened its eyelids, and regarded it attentively.

" Your horse has had a stroke," he said a moment later. " Let me act."

" Oh ! " the other exclaimed, " do you think you can save him ? "

" I hope so," the first speaker laconically remarked.

" *Carai !* if you do that, we shall be friends for life. Poor Negro ! my old comrade ! "

The horseman bathed the animal's temples and nostrils with rum and water. At the end of a few moments the horse appeared slightly recovered, its faded eyes began to sparkle again, and it tried to rise.

"Hold him tight," the improvised surgeon said.

"Be quiet, then, my good beast. Come, Negro, my boy, *quieto, quieto;* it is for your good," he said soothingly.

The intelligent animal seemed to understand. It turned its head toward its master, and answered him with a plaintive neigh. The horseman, during this period, had been feeling in his girdle; and bending again over the horse,—

"Mind and hold him tightly," he again recommended.

"What are you going to do?"

"Bleed him."

"Yes, that is it. I knew it; but unfortunately I did not dare risk doing it myself, through fear of killing the horse."

"All right?"

"Go on."

The horse made a hasty move, caused by the coldness of the wound; but its master held it down and checked its struggles. The two men suffered a moment of anxiety: the blood did not issue. At last a black drop appeared in the wound, then a second, speedily followed by a long jet of black and foaming blood.

"He is saved," the stranger said, as he wiped his lancet, and returned it to his fob.

"I will repay you this, on the word of Belhumeur!" the owner of the horse said with much emotion. "You have rendered me one of those services which are never forgotten."

And, by an irresistible impulse, he held out his hand to the man who had so providentially crossed his path. The latter warmly returned the vigorous pressure. Henceforth all was arranged between them. These two men, who a few moments previously were ignorant of each other's existence, were friends, attached by one of those services which in American countries possess an immense value.

The blood gradually lost its black tinge; it became vermilion, and flowed abundantly. The breathing of the panting steed had grown easy and regular. The first stranger made a copious bleeding, and when he considered the horse in a fair way of recovery he stopped the effusion.

"And now," he said, "what do you propose doing?"

"My faith, I don't know. Your help has been so useful to me that I should like to follow your advice."

"Where were you going when this accident occurred?"

"To the Rancho."

"I am going there too. We are only a few yards from it. You will get up behind me. We will lead your horse, and start when you please."

"I ask nothing better. You believe that my horse cannot carry me?"

"Perhaps he could do so, for he is a noble animal; but it would be imprudent, and you would run a risk of killing him. It would be better, believe me, to act as I suggested."

"Yes; but I am afraid——"

"What of?" the other sharply interrupted him. "Are we not friends?"

"That is true. I accept."

The horse sprang up somewhat actively, and the two men who had met so strangely started at once, mounted on one horse. Twenty minutes later they reached the first buildings of the Rancho. At the entrance of the village the owner of the horse stopped, and turning to his companion, said,—

"Where will you get down?"

"That is all the same to me; let us go first where you are going."

"Ah!" the horseman said, scratching his head, "the fact is, I am going nowhere in particular."

"What do you mean?"

"Oh! you will understand me in two words. I landed to-day at Guaymas; the Rancho is only the first station of a journey I meditate in the desert, and which will probably last a long time."

By the moonlight, a ray of which now played on the stranger's face, his companion attentively regarded his noble and pensive countenance, on which grief had already cut deep furrows.

"So that," he at length said, "any lodging will suit you?"

"A night is soon spent. I only ask a shelter for horse and self."

"Well, if you will permit me to act in my turn as guide, you shall have that within ten minutes."

"Agreed."

"I do not promise you a palace, but will take you to a *pulqueria*, where I am accustomed to put up when accident brings me to these parts. You will find the society rather mixed, but what would you have? and, as you said yourself, a night is soon spent."

"In Heaven's name, then, proceed."

Then, passing his arm through that of his comrade, the new guide seized the horse's reins, and steered to a house standing about two-thirds of the way down the street where they were, whose badly-fitting windows gleamed in the night like the stoke-holes of a furnace, while cries, laughter, songs, and the shrill sound of the *jarabés*, indicated that, if the rest of the *pueblo* were plunged in sleep, there, at least, people were awake.

The two strangers stopped before the door of this pot-house.

" Have you quite made up your mind ?" the first said.

" Perfectly," the other answered.

The guide then rapped furiously at the worm-eaten door. It was long ere any one answered. At length a hoarse voice shouted from inside, while the greatest silence succeeded, as if by enchantment, the noise that had hitherto prevailed.

" *Quien vive !* "

" *Gente de paz,*" the stranger replied.

" Hum !" the voice went on, "that is not a name. What sort of weather is it ?"

" One for all—all for one. The *cormuel* is strong enough to blow the horns off the oxen on the top of the Cierro del Herfuano."

The door was immediately opened, and the strangers entered. At first they could distinguish nothing through the thick and smoky atmosphere of the room, and walked hap-hazard. The companion of the first horse-man was well known in this den ; for the master of the house and several other persons eagerly collected round him.

" Caballeros," he said, pointing to the person who followed him, " this senor is my friend, and I must request your kindness for him."

" He shall be treated like yourself, Belhumeur," the host replied. " Your horses have been led to the corral, where a truss of alfalfa has been put before them. As for yourselves, the house belongs to you, and you can dispose of it as you please."

During this exchange of compliments the strangers had contrived to find their way through the crowd. They crossed the room, and sat down in a corner before a table on which the host himself placed pulque, mezcal, chinguirito, Catalonian refino, and sherry.

" Caramba, Senor Huesped!" the man whom we had heard called frequently Belhumeur said with a laugh, " you are generous to-day."

" Do you not see that I have an angelito?" the other answered gravely.

" What, your son Pedrito——?"

" Is dead. I am trying to give my friends a cordial welcome, in order the better to feast the entrance into heaven of my poor boy, who, having never sinned, is an angel by the side of God."

" That 's very proper," Belhumeur said, hobnobbing with the rather stoical parent.

The latter emptied his glass of refino at a draught, and withdrew. The strangers, by this time accustomed to the atmosphere in which they found themselves, began to look around them. The room of the pulqueria offered them a most singular sight.

In the centre some ten individuals, with faces enough to hang them, covered with rags, and armed to the teeth, were furiously playing at montè. It was a strange fact, but one which did not appear to astonish any of the honourable gamblers, that a long dagger was stuck in the table to the right of the banker, and two pistols lay on his left. A few steps further on, men and women, more than half intoxicated, were dancing and singing, with lubricious gestures and mad shouts, to the shrill sounds of two or three *vihuelas* and *jarabès*. In a corner of the room thirty people were assembled round a table, on which a child, four years of age at the most, was seated in a wicker chair. This child presided over the meeting. He was dressed in his best clothes, had a crown of flowers on his head, and a pro-

D

fusion of nosegays was piled up on the table all round him.

But alas! the child's brow was pale, his eyes glassy, his complexion leaden, and marked with violet spots. His body had the peculiar stiffness of a corpse. He was dead. He was the angelito, whose entrance into heaven the worthy pulquero was celebrating.

Men, women, and children were drinking and laughing, as they reminded the poor mother, who made heroic efforts not to burst into tears, of the precocious intelligence, goodness, and prettiness of the little creature she had just lost.

"All this is hideous," the first traveller muttered, with signs of disgust.

"Is it not so?" the other assented. "Let us not notice it, but isolate ourselves amid these scoundrels, who have already forgotten our presence, and talk."

"Willingly, but unhappily we have nothing to say to each other."

"Perhaps we have. In the first place, we might let each other know who we are."

"That is true."

"You agree with me? Then I will give you the example of confidence and frankness."

"Good. After that my turn will come."

Belhumeur looked round at the company. The orgie had recommenced with fresh fury; it was evident that no one troubled himself about them. He rested his elbows on the table, leant over to his comrade, and began :—

"As you already know, my dear mate, my name is Belhumeur. I am a Canadian; that is to say, almost a Frenchman. Circumstances too long to narrate at present, but which I will tell you some day, brought me, when a lad, into this country. Twenty years of my life have passed in traversing the desert in every direction : there is not a stream or a by-path which I do not know. I could, if I would, live quietly and free from care with a very dear friend, an old companion, who has retired to a magnificent hacienda which he possesses a few leagues from Hermosillo ; but the existence of a hunter has charms which only those who have lived it can understand : it always compels them to renew it in spite of themselves. I am still a young man, hardly five-and-forty years of age. An old friend of mine, an Indian chief of the name of Eagle-head, proposed to me to accompany him on an excursion he wished to make in Apacheria. I allowed myself to be tempted ; said good-by to those I love, and who tried in vain to hold me back ; and free from all ties, without regret for the past, happy in the present, and careless of the future, I went gaily ahead, bearing with me those inestimable treasures for the hunter, a strong heart, a gay character, excellent arms, and a horse accustomed, like his master, to good fortune and ill ; and so here I am. And now, mate, you know me as well as if we had been friends for the last ten years."

The other had listened attentively to this story, fixing a thoughtful glance on the bold adventurer, who sat smiling before him. He gazed with interest on this man, with the loyal face and sharply-cut features, whose countenance exhaled the rude and noble frankness of a man who is really good and great.

When Belhumeur was silent he remained for some moments without replying, doubtlessly plunged in profound and earnest reflections ; then, offering him across the table a white, elegant, and delicate hand, he replied with great emotion, and in the best French ever spoken in these distant regions,—

"I thank you, Belhumeur, for the confidence you have placed in me. My history is not longer, but more mournful than yours. You shall have it in a few words."

"Eh?" the Canadian exclaimed, vigorously pressing the hand offered him. "Do you happen to be a Frenchman?"

"Yes, I have that honour."

"By Jove! I ought to have suspected it," he burst out joyously. "Only to think that for an hour we have been stupidly talking bad Spanish, instead of employing our own tongue; for I come from Canada, and the Canadians are the French of America, are they not?"

"You are right."

"Well, then, it is agreed, no more Spanish between us?"

"No, nothing but French."

"Bravo! Here's your health, my worthy fellow-countryman! And now," he added, returning his glass to the table after emptying it, "let us have your story. I am listening."

"I told you that it is not long."

"No matter; go on ahead. I am certain 'twill interest me enormously."

The Frenchman stifled a sigh.

"I, too, have lived the life of a wood-ranger," he said; "I, too, have experienced the intoxicating charms of that feverish existence, full of moving incidents, no two of which are alike. Far from the country where we now are, I have traversed vast deserts, immense virgin forests, in which no man prior to myself had left the imprint of his footstep. Like you, a friend accompanied me in my adventurous travels, sustaining my courage, maintaining my gaiety by his inexhaustible humour and his unbounded courage. Alas! that was the happiest period of my life.

"I fell in love with a woman, and married her. So soon as my friend saw me rich and surrounded by a family he left me. His departure was my first grief— a grief from which I never recovered, which each day rendered more poignant, and which now tortures me like a remorse. Alas! where is now that strong heart, that devoted friend who ever interposed between danger and myself, who loved me like a brother, and for whom I felt a son's affection? He is probably dead!"

In uttering the last words the Frenchman let his head sink in his hands, and yielded to a flood of bitter thoughts, which rose from his heart with every reminiscence he recalled. Belhumeur looked at him in a melancholy manner, and pressing his hand, said in a low and sympathising voice, "Courage, my friend."

"Yes," the Frenchman continued, "that was what he always said to me when, prostrated by grief, I felt hope failing me. 'Courage,' he would say to me in his rough voice, laying his hand on my shoulders; and I would feel galvanised by the touch, and draw myself up at the sound of that cherished voice, ready to recommence the struggle, for I felt myself stronger. Several years passed in the midst of a felicity which nothing came to trouble. I had a wife I adored, charming children for whom I formed dreams of the future; in short, I wanted for nothing save my poor comrade, about whom I could discover nothing from the moment he left me, in spite of my constant inquiries. Now my happiness has faded away never to return. My wife, my children are dead—cruelly murdered in their sleep by Indians, who carried my hacienda by storm. I alone remained alive amid the smoking ruins of that abode where I had spent so many happy days. All I loved was eternally buried beneath the ashes. My heart was broken, and I did not wish to survive all that was dear to me; but a friend, the only one who remained to me, saved me. He carried me off by main force to his tribe, for he was an Indian. By his care and devotion he recalled me to life, and restored me, if not the hope of a happiness henceforth impossible for me, at least the courage to struggle against that destiny whose blows had been so rude. He died only a few months back. Before closing his eyes for ever he made me swear to do all he asked of me. I promised him. 'Brother,' he said, 'every man must proceed in life toward a certain object. So soon as I am dead, go in search of that friend from whom you have so long been separated. You will find him, I feel convinced. He will trace your line of conduct.' Two hours later the worthy chief died in my arms. So soon as his body was committed to the earth I set out. This very day, as I told you, I reached Guaymas. My intention is to bury myself immediately in the desert; for if my poor friend be still alive, I can only find him there."

There was a lengthened silence, at length broken by Belhumeur.

"Hum! all that is very sad, mate, I must allow," he said, tossing his head. "You are rushing upon a desperate enterprise, in which the chances of success are almost null. A man is a grain of sand lost in the desert. Who knows, even supposing he still lives, at what place he may be at this moment; and if, while you are seeking him on one side, he may not be on the other? Still, I have a proposition to make to you, which, I believe, can only be advantageous."

"I know it, my friend, before you tell it me. I thank you, and accept it," the Frenchman replied quickly.

"It is agreed, then. We will start together. You will come with me into Apacheria?"

"Yes."

"By Jove! I am in luck. I have hardly separated from Loyal Heart ere Heaven brings me together with a friend as precious as he is."

"Who is that Loyal Heart you mention?"

"The friend with whom I lived so long, and whom you shall know some day. But come, we will start at daybreak."

"Whenever you please."

"I have the meeting with Eagle-head two days' journey from here. I am much mistaken, or he is waiting for me by this time."

"What are you going to do in Apacheria?"

"I do not know. Eagle-head asked me to accompany him, and I am going. It is my rule never to ask my friends more of their secrets than they are willing to tell me. In that way we are more free."

"Excellent reasoning, my dear Belhumeur; but, as we shall be together for a long time, I hope at least——"

"I, too."

"It is right," the Frenchman continued, "that you should know my name, which I have hitherto forgotten to tell you."

"That need not trouble you; for I could easily give you one if you had reasons for preserving your incognito."

"None at all: my name is Count Louis de Prébois Crancé."

Belhumeur rose as if moved by a spring, took off his fur cap, and bowing before his new friend, said,—

"Pardon me, sir count, for the free manner in which I have addressed you. Had I known in whose company I had the honour of being, I should certainly not have taken so great a liberty."

"Belhumeur, Belhumeur," the count said with a mournful smile, and seizing his hand quickly, "is our friendship to commence in that way? There are here only two men ready to share the same life, run the same dangers, and confront the same foes. Let us leave to the foolish inhabitants of cities those vain distinctions which possess no significance for us; let us be frankly and loyally brothers. I only wish to be to you Louis, your good comrade, your devoted friend, in the same way as you are to me only Belhumeur, the rough wood-ranger."

The Canadian's face shone with pleasure at these words.

"Well spoken," he said gaily, "well spoken, on my soul! I am but a poor ignorant hunter; and, by my faith, why should I conceal it? What you have just said to me has gone straight to my heart. I am yours, Louis, for life and death; and I hope to prove to you soon, comrade, that I have a certain value."

"I am convinced of it; but we understand each other now, do we not?"

"By Jove——!"

At this moment there was such a tremendous disturbance in the street, that it drowned that in the room. As always happens under such circumstances, the adventurers assembled in the pulqueria were silent of a common accord, in order to listen. Shouts, the clashing of sabres, the stamping of horses, drowned at intervals by the discharge of fire-arms, could be clearly distinguished.

"Caraï!" Belhumeur exclaimed, "there's fighting going on in the street."

"I am afraid so," the pulquero laconically answered, who was more than half drunk, as he swallowed a glass of refino.

Suddenly blows from sabre hilts and pistol buts resounded vigorously on the badly-joined planks of the door, and a powerful voice shouted angrily,—

"Open, in the devil's name, or I'll smash in your miserable door!"

CHAPTER IV.

COUNT MAXIME GAETAN DE LHORAILLES.

BEFORE explaining to the reader the cause of the infernal noise which suddenly rose to disturb the tranquillity of the people assembled in the pulqueria, we are obliged to go back a little distance.

About three years before the period in which our story opens, on a cold and rainy December night, eight men, whose costumes and manners showed them to belong to the highest Parisian society, were assembled in an elegant private room of the Café Anglais.

The night was far advanced; the wax candles, two-thirds consumed, only spread a mournful light; the rain lashed the windows, and the wind howled lugubriously. The guests, seated round the table and the relics of a splendid supper, seemed, in spite of themselves, to have been infected by the gloomy melancholy that brooded over nature, and, lying back on their chairs, some slept, while others, lost in thought, paid no attention to what was going on around them.

The clock on the mantel-piece slowly struck three, and the last sound had scarcely died away ere the repeated clacking of a postilion's whip could be heard beneath the windows of the room.

The door opened and a waiter came in.

" The post-chaise the Count de Lhorailles ordered is waiting," he said.

" Thanks," one of the guests said, dismissing the waiter by a sign.

The latter went out, and closed the door after him. The few words he had uttered had broken the charm which enchained the guests ; all sat up, as if aroused from sleep suddenly ; and turning to a young man of about thirty, they said,—

" It is really true that you are going ?"

" I am," he answered, with a nod of affirmation.

" Where to, though ?   People do not usually part in this mysterious way," one of the guests continued.

The gentleman to whom the remark was addressed smiled sorrowfully.

The Count de Lhorailles was a handsome man, with expressive features, energetic glance, and disdainful lip ; he belonged to the most ancient nobility, and his reputation was perfectly established among the " lions " of the day. He rose, and looking round the circle, said,—

" Gentlemen, I can perfectly well understand that my conduct appears to you strange You have a right to an explanation from me, and I am most desirous to give it you. It was, indeed, for that purpose that I invited you to the last supper we shall enjoy together. The hour for my departure has struck—the chaise is waiting. To-morrow I shall be far from Paris, and within a week I shall have left France never to return. Listen to me."

The guests made a marked movement as they gazed on the count.

"Do not be impatient, gentlemen," he said; "the story I have to tell you is not long, for it is my own. In two words, here it is:—

"I am completely ruined. I have only a small sum of money left, on which I should starve in Paris, and end in a month by blowing out my brains—a gloomy perspective which possesses no attractions for me, I assure you. On the other hand, I have such a fatal skill with arms, that, without any fault of my own, I enjoy a reputation as a duellist, which weighs on me fearfully, especially since my deplorable affair with that poor Viscount de Morsens, whom I was obliged to kill against my will, in order to close his mouth and put a stop to his calumnies. In fine, for the reasons I have had the honour of imparting to you, and an infinity of others it is needless for you to know, and which I am convinced would interest you very slightly, France has become odious to me to such a degree that I am most anxious to quit it. So now a parting glass of champagne, and good-by to all."

"A moment," the guest remarked who had already spoken. "You have not told us, count, to what country you intend to proceed."

"Cannot you guess it? To America. I am allowed to possess a certain amount of courage and intelligence, and therefore am going to a country where, if I may believe all I hear, those two qualities are sufficient to make the fortune of their possessor. Have you any more questions to ask me, baron?" he added, turning to his questioner.

The latter, ere replying, remained for some moments plunged in serious reflections; at length he raised his head, and fixed a cold and searching glance on the count.

"You really mean to go, my friend?" he said quite seriously. "You will swear it on your honour?"

"Yes, on my honour."

"And you are really resolved to make for yourself, in America, a position at the least equal to that you held here?"

"Yes," he said sharply, "by all the means possible."

"That is good. In your turn listen to me, count, and if you will profit by what I am about to reveal to you, you may, perhaps, by the help of Heaven, succeed in accomplishing the wild projects you have formed."

All the guests drew round curiously: the count himself felt interested in spite of himself.

The Baron de Spurtzheim was a man of about five-and-forty. His bronzed complexion, his marked features, and the strange expression of his eye gave him a peculiar aspect, which escaped the notice of the vulgar herd, and caused him to be regarded as a really remarkable man by all intelligent persons.

The only thing known about the baron was his colossal fortune, which he spent royally. As for his antecedents, every one was ignorant of them, although he was received in the first society. It was merely remarked vaguely that he had been a great traveller, and had resided for several years in America; but nothing was more uncertain than these rumours, and they would not have been sufficient to open the *salons* of the noble suburb to him, had not the Austrian ambassador, without his knowledge, served as his guarantee most warmly in several delicate circumstances.

The baron was more intimately connected with the count than with his other companions. He seemed to feel a certain degree of interest in him; and several times, guessing his friend's embarrassed circumstances, he had delicately offered him his assistance. The Count de Lhorailles, though too proud to accept these offers, felt equally grateful to the baron, and had allowed him to assume a certain influence over him, without suspecting it.

"Speak, but be brief, my dear baron," the count said. "You know that the chaise is waiting for me."

Without replying, the baron rang the bell. The waiter came in.

"Dismiss the postilion, and tell him to return at five o'clock. You can go."

The waiter bowed and went out.

The count, more and more amazed at his friend's strange conduct, did not make the least observation. However, he poured out a glass of champagne, which he emptied at a draught, crossed his arms, leant back in his chair, and waited.

"And now, gentlemen," the baron said in his sarcastic and incisive voice, "as our friend De Lhorailles has told us his history, and we are becoming confidential, why should not I tell you mine? The weather is fearful—it is raining torrents. Here we are, comfortably tiled in : we have champagne and regalias—two excellent things when not abused. What have we better to do? 'Nothing,' I hear you say. Listen to me, then, for I believe what I have to tell you will interest you the more, because some among you will not be vexed to know the whole truth about me."

The majority of the guests burst into a laugh at this remark. When their hilarity was calmed the baron began :—

"As for the first part of my story, I shall imitate the count's brevity. In the present age gentlemen find themselves so naturally beyond the pale of the law through the prejudices of blood and education, that they all are fated to pass through a rough apprenticeship to life, by devouring in a few years, they know not how, the paternal fortune. This happened to me, gentlemen, as to yourselves. My ancestors in the middle ages were, to a certain extent, freebooters. True blood always shows itself. When my last resources were nearly exhausted, my instincts were aroused, and my eyes fixed on America. In less than ten years I amassed there the colossal fortune which I now have the distinguished honour, not of dissipating—the lesson was too rude, and I profited by it—but of spending in your honourable company, while careful to keep my capital intact."

" But," the count exclaimed impatiently, " how did you amass this colossal fortune, as you yourself term it?"

" About a million and a half," the baron coolly remarked.

A shudder of covetousness ran through the party.

" A colossal fortune indeed," the count continued; " but, I repeat, how did you acquire it?"

" If I had not intended to reveal it to you, my dear fellow, you may be sure I would not have abused your patience by making you listen to the trivialities you have just heard."

" We are listening," the guests shouted.

The baron coolly looked at them all.

" In the first place let us drink a glass of champagne to our friend's success," he said in his sarcastic tone.

The glasses were filled and emptied again in a twinkling, so great was the curiosity of the auditors. After putting down his glass before him the baron lighted a regalia, and, turning to the count, said to him,—

" I am now addressing myself more particularly to

you, my friend. You are young, enterprising, gifted
with an iron constitution and an energetic will. I am
convinced that, if death does not thwart your plans, you
will succeed, whatever may be the enterprises you
undertake, or the objects you propose to yourself. In
the life you are about to begin, the principal cause of
success, I may say almost the only one, is a thorough
knowledge of the ground on which you are about to
manœuvre, and the society you propose entering. If,
on my entrance upon that adventurous life, I had possessed the good fortune of meeting a friend willing to
initiate me into the mysteries of my new existence, my
fortune would have been made five years earlier. What
no one did for me I am willing to do for you. Perhaps,
at a later date you will be grateful for the information
I have given you, and which will serve as your guide in
the inextricable maze you are about to enter. In the
first place, lay down this principle : the people among
whom you are going to live are your natural enemies.
Hence you will have to support a daily, hourly struggle.
All means must appear to you good to emerge from the
battle a victor. Lay on one side your notions of honour
and delicacy. In America they are vain words, useless
even to make dupes, from the very simple reason that
no one believes in them. The sole deity of America
is gold. To acquire gold the American is capable of
everything; but not, as in old Europe, under the cloak
of honesty, and by a roundabout process, but frankly,
openly, without shame, and without remorse. This laid
down, your line of conduct is ready traced. There is no project, however extravagant it may appear, which in that
country does not offer chances of success ; for the means
of execution are immense, and almost impossible of
control. The American is the man who has best compre-

hended the strength of association : hence it is the lever by means of which all his schemes are carried out. On arriving there alone. without friends or acquaintances, however intelligent and determined you may be. you will be lost, because you find yourself alone in the face of all."

" That is true," the count muttered with conviction.

" Patience!" the baron replied with a smile. " Do you think I intend to send you into action without a cuirass? No, no, I will give you one, and magnificently tempered, too, I assure you."

All those present looked with amazement on this man. who had grown enormously in their esteem in a few moments. The baron feigned not to perceive the impression he produced, and in a minute or so he continued. laying a stress on every word, as if wishful to engrave it more deeply on the count's memory :——

" Remember what I am about to tell you; it is of the utmost importance for you not to forget a word, my friend : from that positively depends the success of your trip to the New World "

" Speak — I am not losing a syllable!" the count interrupted him with a species of febrile impatience.

" When strangers began to flock to America. a company of bold fellows was formed, without faith or law, without pity as without weakness, who, denying all nationality, as they issued from every people, only recognised one government, that which they themselves instituted on Tortoise Island. a desolate rock, lost in the middle of the mighty ocean——a monstrous government; for violence was its basis, and it only admitted of right being might. These bold companions, attached to each other by a Draconian charter, assumed the name of Brethren of the Coast. and were divided into two classes——the Buccaneers and the Filibusters.

" The buccaneers, wandering through the primeval forests, hunted oxen, while the filibusters scoured the seas, attacking every flag, plundering every vessel under the pretext of making war on the Spaniards, but in reality stripping the rich for the benefit of the poor—the only means they discovered to restore the balance between the two classes. The Brethren of the Coast, continually recruited from all the rogues of the old world, became powerful; so powerful, indeed, that the Spaniards trembled for their possessions, and a glorious King of France did not disdain to treat with them, and send an ambassador to them. At last, through the very force of circumstances, like all powers which are the offspring of anarchy, and consequently possess no inherent vitality, when the maritime nations recognised their own strength, the Brethren of the Coast grew gradually weaker, and finally disappeared entirely. By forcing them into obscurity, it was supposed that they were not merely conquered, but annihilated; but it was not so, as you shall now see. I ask your pardon for this long and tedious prologue, but it was indispensable, so that you should better comprehend the rest I have to explain to you."

" It is nearly half-past four," the count observed; " we have not more than forty minutes left us."

" That period, though so short, will be sufficient," the baron answered. " I resume my narrative. The Brethren of the Coast were not destroyed, but transformed. They yielded with extraordinary cleverness to the exigencies of that progress which threatened to outstrip them : they had changed their skin—from tigers they had become foxes. The Brethren of the Coast were converted into *Dauph'yeers*. Instead of boldly boarding the enemies' ships, sword and hatchet in hand, as they

B

formerly did, they became insignificant, and dug mines,
At the present day the Dauph'yeers are the masters and
kings of the New World; they are nowhere and everywhere, but they reign; their influence is felt in all ranks
of society; they are found on every rung of the ladder, but
are never seen. They detached the United States from
England; Peru, Chili, and Mexico, from Spain. Their
power is immense, the more so because it is secret,
ignored, and almost denied, which displays their
strength. For a secret society to be denied existence
is a real power. There is not a revolution in America
in which the influence of the Dauph'yeers does not step
forward valorously, either to insure its triumph or to
crush it. They can do everything—they are everything:
without their circle nothing is possible. Such have the
Brethren of the Coast become, in less than two centuries,
by the force of progress! They are the axis round which
the New World revolves, though it little suspects it. It
is a wretched lot for that magnificent country to have
been condemned, ever since its discovery, to undergo
the tyranny of bandits of every rank, who seem to have
undertaken the mission of exhausting her in every way,
while never giving her the chance of liberating herself."

There was a lengthened silence: each was reflecting
on what he had just heard. The baron himself had
buried his face in his hands, and was lost in that world
of ideas which he had evoked, and which now assailed
him in a mass with sensations of mingled pain and
bitterness.

The distant sound of a rapidly approaching vehicle
recalled the count to the gravity of the situation.

"Here is my chaise," he said. "I am about to set
out, and I know nothing."

" Patience !" the baron replied. " Take leave of your friends, and we will start."

Yielding, in spite of himself, to the influence of this singular man, the count obeyed, without dreaming of offering the slightest opposition. He rose, embraced each of his old friends, exchanged with them hearty hand-shakings, received their auguries of success, and left the room, followed by the baron.

The post-chaise was waiting in front of the house. The young men had opened the windows, and were waving fresh adieux to their friend. The count turned a long look on the Boulevard. The night was gloomy, though the rain no longer fell; the sky was black; and the gas-jets glinted feebly in the distance like stars lost in a fog.

" Farewell," he said in a stifled voice, " farewell ! Who knows whether I shall ever return ? "

" Courage ! " a stern voice whispered in his ear.

The young man shuddered: the baron was at his side.

" Come, my friend," he said, as he helped him to enter the carriage, " I will accompany you to the barrier."

The count got in and fell back on a cushion.

" The Normandy road," the baron shouted to the postilion, as he shut the door.

The driver cracked his whip, and the chaise started at a gallop.

" Good-by ! good-by ! " the young men shouted as they leant out of the windows of the Café Anglais.

For a long time the two men remained silent. At length the baron took the word.

" Gaëtan ! " he said.

" What would you ? " the latter replied.

" I have not yet finished my narrative."

"It is true," he muttered distractedly.

"Do you not wish me to end it?"

"Speak, my friend."

"In what a tone you say that, my good fellow! Your mind is wandering in imaginary space; you are doubtlessly dreaming of those you are leaving."

"Alas!" the count murmured with a sigh, "I am alone in the world. What have I to regret? I possess neither friends nor relations."

"Ungrateful man!" the baron said in a reproachful tone.

"It is true. Pardon me, my dear fellow; I did not think of what I was saying"

"I pardon you, but on condition that you listen to me."

"I promise it."

"My friend, if you desire success, the friendship and protection of those Dauph'yeers I mentioned are indispensable for you."

"How can I obtain them—I, a wretched stranger? How I tremble on thinking of the country in which I dreamed of creating such a glorious future! The veil that covered my eyes is fallen. I see the extravagance of my projects, and all hope abandons me."

"Already?" the baron exclaimed sternly. "Child without energy, to abandon a contest even before having engaged in it! man without strength and courage! I will give you the means, if you like, of obtaining the friendship and protection so necessary for you."

"You!" the count said, quivering with excitement.

"Yes, I! Do you fancy that I have been amusing myself with torturing your mind for the last two hours, like the jaguar plays with the lamb, for the mere pleasure of deriding you? No, Gaëtan. If you had that thought, you were wrong, for I am fond of you. When I learned your scheme I applauded, from the bottom of my heart, that resolution which restored you to your proper place in my mind. When you this night frankly avowed to us your position, and explained your plans, I found myself again in you; my heart beat; for a moment I was happy; and then I vowed to open to you that path so wide, so great, and so noble, that if you do not succeed, it will be because you do not desire to do so."

"Oh!" the count said energetically, "I may succumb in the contest which begins this day between myself and humanity at large, but fear nothing, my friend; I will fall nobly and like a man of courage."

"I am persuaded of it, my friend. I have only a few more words to say to you. I, too, was a Dauph'yeer, and am so still. Thanks to my brethren, I gained the fortune I now possess. Take this portfolio; put round your neck this chain, from which a medallion hangs; then, when you are alone, read the instructions contained in the portfolio, and act as they prescribe. If you follow them point for point, I guarantee your success. That is the present I reserved for you, and which I would not give you till we were alone."

"O heavens!" the count said with effusion.

"Here we are at the barrier," the baron remarked, as he stopped the carriage. "It is time for us to separate. Farewell, my friend! Courage and good-will! Embrace me. Above all, remember the portfolio and the medallion."

The two men remained for a long time in each other's arms. At length the baron freed himself by a vigorous effort, opened the door, and leaped out on the pavement.

"Farewell!" he cried, for the last time; "farewell, Gaëtan! Remember me."

The post-chaise was bowling along the high road at full speed. Strange to say, both men muttered the same word, shaking their heads with discouragement, when they found themselves alone—one walking at full speed along the footpath, the other buried in the cushions.

That word was " Perhaps ! "

The reason was that, despite all their efforts to deceive each other, neither of them hoped.

CHAPTER V.

THE DAUPH'YEERS.

Now let us quit the old world, and, taking an immense stride, transport ourselves to the new one at a single leap.

There is in America a city which possibly cannot be compared to any other in the whole world. That city is Valparaiso.

Valparaiso! The word resounds in the enchanted ear like the gentle and soft notes of a love song.

A coquettish, smiling, and mad city, softly reclining, like a careless Creole, round a delicious bay, at the foot of three majestic mountains, lazily bathing her rosy and dainty feet in the azure waves of the Pacific, and veiling her dreamy brow in the storm-laden clouds which escape from Cape Horn, and roll with a sinister sound round the peaks of the Cordilleras, to form a splendid glory for them.

Although built on the Chilian coast, this strange city belongs, in fact, to no country, and recognises nc nationality; or, to speak more correctly, it admits all into its bosom.

At Valparaiso the adventurers of every clime have

given each other the meeting. All tongues are spoken there, every branch of trade carried on. The population is the quaintest amalgam of the most eccentric personalities, who have rushed from the most remote parts of the four quarters of the world, to attack fortune in this city, the advanced sentinel of Transatlantic civilisation, and whose occult influence governs the Hispano-American republic.

Valparaiso, like nearly all the commercial centres of South America, is a pile of shapeless dens and magnificent palaces jostling each other, and hanging in abrupt clusters on the abrupt flanks of the three mountains.

At the period the event occurred which we are about to describe, the streets were narrow, dirty, deprived of air and sun. The paving, being perfectly ignored, rendered them perfect morasses, in which the wayfarer sank to the knee when the winter's rains had loosened the soil. This rendered the use of a horse indispensable, even for the shortest passage.

Deleterious exhalations incessantly escaped from these mud holes, heightened by the filth of every description which the daily cleaning of the inhabitants accumulated, while no one dreamed of draining these permanent abodes of pernicious fevers.

At the present day, we are told, this state of things has been altered, and Valparaiso no longer resembles itself. We should like to believe it; but the carelessness of the South American, so well known to us, compels us to be very circumspect in such a matter.

In one of the dirtiest and worst-famed streets of Valparaiso was a house, which we ask the reader's permission to describe in a few words.

We are compelled, at the outset, to confess that if

the architect intrusted with its construction had shown himself more than sober in the distribution of the ornaments, he had built it perfectly to suit the trade of the various tenants destined in future to occupy it one after the other.

It was a clay-built hovel. The *façade* looked upon the Street de la Merced ; the opposite side had an outlook of the sea, above which it projected for a certain distance upon posts.

This house was inhabited by an innkeeper. Contrary to European buildings, which grow smaller the higher they rise from the ground, this house grew larger ; so that the upper part was lofty and well lighted, while the shop and other ground-floor rooms were confined and gloomy.

The present occupier had skilfully profited by this architectural arrangement to have a room made in the wall between the first and second floors, which was reached by a turning staircase, concealed in the masonry.

This room was so built that the slightest noise in the street distinctly reached the ears of persons in it, while stifling any they might make, however loud it might be.

The worthy landlord, occupier of this house, had naturally a rather mixed custom of people of every description — smugglers, *rateros*, rogues, and others, whose habits might bring them into unpleasant difficulties with the Chilian police ; consequently, a whale-boat constantly fastened to a ring under a window opening on the sea, offered a provisional but secure shelter to the customers of the establishment whenever, by any accident, the agents of government evinced a desire to pay a domiciliary visit to this den.

This house was known—and probably is still known, unless an earthquake or a fire has caused this rookery to disappear from the face of the earth of Valparaiso— by the name of the *Locanda del Sol.*

On an iron plate suspended from a beam, and creaking with every breath of wind, there had been painted by a native artist a huge red face, surrounded by orange beams, possibly intended as an explanation of the sign to which I have alluded above.

Senor Benito Sarzuela, master of the Locanda del Sol, was a tall, dry fellow, with an angular face and crafty look—a mixture of the Araucano, Negro, and Spaniard, whose *morale* responded perfectly to his *physique ;* that is to say, he combined in himself the vices of the three races to which he belonged—red, black, and white— without possessing one single virtue of theirs, and that beneath the shadow of an avowed and almost honest trade he carried on clandestinely some twenty, the most innocent of which would have taken him to the *presidios* or galleys for life, had he been discovered.

Some two months after the events we described in a previous chapter, about eleven of the clock on a cold and misty night, Senor Benito Sarzuela was seated in melancholy mood within his bar, contemplating with mournful eye the deserted room of his establishment.

The wind blowing violently, caused the sign of the *meson* to creak on its hinges with gloomy complaints, and the heavy black clouds coming from the south moved weightily athwart the sky, dropping at intervals heavy masses of rain on the ground loosened by previous storms.

" Come," the unhappy host muttered to himself with a piteous air, " there is another day which finishes as badly as the others. *Sangre de Dios !* for the last week I have had no luck. If it continues only a fortnight longer I shall be a ruined man."

In fact, through a singular accident, for about a month the Locanda del Sol had been completely shorn of its old brilliancy, and the landlord did not know any reason for its eclipse.

The sound of clanking glasses and cups was no longer heard in the room usually affected by the thirsty souls. Strange change in human things! Abundance had been too suddenly followed by the most perfect vacuum. It might be said that the plague reigned in this deserted house. The bottles remained methodically arranged on the shelves, and hardly two passers-by had come in during the past day to drink a glass of *pisco,* which they hastily paid for, so eager were they to quit this den, in spite of the becks, and nods, and wreathed smiles of the host, who tried in vain to keep them to talk of public affairs, and, above all, cheer his solitude.

After the few words we have heard him utter, the worthy Don Benito rose carelessly, and prepared, with many an oath, to close his establishment, so as at any rate to save in candles, when suddenly an individual entered, then two, then three, then six, then ten, and at last such a number that the locandero gave up all attempts at counting them.

These men were all wrapped up in large cloaks; their heads were covered by felt hats, whose broad brims, pulled down carefully over their eyes, rendered them perfectly unrecognisable.

The room was soon crowded with customers drinking and smoking, but not uttering a word.

The extraordinary thing was that, although all the tables were lined, such a religious silence prevailed among these strange bibbers that the noise of the rain pattering outside could be distinctly heard, as well as the footfalls of the horses ridden by the serenos, which resounded hoarsely on the pebbles, or in the muddy ponds that covered the ground.

The host, agreeably surprised by this sudden turn of fortune, had joyfully set to work serving his unexpected customers; but all at once a singular thing happened, which Senor Sarzuela was far from anticipating. Although the proverb says that you can never have enough of a good thing—and proverbs are the wisdom of nations —it happened that the affluence of people, who appeared to have made an appointment at his house, became so considerable, and assumed such gigantic proportions, that the landlord himself began to feel terrified; for his hostelry, empty a moment previously, was now so crammed that he soon did not know where to put the new arrivals who continued to flock in. In fact, the crowd, after filling the common room, had, like a rising tide, flowed over into the adjoining room, then it escaladed the stairs, and spread over the upper floors.

At the first stroke of eleven more than two hundred customers occupied the Locanda del Sol.

The locandero, with that craft which was one of the most salient points of his character, then comprehended that something extraordinary was about to happen, and that his house would be the scene.

At the thought a convulsive tremor seized upon him, his hair began to stand on end, and he sought in his brain for the means he must employ to get rid of these sinister and silent guests.

In his despair he rose with an air which he sought to render most resolute, and walked to the door as if for the purpose of closing his establishment. The customers, still silent as fish, did not make a sign of moving; on the contrary, they pretended they noticed nothing.

Don Benito felt his nervousness redoubled.

Suddenly the voice of a sereno rising in the distance furnished him with the pretext he vainly sought, by shouting as he passed the locanda,—

"*Ave Maria purissima!   Las onze han dado y lluve.*"*

Although accompanied by modulations capable of making a dog weep, the sacramental cry of the sereno absolutely produced no impression on mine host's customers.   The force of terror at length restoring him a slight degree of courage, Senor Sarzuela decided on directly addressing his obstinate customers.   For this purpose he deliberately posted himself in the centre of the room, thrust his fist in his side, and raising his head, said in a voice which he tried in vain to render firm, but whose tremor he could not hide,—

"Senores caballeros, it is eleven o'clock.   The police regulations forbid me keeping open longer.   Have the goodness, I beg you, to withdraw without delay, so that I may close my establishment."

This harangue, from which he promised himself the greatest success, produced an effect exactly contrary to what he expected.   The strangers vigorously smote the table with their glasses, shouting unanimously,—

"Drink!"

The landlord bounded back at this fearful disturbance.

"Still, caballeros," he ventured to remark, after a moment's hesitation, "the police regulations are severe. It is eleven, and——"

* I salute you, most pure Mary! Eleven has struck, and it rains.

He could say no more: the noise recommenced with even greater intensity, and the customers shouted together, in a voice of thunder, "Drink!"

A reaction, easy to comprehend, then took place in the mind of mine host. Fancying that a personal attack was made on himself, persuaded that his interests were at stake, the coward disappeared to make room for the miser, threatened in what is dearest to him—his property.

"Ah," he shouted in feverish exasperation, "that is the game! Well, we will see if I am master in my own house. I will go and fetch the alcade."

This threat of justice from the mouth of the worthy Sarzuela appeared so droll, that the customers broke out, with a unanimity which did them all credit, into a burst of Homeric laughter right under the poor fellow's nose. This was the *coup de grâce*. The host's anger was converted into raving madness, and he rushed head foremost at the door, under the laughter and inextinguishable shouts of his persecutors. But he had hardly crossed the threshold of his house ere a new arrival seized him unceremoniously by the arm, and hurled him back roughly into the room, saying in a bantering voice,—

"What fly has stung you, my dear landlord? Are you mad to go out bare-headed in such weather, at the risk of catching a pleurisy?"

And then, while the locandero, terrified and confounded by this rude shock, tried to regain his balance and re-establish a little order in his ideas, the unknown, as coolly as if he were at home, had, with the help of some of the customers, to whom he made signs, shut the shutters and bolted the door with as much care as Sarzuela himself usually devoted to this delicate operation.

" There, now that is done," the stranger said, turning to the amazed host, " suppose we have a chat, *compadre?* Ah! I suppose you do not recognise me?" he added, as he removed his hat and displayed a fine intelligent face, over which a mocking smile was at this moment playing.

" Oh, el Senor Don Gaëtano!" said Sarzuela, whom this meeting was far from pleasing, and who tried to conceal a horrible grimace.

" Silence!" the other said. " Come hither."

With a gesture he drew the landlord into a corner of the room, and, leaning down to his ear, said in a low voice,—

" Are there any strangers in your house?"

" Look!" he said with a piteous glance, as he pointed to the still drinking customers, " that legion of demons invaded my house an hour back. They drink well, it is true; but there is something suspicious about them not at all encouraging to an honest man."

" The more reason that you should have nothing to fear. Besides, I am not alluding to them. I ask you if you have any strange lodgers? As for those men, you know them as well as I do, perhaps better."

" From top to bottom of my house I have no other persons than these caballeros, whom you say I know. It is very possible; but as ever since they have been here, thanks to the way in which they are muffled, it has been impossible for me to see the tip of a nose, I was utterly unable to recognise them."

" You are a donkey, my good friend. These men who bother you so greatly are all Dauph'yeers."

" Really!" the amazed host exclaimed; " then why do they hide their faces?"

" My faith, Master Sarzuela, I fancy it is probably because they do not wish to have them seen."

And laughing at the landlord, who was sadly out of countenance. the stranger made a sign. Two men rose, rushed on the poor fellow, and before he could even guess what they intended, he found himself so magnificently garotted that he could not even cross himself.

"Fear nothing, Master Sarzuela; no harm will befall you," the stranger continued. "We only want to talk without witnesses, and as you are naturally a chatterer, we take our precautions, that is all. So be calm; in a few hours you will be free. Come, look sharp, you fellows," he continued, addressing his men. "Gag him, lay him on his bed, and turn the key in his door. Good-by, my worthy host, and pray keep calm."

The stranger's orders were punctually executed; the luckless Sarzuela, tied and gagged, was carried from the room on the shoulders of two of his assailants, borne upstairs, thrown on his bed, and locked in in a twinkling, before he had even time to think of the slightest resistance.

We will leave him to indulge in the gloomy reflections which probably assailed him in a throng so soon as he was alone, face to face with his despair, and return to the large room of the locanda, where persons far more interesting to us than the poor landlord are awaiting us.

The Dauph'yeers, so soon as they found themselves masters of the hostelry, ranged the tables one on the other against the walls, so as to clear the centre of the room, and drew up the benches in a line, on which they then seated themselves.

The Locanda del Sol, owing to the changes it underwent, was in a few moments completely metamorphosed into a club.

The last arrival, the man who had given the order to

gag the host, enjoyed, according to all appearances, a certain influence over the honourable company collected at this moment in the ground-floor room of the hostelry. So soon as the master of the house had disappeared he took off his cloak, made a sign commanding silence, and speaking in excellent French, said in a clear and sonorous voice,—

" Brethren, thanks for your punctuality."

The Dauph'yeers politely returned his salute.

" Gentlemen," he continued, " our projects are advancing. Soon, I hope, we shall attain the object to which we have so long been tending, and quit that obscurity in which we are languishing, to conquer our place in the sunshine. America is a marvellous land, in which every ambition can be satisfied. I have taken all the necessary measures, as I pledged myself to you to do a fortnight ago, when I had the honour of convening you for the first time. We have succeeded. You were kind enough to appoint me director of the Mexican movement, and I thank you for it, gentlemen. A concession of three thousand acres of land has been made me at Guetzalli, in Upper Sonora. The first step has been taken. My lieutenant, De Laville, started yesterday for Mexico, to take possession of the granted territory. I have to-day another request to make of you. You who listen to me here are all Europeans or North Americans, and you will understand me. For a very long time the Dauph'yeers, the successors of the Brethren of the Coast, have been calmly watching, as apparently disinterested spectators of the endless drama of the American republics, the sudden changes and shameless revolutions of the old Spanish colonies. The hour has arrived to throw ourselves into the contest. I need one hundred and fifty devoted men. Guetzalli will serve them as a temporary refuge. I shall soon tell them what I expect from their courage ; but you must strive to carry out what I attempt. The enterprise I meditate, and in which I shall possibly perish, is entirely in the interest of the association. If I succeed, every man who took part in it will have a large reward and splendid position insured him. You know the man who introduced me to you, and he had gained your entire confidence. The medal he gave me, and which I now show you, proves to you that he entirely responds for me. Will you, in your turn, trust in me as he has done ? Without you I can do nothing. I await your reply."

He was silent. His auditors began a long discussion among themselves, though in a low voice, which they carried on for some time. At length silence was restored, and a man rose.

" Count Gaëtan de Lhorailles," he said, " my brethren have requested me to answer you in their name. You presented yourself to us, supported by the recommendation of a man in whom we have the most entire confidence. Your conduct has appeared to confirm this recommendation. The one hundred and fifty men you ask for are ready to follow you, no matter whither you may lead them, persuaded as they are that they can only gain by seconding your plans. I, Diégo Léon, inscribe myself at the head of the list."

" And I !"
" And I !"
" And I !"

The Dauph'yeers shouted, outvying each other. The count gave a signal, and the silence was re-established.

" Brothers, I thank you," he said. " The nucleus of our association will remain at Valparaiso, and if I need them I will draw from that city the resolute men I may presently want. For the moment one hundred and fifty men are sufficient for me. If my plans succeed, who knows what the future may have in store for us? I have drawn up a charter-party, all the stipulations of which will be rigorously kept by myself, and by you, I have no doubt. Read and sign. In two days I start for Talca; but in six weeks I will meet here those among you who consent to follow me, and then I will communicate to them my plans in their fullest details."

"Captain de Lhorailles," Diégo Léon replied, " you say that you have only need of one hundred and fifty men. Draw them by lots, then ; for all wish to accompany you."

"Thank you once again, my brave comrades. Believe me, each shall have his turn. The project I have formed is grand and worthy of you. Selection would only arouse jealousy among men all equally worthy. Diégo Léon, I intrust to you the duty of drawing lots for the names of those who are to form part of the first expedition."

"It shall be done," said Léon, a methodical and steady Bearnese, and ex-corporal of the Spahis.

"And now, my friends, one last word. Remember that in three months I shall expect you at Guetzalli; and, by the aid of Heaven, the star of the Dauph'yeer shall not be dimmed. Drink, brothers, drink to the success of our enterprise !"

"Let us drink!" all the Brethren of the Coast shouted, quite electrified.

The wine and brandy then began flowing. The whole night was spent in an orgie, whose proportions became, towards morning, gigantic. The Count de Lhorailles—thanks to the talisman the baron gave him on parting—had found himself, immediately on his arrival in America, at the head of resolute and unscrupulous men, by whose help it was easy for an intellect like his to accomplish great things.

Two months after the meeting to which we have introduced the reader, the count and his one hundred and fifty Dauph'yeers were assembled at the colony of Guetzalli—that magnificent concession which M. de Lhorailles had obtained through his occult influences.

The count appeared to command good fortune, and everything he undertook succeeded. The projects which appeared the wildest were carried out by him. His colony prospered, and assumed proportions which delighted the Mexican government. The count, with the tact and knowledge of the world he thoroughly possessed, had caused the jealous and the curious to be silent. He had created a circle of devoted friends and useful acquaintances, who on various occasions pleaded in his behalf, and supported him by their credit.

Our readers can judge of the progress he had made in so short a time—scarce three years—when we say that, at the moment we introduce him on the stage, he had almost attained the object of his constant efforts. He was about to gain an honourable rank in society by marrying the daughter of Don Sylva de Torrès, one of the richest hacienderos in Sonora; and through the influence of his future father-in-law he had just received a commission as captain of a free corps, intended to repulse the incursions of the Comanches and Apaches on the Mexican territory, and the right of forming this company exclusively of Europeans if he thought proper.

We will now return to the house of Don Sylva de Torrès, which we left almost at the moment the Count de Lhorailles entered it.

CHAPTER VI.

BY THE WINDOW.

WHEN the young lady left the sitting-room to retire to her sleeping apartment, the count followed her with a lengthened look, apparently not at all understanding the extraordinary conduct of his betrothed, especially under the circumstances in which they stood to each other, as they were so shortly to be married; but, after a few moments' reflection, the count shook his head, as if to dispel the mournful thoughts by which he was assailed, and, turning to Don Sylva, said,—

"Let us talk about business matters. Are you agreeable?"

"Have you anything new, then, to tell me?"

"Many things."

"Interesting?"

"You shall be the judge."

"Go on, then. I am all impatience to hear them."

"Let us proceed in rotation. You are aware, my friend, why I left Guetzalli?"

"Perfectly. Well, have you succee ed?"

"As I expected. Thanks to certain letters of which I was the bearer, and, above all, your kind recommendation, General Marcos received me in the most charming manner. The reception he deigned to accord me was most affectionate. In short, he gave me *carte blanche*, authorising me to raise, not merely one hundred and fifty men, but double the number if I considered it necessary."

"Oh! that is magnificent."

"Is it not? He told me also that in a war like that I was about to undertake—for my chase of the Apaches is a real war—he left me at liberty to act as I pleased, ratifying beforehand all I might do, being persuaded, as he added, that it would ever be for the interest and glory of Mexico."

" Come, I am delighted with the result. And now, what are your intentions ? "

" I have resolved on quitting you to proceed, in the first place, to Guetzalli, whence I have now been absent nearly three weeks. I want to revisit my colony, in order to see if all goes on as I would wish, and if my men are happy. On the other hand, I shall not be sorry, before departing for possibly a long period with the greater part of my forces, to protect my colonists from a *coup de main*, by throwing up round the establishment earth-works strong enough to repulse an assault of the savages. This is the more important, because Guetzalli must always remain, to a certain extent, my head quarters."

" All right ; and you start ? "

" This very evening."

" So soon ? "

" I must. You are aware how time presses at present."

" It is true. Have you nothing more to say to me ? "

" Pardon me, I have one other point which I expressly reserved for the last."

" You attach a great interest to it, then ? "

" Immense."

" Oh, oh ! I am listening to you, then, my friend. Speak quickly."

" On my arrival in this country, at a period when the enterprises I have since successfully carried out were only in embryo, you were good enough, Don Sylva, to place at my disposal not only your credit, which is immense, but your riches, which are incalculable."

"It is true," the Mexican said with a smile.

"I availed myself largely of your offers, frequently assailing your strong box, and employing your credit whenever the occasion presented itself. Permit me now to settle with you the only part of the debt I can discharge, for I am incapable of repaying the other. Here," he added, taking a paper from his portfolio, "is a bill for 100,000 piastres, payable at sight on Walter Blount and Co., bankers, of Mexico. I am happy, believe me, Don Sylva, to be able to pay this debt so promptly, not because——"

"Pardon me," the haciendero quickly interrupted him, and declining with a gesture the paper the count offered him, "we no longer understand each other, it seems to me."

"How so?"

"I will explain. On your arrival at Guaymas, you presented yourself to me, bearer of a pressing letter of recommendation from a man to whom I owed very great obligations a few years back. The Baron de Spurtzheim described you to me rather as a beloved son than as a friend in whom he took interest. My house was at once opened to you—it was my duty to do so. Then, when I knew you, and could appreciate all that was noble and grand in your character, our relations, at first rather cold, became closer and more intimate. I offered you my daughter's hand, which you accepted."

"And gladly so," the count explained.

"Very good," the haciendero continued with a smile. "The money I could receive from a stranger—money which he honestly owes me—belongs to my son-in-law. Tear up that paper, then, my dear count, and pray do not think of such a trifle."

"Ah!" the count said, in a tone of vexation, "that

was exactly what troubled me. I am not your son-in-law yet, and may I confess it? I fear I never shall be."

"What can make you fancy that? Have you not my promise? The word of Don Sylva de Torrès, Sir Count de Lhorailles, is a pledge which no one has ever yet dared to doubt."

"And for that reason I have no such idea. It is not you I am afraid of."

"Who, then?"

"Dona Anita."

"Oh, oh! my friend, you must explain yourself, for I confess I do not understand you at all," Don Sylva said sharply, as he rose and began walking up and down the room in considerable agitation.

"Good gracious, my friend, I am quite in despair at having produced this discussion! I love Dona Anita. Love, as you know, easily takes umbrage. Although my betrothed has ever been amiable, kind, and gracious to me, still I confess that I fancy she does not love me."

"You are mad, Don Gaëtano. Young girls know not what they like or dislike. Do not trouble yourself about such childish things. I promised that she shall be your wife, and it shall be so."

"Still, if she loved another, I should not like——"

"What! Really what you say has not common sense. Anita loves no one but you, I am sure; and stay, would you like to be quite reassured? You say that you start for Guetzalli this evening?"

"Yes."

"Very good. Prepare apartments for my daughter nd myself. In a few days we will join you at your hacienda."

"Is it possible?" the count said joyfully.

" To-morrow at daybreak we will start; so make haste."

" A thousand thanks."

" Come, you are now easier? "

" I am the happiest of mortals."

" All the better."

The two men exchanged a few words further, and separated with renewed promises of meeting again soon.

Don Sylva, accustomed to command despotically in his establishment, and to allow no one to discuss his will, told his daughter, through a waiting-maid, that she must prepare for a rather long journey the next morning, and felt certain of her obedience.

The news was a thunderbolt for the young lady She sank half fainting into an easy chair, and melted into tears. It was evident to her that this journey was only a pretext to separate her from the man she loved, and place her, a defenceless victim, in the power of the man she abhorred, and who was to be her husband. The poor child remained thus for several hours, a prey to violent despair, and not dreaming of seeking impossible repose; for, in the state in which she found herself, she knew that sleep would not close her eyes, all swollen with tears, and red with fever.

Gradually the sounds of the town died away one after the other. All slept, or seemed to sleep. Don Sylva's house was plunged into complete darkness; a weak light alone glistened like a star through the young girl's windows, proving that there at least some one was watching.

At this moment two hesitating shadows were cast on the wall opposite the haciendero's house. Two men, wrapped in long cloaks, stopped and examined the dimly-lighted window with that attention only found in thieves and lovers. The two men to whom we allude incontestably belonged to the latter category.

"Hum!" the first said in a sharp but suppressed voice, "you are certain of what you assert, Cucharès?"

"As of my eternal salvation, Senor Don Martial," the scamp replied in the same tone. "The accursed Englishman entered the house while I was there. Don Sylva appeared on the best terms with the heretic. May his soul be confounded!"

We may here remark that a few years ago, and possibly even now, in the eyes of the Mexicans all foreigners were English, no matter the nation to which they belonged, and consequently heretics. Hence they naturally ranked, though little suspecting it, with the men whom it is no crime to kill, but whose assassination is rather looked upon as a meritorious action. We are bound to add, to the credit of the Mexicans, that whenever the occasion offered, they killed the English with an ardour which was a sufficient proof of their piety.

Don Martial continued :—

"On the faith of the Tigrero, this man has twice crossed my path, and I have spared him; but let him be careful against the third meeting."

"Oh!" Cucharès said, "the reverend Fray Becchico says that a man gains splendid indulgences by 'cutting' an Englishman. I have not yet had the luck to come across one, although I owe about eight dead men. I am much inclined to indulge myself with this one; it would be so much gained."

"On thy life, picaro, let him alone. That man belongs to me."

"Well, we 'll not mention it again," he replied, stifling a sigh; "I will leave him to you. For all that it annoys me, although the nina seems to detest him cordially."

" Have you any proof of what you say ? "

" What better proof than the repugnance she displays so soon as he appears, and the pallor which then covers her face without any apparent cause? "

" Ah ! I would give a thousand ounces to know what to believe."

" What prevents you ?   Everybody is asleep—no one will see you.   The story is not high—fifteen feet at the most.   I am certain that Dona Anita would be delighted to have a chat with you."

" Oh, if I could but believe it !" he muttered with hesitation, casting a side glance at the still lighted window.

" Who knows ? perhaps she is expecting you."

" Silence, you scoundrel !"

" By 'r Lady, only listen ! If what is said be true, the poor child must be in a perplexity, if not worse: she has probably great need of assistance."

" What do they say ?   Come, speak, but be brief."

" A very simple thing—that Dona Anita de Torrès marries within a week the Englishman, Don Gaëtano."

" You lie, villain !" the Tigrero said with badly-restrained wrath.   " I know not what prevents me thrusting down your throat with my dagger the odious words you have just uttered."

" You would do wrong," the other said, without being in the least disconcerted.   " I am only an echo that repeats what it hears, nothing more.   You alone in all Guaymas are ignorant of this news.   After all, there is nothing astonishing in that, as you have only returned to town this day, after an absence of more than a month."

" That is true ; but what is to be done?"

" Caraï ! follow the advice I give you."

The Tigrero turned another long glance on the window, and let his head sink with an irresolute air.

" What will she say on seeing me ?" he muttered.

" Caramba ! " the lepero said in a sarcastic tone, " she will cry, ' You are welcome, *alma mia !*' It is clear, caraï ! Don Martial, have you become a timid child, that a woman's glance can make you tremble? Opportunity has only three hairs, in love as in war. You must seize her when she presents herself : if you do not, you run a risk of never meeting her again."

The Mexican approached the lepero near enough to touch him, and, fixing his glance on his tiger-cat eyes, said in a low and concentrated voice,—

" Cucharès, I trust in you. You know me. I have often come to your assistance. Were you to deceive my confidence I would kill you like a coyote."

The Tigrero pronounced these words with such an accent of dull fury, that the lepero, who knew the man before whom he was standing, turned pale in spite of himself, and felt a shudder of terror pass through his limbs.

" I am devoted to you, Don Martial," he replied in a voice, which he tried in vain to render firm. " Whatever may happen, count on me. What must I do ? "

" Nothing; but wait, watch, and at the least suspicious sound, the first hostile shadow that appears in the darkness, warn me."

" Count on me. Go to work. I am deaf and dumb, and during your absence I will watch over you like a son over his father."

" Good !" the Tigrero said.

He drew a few steps nearer, undid the reata fastened round his loins, and held it in his right hand. Then he raised his eyes, measured the distance, and turning the reata forcibly round his head, hurled it into Dona Anita's balcony. The running knot caught in an iron hook, and remained firmly attached.

"Remember!" the Tigrero said, as he turned toward Cucharès.

"Go on," the latter said, as he leaned against the wall and crossed his legs; "I answer for everything."

Don Martial was satisfied, or feigned to be satisfied, with this assurance. He seized the reata, and taking a leap, like one of those panthers he had so often tracked on the prairies, he raised himself by the strength of his wrists, and speedily reached the balcony. He climbed over and went up to the window.

Dona Anita was asleep, half reclining in an easy chair. The poor girl, pale and exhausted, her eyes swollen with tears, had been conquered by sleep, which never gives up its claim on young and vigorous constitutions. On her marbled cheeks the tears had traced a long furrow, which was still humid. Martial surveyed with a tender glance the woman he loved, though not daring to approach her. Surprised thus during her sleep, Anita appeared to him even more beautiful; a halo of purity and candour seemed to surround her, watch over her repose, and render her holy and unassailable.

After a long and voluptuous contemplation, the Tigrero at length decided on advancing. The window, which was only leaned to (for the young girl had not dreamed of falling to sleep, as she had done), opened at the slightest push. Don Martial took one step, and found himself in the room. At the sight of this virginal chamber a religious respect fell on the Tigrero: he felt his heart beat rebelliously; and tottering, mad with fear and love, he fell on his knees by the side of the being he adored.

Anita opened her eyes.

"Oh!" she exclaimed, on seeing Don Martial,

" blessed be God, since He sends you to my assistance ! "

The Tigrero surveyed her with moistened eye and
panting chest. But suddenly the girl drew herself up;
her memory returned, and with it that timid modesty
innate in all women.

" Begone," she said, recoiling to the extremity of the
room, " begone, caballero ! How are you here ? Who
led you to my room ? Answer, I command you."

The Tigrero humbly bowed his head.

" God," he said, in an inarticulate voice, " God alone
has conducted me to your side, senorita, as you yourself
said. Oh, pardon me for having dared to surprise you
thus ! I have committed a great fault, I am aware ;
but a misfortune menaces you—I feel it, I guess it.
You are alone, without support, and I have come to say
to you, ' Madam, I am very low, very unworthy to serve
you, but you have need of a firm and devoted heart.
Here I am ! Take my blood, take my life. I would be
so happy to die for you !' In the name of Heaven,
senora, in the name of what you love most on earth, do
not reject my prayer. My arm, my heart, are yours :
dispose of them."

These words were uttered by the young man in a
choking voice, as he knelt in the middle of the room,
his hands clasped, and fixing on Dona Anita his eyes,
into which he had thrown his entire soul.

The haciendero's daughter turned her limpid glance
on the young man, and, without removing her eyes,
approached him with short steps, hesitating and trembling despite herself. When she arrived near him
she remained for a moment undecided. At length she
laid her two small, dainty hands on his shoulders, and
placed her gentle face so near his, that the Tigrero felt

on his forehead the freshness of her embalmed breath, while her long, black, and perfumed tresses gently caressed him.

"It is true, then," she said in an harmonious voice, "you love me, Don Martial?"

"Oh!" the young man murmured, almost mad with love at this delicious contact.

The Mexican girl bent over him still more, and grazing with her rosy lips the Tigrero's moist brow,—

"Now," she said to him, starting back with the ravishing movement of a startled fawn, while her brow turned purple with the effort she had made to overcome her modesty, "now defend me, Don Martial; for in the presence of God, who sees us and judges us, I am your wife!"

The Tigrero leaped on his feet beneath the corrosive sting of this kiss. With a radiant brow and sparkling eyes, he seized the girl's **arm**, and drawing her to a corner of the room, where was a statue of the Virgin, before which perfumed oil was burning,—

"On your knees, senorita," he said in an inspired voice, and himself bowed the knee.

The girl obeyed him.

"Holy Mother of Sorrow!" Don Martial went on, *Nuestra Senora de la Soledad!* divine succour of the afflicted, who soundest all hearts! thou seest the purity of our souls, the holiness of our love. Before thee I take for my wife Dona Anita de Torrès. I swear to defend and protect her, before and against everybody, even if I lose my life in the contest I commence this day for the happiness of her I love, and who from this day forth is really my betrothed."

After pronouncing this oath in a firm voice the Tigrero turned to the maiden.

" It is your turn now, senorita," he said to her.

The girl fervently clasped her hands, and raising her tear-laden eyes to the holy image,—

" Nuestra Senora de la Soledad," she said in a voice broken with emotion, " thou, my only protector since the day of my birth, knowest how truly I am devoted to thee ! I swear that all this man has said is the truth. I take him for my husband in thy sight, and will never have another."

They rose, and Dona Anita led the Tigrero to the balcony.

" Go !" she said to him. " Don Martial's wife must not be suspected. Go, my husband, my brother ! The man to whom they want to deliver me is called the Count de Lhorailles. To-morrow at daybreak we leave this place, probably to join him."

" And he ? "

" Started this night."

" Where is he going ? "

" I know not."

" I will kill him."

" Farewell, Don Martial, farewell ! "

" Farewell, Dona Anita ! Take courage; I am watching over you."

And after imprinting a last and chaste kiss on the pure brow of the young girl he clambered over the balcony, and hanging by the reata, glided down into the street. The haciendero's daughter unfastened the running knot, leant out, and followed the Tigrero so long as she could see him; then she closed the window again.

" Alas, alas ! " she murmured, suppressing a sigh, " what have I done ? Holy Virgin, thou alone canst restore me the courage which is deserting me."

She let the curtain fall which veiled the window, and turned to go and kneel before the Virgin; but suddenly she recoiled, uttering a cry of terror. Two paces from her Don Sylva was standing with frowning brow and stern face.

"Dona Anita, my daughter," he said, in a slow and stern voice, "I have seen and heard everything; spare yourself, then, I beg you, all useless denial."

"My father!" the poor child stammered in a broken voice.

"Silence!" he continued. "It is three o'clock: we set out at sunrise. Prepare yourself to marry in a fortnight Don Gaëtano de Lhorailles."

And, without deigning to add a word, he walked out slowly, carefully closing the door after him.

So soon as she was alone the young girl bent down as if listening, tottered a few steps forward, raised her hands with a nervous gesture to her contracted throat—then uttering a piercing cry, fell back on the floor.

She had fainted.

CHAPTER VII.

A DUEL.

It was about eight in the evening when the Count de Lhorailles left the residence of Don Sylva de Torrès. The *feria de plata* was then in all its splendour. The streets of Guaymas were thronged with a joyful and motley crowd; the shouts of songs and laughter rose on every side. The piles of gold heaped on the monté tables emitted their yellow and intoxicating reflection in the dazzling gleams of the lights that shone in every door and window: here and there the sounds of the *vihuelas* and *jarabès* escaped from the pulquerias, invaded by the drinkers. The count, elbowed and elbowing, traversed as quickly as was possible the dense groups which at every instant barred his passage; but the conversation he had had with Don Sylva had put him in too happy a temper for him to dream of being vexed at the numerous collisions he endured at every moment.

At length, after numberless difficulties, and wasting at least thrice the time he would have employed under other circumstances, he reached at about ten in the evening, the house where he lodged. He had spent about two hours in covering less than six hundred yards.

On arriving at the meson, the count proceeded first to the corral to see his horse, to which he gave, with his own hand, two trusses of alfalfa; then, after ordering that he should be called at one o'clock, if by accident (which was most improbable) he was not up by that time, he retired to his *cuarto* to take a few hours' rest.

The count intended to start at such an early hour in order to avoid the heat of the day, and travel more quickly. Besides, after his lengthened conversation with Don Sylva, the noble adventurer was not sorry to find himself alone, in order to go over in his mind all the happy things that had happened during the past evening.

From the moment he had landed in America the count had enjoyed—to employ a familiar term—a shameful good luck: everything succeeded with him. In a few months his fortune might be thus summed up: —A colony founded under the most favourable auspices, and already on the road of progress and improvement: while keeping his nationality intact—that is to say, his liberty of action and an inviolable neutrality—he was

G

in the service of the Mexican Government, as captain
of a free corps of one hundred and fifty devoted men,
with whom he could attempt, if not carry out, the
wildest enterprises. In the last place, he was on the
point of marrying the daughter of a man twenty times a
millionaire, as far as he had opportunity of judging;
and what in no way spoiled the affair, his betrothed was
delightful.

Unfortunately, or fortunately, according to the stand-
point our readers may think proper to take in judging
of our hero, this man, worn out by the enervating
eccentricities of Parisian life, no longer felt his heart
beat from any emotion of joy, sorrow, or fear: all was
dead within him. He was exactly the man wanted
to succeed in the country to which accident had sent
him. In the great duel of life he had begun in
America he had an immense advantage over his adversaries—that of never allowing himself to be directed
by passion; and consequently, owing to his unalterable
coolness, he was enabled to evade the pitfalls incessantly laid for him, over which he triumphed without
appearing to notice them.

After what we have said we have hardly need to add
that he did not love the woman whose hand he sought.
She was young and lovely—all the better. Had she
been old and ugly he would have accepted her hand
all the same. What did he care? He only sought
one thing in marriage—a brilliant and envied position.
In fine, the Count de Lhorailles was all calculation.
We have made a mistake, however, in affirming that
he had not a weak point. He was ambitious. This
passion, one of the most violent of those with which
Heaven has afflicted the human race, was possibly the
only link by which the count was still attached to

humanity. Ambition in him had reached such a pitch, especially during the last few months—it had taken such an immense development—that he would have sacrificed all to it.

Now let us see what was the object of this man's ambition. What future did he dream of ? It is probable that we may explain this to the reader in fuller detail presently.

The count went to bed ; that is to say, after wrapping himself carefully in his zarapè, he stretched himself on the leathern frame which throughout Mexico is the substitute for beds, whose existence is completely ignored. So soon as he lay down he fell asleep, with that conscience peculiar to the adventurer whose every hour is claimed beforehand, and who, having but a few moments to grant to rest, hastens to profit by them, and sleeps, as the Spaniards say, *a la pierna suelta*, which we may translate nearly by sleeping with closed fists.

At one in the morning the count, as he had promised, awoke, lighted the *cebo* which served him as candle, arranged his toilette to a certain extent, carefully examined his pistols and rifle, and assured himself that his sabre left the scabbard easily ; then, when all these various preparations, indispensable for every traveller careful for his safety, were ended, he opened the door of the cuarto and proceeded to the corral.

His horse was eating heartily, and gaily finishing its alfalfa. The count himself gave it a measure of oats, which he saw it dispose of with neighs of pleasure, and then put on the saddle. In Mexico especially, horsemen, whatever the class of society to which they belong, never leave to others the care of attending to their steeds · for in those semi-savage countries the life of the rider depends nearly always upon the vigour and speed of his animal.

The door of the meson was only leaned to, so that the travellers might start whenever they pleased without disturbing anybody. The count lit his cigar, leaped into the saddle, and started on a trot along the road leading to the Rancho. Nothing is so agreeable as night travelling in Mexico. The earth, refreshed by the night breeze, and bedewed by the copious dew, exhales acrid and perfumed scents, whose beneficent emanations restore the body all its vigour, and the mind its lucidity. The moon, just on the point of disappearing, profusely scattered its oblique rays, which lengthened immoderately the shadow of the trees growing at intervals along the road, and made them in the obscurity resemble a legion of fleshless spectres. The sky, of a deep azure, was studded with an infinite number of glistening stars, in the midst of which flashed the dazzling southern cross, to which the Indians have given the name of *Poron Chayké*. The wind breathed gently through the branches, in which the blue jay uttered at intervals the melodious notes of its melancholy song, with which were mingled at times, in the profundities of the desert, the howling of the couguar, the sharp miauw of the panther or the ounce, and the hoarse bark of the coyotes in search of prey.

The count, on leaving Guaymas, had hurried on his horse ; but subjugated, in spite of himself, by the irresistible attractions of this autumn night, he gradually checked the pace of his steed, and yielded to the flood of thoughts which mounted incessantly to his brain, and plunged him into a gentle reverie. The descendant of an ancient and haughty Frank race, alone in this desert, he mentally surveyed the splendour of his name so long eclipsed, and his heart expanded with joy and pride on reflecting that the task was reserved for him perhaps to rehabilitate those from whom he descended, and restore, this time eternally, the fortunes of his family, of which he had hitherto proved such a bad guardian.

This land, which he trampled under foot, would restore him what he had lost and madly squandered a hundredfold. The moment had at length arrived when, free from all hobbles, he was about to realise those plans for the future so long engraved on his brain. He went on thus, travelling in the country of chimeras, and so absorbed in his thoughts, that he no longer troubled himself with what went on around him.

The stars were beginning to turn pale in the heavens, and be extinguished in turn. The dawn was tracing a white line, which gradually assumed a reddish tint on the distant obscurity of the horizon. On the approach of day the air became fresher; then the count, aroused—if we may employ the term—by the icy impression produced on him by the bountiful desert dew, pulled the folds of his zarapè over his shoulders with a shudder, and started at a gallop, directing a glance to the sky, and muttering,—

" I will succeed, no matter the odds."

A haughty defiance, to which the heavens seemed prepared to respond immediately.

The day was on the brink of dawning, and, in consequence of that, the night, owing to its struggle with the twilight, had become more gloomy, as always happens during the few moments preceding the apparition of the sun. The first houses of the Rancho were standing out from the fog, a short distance before him, when the count heard, or fancied he heard, the sound of several horses' hoofs re-echoing on the pebbles behind him.

In America, by night, and on a solitary road, the presence of man announces always, or nearly always, a peril.

The count stopped and listened. The sound was rapidly approaching. The Frenchman was brave, and had proved it in many circumstances; still he did not at all desire to be assassinated in a corner of the road, and perish miserably through an ambuscade. He looked around, in order to study the chances of safety offered him in the probable event that the arrivals were enemies.

The plain was bare and flat : not a tree, not a ditch, nor any elevation behind which he could intrench himself. Two hundreds yards in front, as we have said, were the first houses of the Rancho.

The count made up his mind on the instant. He dug his spurs into his horse's flanks, and galloped at full speed in the direction of San José. It seemed to him as if the strangers imitated him, and pressed on their horses too.

A few minutes passed thus, during which the sound grew more and more distinct. It was, therefore, evident to the Frenchman that the strangers were after him. He threw a glance behind him, and perceived two shadows, still distant, rushing at full speed towards him. By this time the count had reached the Rancho. Reassured by the vicinity of houses, and not caring to fly from a perhaps imaginary danger, he turned back, drew his horse across the road, took a pistol in each hand, and waited. The strangers were still pressing on without checking the speed of their horses, and were soon within twenty yards of the count.

"Who goes there?" he shouted in a loud and firm voice.

The unknown made no reply, and appeared to redouble their speed.

"Who's there?" the count repeated. "Stop, or I fire!"

He uttered these words with such a determined accent, his countenance was so intrepid, that, after a few moments' hesitation, the strangers stopped.

There were two of them. The day, just feebly breaking, permitted the count to distinguish them perfectly. They were dressed in Mexican costume; but, strangely enough in this country, where, under similar circumstances, the bandits care very little about showing their faces, the strangers were masked.

"Hold, my masters!" the count shouted. "What means this obstinate pursuit?"

"That we probably have an interest in catching you up," a hoarse voice sarcastically replied.

"Then you really are after me?"

"Yes, if you are the stranger known as the Count de Lhorailles."

"I am he," he said without any hesitation.

"Very good; then we can come to an understanding."

"I ask nothing better, though, from your suspicious conduct, you appear to me to be bandits. If you want my purse, take it, and be off, for I am in a hurry."

"Keep your purse, caballero; we want to take your life, and not your money."

"Ah, ah! 'tis, then, a trap, followed by an assassination."

"You are mistaken. I offer you a fair fight."

"Hum!" the count said, "a fair fight: two against one—that is rather disproportionate."

"You would be correct if matters were as you assume," the man haughtily replied who had hitherto taken the word; "but my companion will content himself with looking on and taking no part in the duel."

The count reflected.

"Pardieu!" he said at last, "it is an extraordinary affair! A duel in Mexico, and with a Mexican! Such a thing as that has never been heard of before."

"It is true, caballero; but all things must have a beginning."

"Enough of jesting. I ask nothing better than to fight, and I hope to prove to you that I am a resolute man; but before accepting your proposition, I should not be sorry to know why you force me to fight you."

"For what end?"

"Corbleu! Why, to know it. You must understand that I cannot waste my time in fighting with every ruffler I meet on the road, and who has a fancy to have his throat cut."

"It will be enough for you to know that I hate you."

"Caramba! I suspected as much; but as you seem determined not to show me your face, I should like to be able to recognise you at another time."

"Enough chattering," the unknown said haughtily. "Time is flying. We have had sufficient discussion."

"Well, my master, if that is the case, get ready. I warn you that I intend to take you both. A Frenchman would never have any difficulty in holding his own against two Mexican bandits."

"As you please."

"Forward!"

"Forward!"

The three horsemen spurred their horses, and charged. When they met they exchanged pistol shots, and then drew their sabres. The fight was brief, but obstinate. One of the strangers, slightly wounded, was carried

away by his horse, and disappeared in a cloud of dust.
The count, grazed by a ball, felt his anger changed to
fury, and redoubled his efforts to master his foe; but he
had before him a rude adversary, a man of surprising
skill, and of strength at least equal to his own.

This man, whose eyes he saw gleaming like live coals
through the holes in his mask, whirled round him with extraordinary rapidity, making his horse perform the boldest
curvets, attacking him incessantly with the point or edge of
his sabre, while bounding out of reach of the counter-blows.

The count exhausted himself in vain against this
indefatigable enemy. His movements began to lose
their elasticity—his sight grew troubled—the perspiration stood in beads on his forehead. His silent adversary increased the rapidity of his attacks: the issue of
the combat was no longer doubtful, when the Frenchman suddenly felt a slip-knot fall on his shoulders.
Before he could even dream of loosening it he was
roughly lifted from his saddle, and hurled to the ground
so violently that he almost fainted, and found it impossible to make an effort to rise. The second stranger,
after a mad course of a few moments, had at length
succeeded in mastering his horse; he returned in all
haste to the scene of action, the two men so furiously
engaged not noticing it; then, thinking it time to put an
end to the duel, he raised his reata and lassoed the count.

So soon as he saw his enemy on the ground, the unknown leaped from his horse and ran up to him. His
first care was to free the Frenchman from the slip-knot
that strangled him, and then tried to restore him to his
senses, which was not a lengthy task.

"Ah!" the count said, with a bitter smile, as he
rose and crossed his arms on his chest, "that is what
you call fair fighting"

" You are alone to blame for what has happened," the other said quietly, " as you would not agree to my propositions."

The Frenchman disdained any discussion. He contented himself with shrugging his shoulders contemptuously.

" Your life belongs to me," his adversary continued.

" Yes, through a piece of treachery; but no matter—assassinate me, and finish the affair."

" I do not wish to kill you."

" What do you want, then ?"

" To give you a piece of advice."

The count laughed sarcastically.

" You must be mad, my good fellow."

" Not so much as you may fancy. Listen attentively to what I have to say to you."

" I will do so, even only for the hope of being promptly freed from your presence."

" Good, Senor Conde de Lhorailles. Your arrival in this country has caused the unhappiness of two persons."

" Nonsense ! You are jesting with me."

" I speak seriously. Don Sylva de Torrès has promised you his daughter's hand."

" How does that concern you ?"

" Answer !"

" It is true. Why should I conceal it ?"

" Dona Anita does not love you."

" How do you know that ?" the count asked with a mocking smile.

" I know it; I know, too, that she loves another."

" Only think of that ! "

" And that the other loves her."

" All the worse for him ; for I swear that I will not surrender her."

"You are mistaken, senor conde. You will sur•render her or die."

"Neither one nor the other," the impetuous French•man shouted, now perfectly recovered from his stun•ning fall. "I repeat that I will marry Dona Anita. If she does not love me, well, that is unfortunate. I hope that she will presently alter her opinion of me. The marriage suits me, and no one will succeed in breaking it off."

The unknown listened, a prey to violent emotion. His eyes flashed lightning, and he stamped his foot furiously; still he made an effort to master the feel•ing which agitated him, and replied in a slow and firm voice,—

"Take care of what you do, caballero. I have sworn to warn you, and have done so honestly. Heaven grant that my words find an echo in your heart, and that you follow the counsel I give you! The first time accident brings us together again one of us will die."

"I will take my precautions, be assured; but you are wrong not to profit by the present occasion to kill me, for it will not occur again."

The two strangers had by this time remounted.

"Count de Lhorailles," the unknown said again, as he bent over the Frenchman, "for the last time, take care, for I have a great advantage over you. I know you, and you do not know me. It will be an easy thing for me to reach you whenever I please. We are the sons of Indians and Spaniards. We feel a burning hatred; so take care."

After bowing ironically to the count he burst into a mocking laugh, spurred his horse, and started at head•long speed, followed by his silent companion. The

count watched them disappear with a pensive air.
When they were lost in the obscurity he tossed his head
several times, as if to shake off the gloomy thoughts
that oppressed him in spite of himself, then picked up
his sabre and pistols, took his horse by the bridle, and
walked slowly toward the pulqueria, near which the
fight had taken place.

The light which filtered through the badly-joined
planks of the door, the songs and laughter that resounded from the interior, afforded a reasonable prospect of obtaining a temporary shelter in this house.

"Hum!" he muttered to himself as he walked along,
"that bandit is right. He knows me, and I have no
way of recognising him. By Jupiter, I have a good
sound hatred on my shoulders! But nonsense!" he
added. "I was too happy. I wanted an enemy. On
my soul, let him do as he will! Even if Hades combine against me, I swear that nothing will induce me to
resign the hand of Dona Anita."

At this moment he found himself in front of the
pulqueria, at the door of which he rapped. Naturally
impatient, angered, too, by the accident which had happened to him, and the tremendous struggle he had been
engaged in, the count was about to carry out his threat
of beating in the door, when it was opened.

"*Valga me Dios!*" he exclaimed wrathfully, "is
this the way you allow people to be assassinated before
your doors, without proceeding to their assistance?"

"Oh, oh!" the pulquero said sharply, "is any one
dead?"

"No, thanks to Heaven!" the count replied; "but I
had a narrow escape of being killed."

"Oh!" the pulquero said with great nonchalance,
"if we were to trouble ourselves about all who shout

for help at night, we should have enough to do; and besides, it is very dangerous on account of the police."

The count shrugged his shoulders and walked in, leading his horse after him. The door was closed again immediately.

The count was unaware that in Mexico the man who finds a corpse, or brings the assassin to trial, is obliged to pay all the expenses of a justice enormously expensive in itself, and which never affords any satisfaction to the victim. In all the Mexican provinces people are so thoroughly convinced of the truth of what we assert, that, so soon as a murder is committed, every one runs off, without dreaming of helping the victim; for, in the case of death supervening, such an act of charity would entail many annoyances on the individual who tried to imitate the good Samaritan.

In Sonora people do better still: so soon as a quarrel begins, and a man falls, they shut all the doors.

CHAPTER VIII.

THE DEPARTURE.

As Don Sylva had announced to his daughter, by daybreak all was ready for the start. In Mexico, and specially in Sonora, where roads are mainly remarkable for their absence, the mode of travelling differs utterly from that adopted in Europe. There are no public vehicles, no relays of post horses; the only means of transport known and practised is on horseback.

A journey of only a few days entails interminable cares and vexations. You must carry everything with you, because you are certain of finding nothing on the road. Beds, tents, provisions, and water before all, must be carried on mule-back. Without these indispensable precautions you would run a risk of dying from hunger or thirst, and sleeping in the open air.

You must also be provided with a considerable and well-armed escort, in order to repulse the attacks of wild beasts, Indians, and specially robbers, with whom all the roads of Mexico swarm, owing to the anarchy in which this unhappy country is plunged. Hence it is easy to comprehend the lively desire Don Sylva felt to quit Guaymas at as early an hour as possible.

The court of the house resembled a hostelry. Fifteen mules laden with bales were waiting while the palanquin in which Dona Anita was to travel was being got ready Some forty steeds, saddled, bridled, with musquetoons attached to the troussequins, and pistols in the holsters, were fastened to rings in the wall, while a peon held in hand a splendid stallion, magnificently harnessed, which stamped and champed its silver bit, which it covered with foam.

In the street a crowd of people, among whom were Don Martial and Cucharès, already returned from their expedition to the Rancho, were curiously regarding this departure, which they could not at all comprehend at such an advanced period of the year, so unpropitious for a country residence, and making all sorts of comments on the reason of the journey

Among all these people, collected by accident or through curiosity, was a man, evidently an Indian, who, leaning carelessly against the wall, never took his eyes off the door of Don Sylva's house, and followed with evident interest all the movements of the haciendero's numerous servants.

This man, still young, appeared to be an Hiaqui Indian, although an observer, after a close inspection, would have asserted the contrary; for there was in the man's wide brow, in his eyes, whose glitter he tried in vain to moderate, in the haughty mouth, and, above all, in the native elegance of his vigorous limbs, which seemed carved on the model of the Greek Hercules, something proud, resolute, and independent, which rather denoted the proud Comanche or ferocious Apache than the stupid Hiaqui; but in this crowd no one dreamed of troubling himself about the Indian, who, for his part, was careful to attract as little attention as possible.

The Hiaquis are accustomed to come to Guaymas, and let themselves out as workmen or servants: hence the presence of an Indian there is not at all extraordinary, and is not noticed.

At last, at about eight o'clock, Don Sylva, giving his hand to his daughter, who was dressed in a charming travelling costume, appeared beneath the portico of the house. Dona Anita was pale as a ghost. Her haggard features, her swollen eyes, testified to the sufferings of the night, and the restraint she was forced to place on herself, even at this moment, to prevent her bursting into tears in the presence of all. At the sight of the young lady, Don Martial and Cucharès exchanged a rapid glance, while a smile of indefinable expression played round the lips of the Indian to whom we have alluded.

On the haciendero's arrival silence was re-established as if by enchantment; the *arrieros* ran to the heads of their mules; the servants, armed to the teeth, mounted; and Don Sylva, after assuring himself by a glance that all was ready, and that his orders had been punctually executed, placed his daughter in the palanquin, where she at once nestled like a humming-bird among rose leaves.

At a sign from the haciendero, the mules, fastened to

each other by the tails, began to leave the house behind the *nana*, whose bells they followed, and escorted by peons. Before mounting his horse Don Sylva turned to an old servant, who, straw hat in hand, respectfully stood near him.

"Adieu, Tio Pelucho!" he said to him. "I intrust the house to you. Keep good watch, and take care of all in it. I leave you Pedrito and Florentio to help you, and you will give them the necessary orders for all to go on properly during my absence."

"You may be at ease, mi amo," the old man answered, saluting his master. "Thanks to Heaven, this is not the first time you have left me alone here, and I believe I have ever done my duty properly."

"You are a good servant, Tio Pelucho," Don Sylva said with a smile; "I start in most perfect ease of mind."

"May God bless you, mi amo, as well as the nina!" the old man continued, crossing himself.

"Good-by, Tio Pelucho," the young lady then said, leaning out of the palanquin, "I know that you are careful of everything belonging to me."

The old man bowed with visible delight. Don Sylva gave the order for departure, and the whole caravan started in the direction of the Rancho de San José.

It was one of those magnificent mornings only known in these blessed regions. The night storm had entirely swept the sky, which was of a pale blue. The sun, already high in the horizon, shot forth its hot beams, which were slightly tempered by the odoriferous vapours exhaling from the ground. The atmosphere, impregnated by acrid and penetrating odours, was of extraordinary transparency; a light breeze refreshed the air at intervals; flocks of birds, glistening with a thousand colours, flew in every direction, and the mules following the bell of the *nena madrina*—the mother mule—were urged on by the songs of the arrieros.

The caravan moved along gaily through the sandy plain, raising round it clouds of dust, and forming a long twining serpent in the endless turnings of the road. A vanguard of ten servants explored the neighbourhood, examining the bushes, and shifting sand-heaps. Don Sylva smoked a cigar while conversing with his daughter; and a rear-guard, formed of twenty resolute men, closed the march, and insured the security of the convoy.

In this country, we repeat it, where the police are a nullity, and consequently surveillance impossible, a journey of four leagues—and the Rancho de San José is only that distance from Guaymas—is a very serious affair, and demands as many precautions as a journey of a hundred leagues with us, the enemies who may be met, and with whom you run a risk of a contest at any moment—Indians, robbers, or wild beasts—being too numerous, determined, and too greedy for plunder and murder to allow the traveller to confide with gaiety of heart in the speed of his horse.

They were already far from Guaymas, the white houses of which town had long ago disappeared in the numerous turnings of the road, when the capataz, leaving the head of the caravan, where he had hitherto remained, galloped back to the palanquin, where Don Sylva was still riding.

" Well, Blas," the latter said, " what is there new? Have you noticed anything alarming ahead of us?"

" Nothing, excellency," the capataz replied : " all is going on well, and in an hour at the latest we shall be at the Rancho."

"Whence, then, the haste you showed to join me again?"

"Oh! excellency, it is not much; but an idea occurred to me—something I wished you to see."

"Ah, ah!" Don Sylva said. "What is it, my lad?"

"Look, excellency," the capataz continued, pointing in a south-western direction.

"Ah! what is that? A fire, if I am not mistaken."

"It is indeed a fire, excellency. Look here;" and he pointed east-south-east.

"There's another. Who on earth has lighted the fires on those scarped points? What can their object be?"

"Oh! it is easy enough to understand that, excellency."

"Do you think so, my boy? Well, then, you will explain it to me."

"I am willing to do so. Stay," he said, pointing to the first fire; "that hill is the Cerro del Gigante."

"It is."

"And that," the capataz continued, pointing to the second fire, "is the Cerro de San Xavier."

"I think it is."

"I am certain of it."

"Well?"

"As we know that a fire cannot kindle itself, and as people do not amuse themselves with a fire when the thermometer is up at a hundred——"

"You conclude from that——?"

"That these fires have been lighted by robbers or Indians, who have had scent of our departure."

"Stay, stay! that is most logical, my friend. Continue your explanation, for it interests me enormously."

Don Sylva's capataz, or steward, was a tall, herculean

fellow of about forty, devoted body and soul to his master, who placed the greatest confidence in him. The worthy man bowed with a smile of satisfaction on hearing the haciendero's kind remarks.

"Oh! now," he went on, "I have not much more to say, except that the ladrones who are watching us know, through that signal, that Don Sylva de Torrès and his daughter have left Guaymas for the Rancho."

"My faith! you are right. I had forgotten all those details. I did not think of all the birds of prey that are watching our passage. Well, after all, though, what do we care if the bandits are at our heels? We do not hide ourselves. Our start took place in the presence of plenty cf persons. We are numerous enough not to fear any insult; but if any of those picaros dare to attack us, cascaras! they will find their work cut out for them, I am convinced. Push on, then, without any fear, Blas, my boy! Nothing unpleasant can happen to us."

The capataz saluted his master, and galloped back to the head of the column. An hour later they reached the Rancho without any accident.

Don Sylva rode at the right-hand door of the palanquin, talking to his daughter, who only answered in monosyllables, in spite of the continued efforts she made to hide her sorrow from her father's clear eyes, when the haciendero heard his name called repeatedly. He turned his head sharply, and uttered an exclamation of surprise on recognising in the man who addressed him the Count de Lhorailles.

"What! senor conde, you here? What singular hazard makes me meet you so near the port, when you should have been so far ahead of us?"

On perceiving the count the Dona felt herself blush,

and fell back, letting the curtains of the palanquin slip from her hand.

"Oh!" the count replied, with a courteous bow, "since last night certain things have happened to me which I must impart to you, Don Sylva—things which will surprise you, I am certain; but the present is not the moment to commence such a story."

" Whatever you think proper, my friend. But say, do you set out again, or remain here?"

" I go, I go! In stopping here my sole object was to await you. If you consent we will travel together. Instead of preceding you at Guetzalli, we shall arrive together—that is the only difference."

" Capital! Let us go," he added, making a sign to the capataz. The latter, on seeing his master conversing with the count, had ordered a halt; but now the caravan started again. The Rancho was speedily traversed, and then the journey commenced in reality.

The desert lay expanded before the travellers in endless sandy plains. On the yellow ground, a long, tortuous line, formed by the whitened bones of mules and horses that had broken down, indicated the road which must be followed so as not to go astray.

About two hundred yards ahead of the caravan a man was trotting on, carelessly seated on the back of a skeleton donkey, swaying from side to side, half lulled to sleep by the burning sunbeams which fell vertically on his bare head.

" Eh?" Don Sylva said, on perceiving the man. " Blas, call the Indian over there. These devils of redskins know the desert thoroughly, and he can serve as our guide. In that way we shall run no risk of losing our road, for he will be sure to put us right."

"Quite true," the count observed; "in these confounded sands no man can be sure of his direction."

"Go to him," Don Sylva commanded.

The capataz put his horse at a gallop. On arriving within a short distance of the solitary traveller, he formed a sort of speaking trumpet with his hands.

"Halloh, José!" he shouted.

In Mexico all the *Mansos*, or civilised Indians, are called José, and reply to this name, which has grown generic. The Indian thus hailed turned round.

"What do you want?" he asked with a careless air.

It was the man whom we saw at Guaymas, watching so attentively the preparations for the haciendero's departure. Was it chance that brought him to this spot? That was a question which none but himself could have answered.

Blas Vasquez was what is called in Mexico a *hombre de a caballo*, versed for a long period in Indian tricks, as in hunting wild beasts. He bent on the traveller an inquiring glance, which the latter supported with perfect ease. With his head timidly bowed, his hands laid on the donkey's neck, his naked legs hanging down on either side, he offered a complete type of the Indian manso, almost brutalised by the vicious contact with the whites. The capataz shook his head with a dissatisfied air; his investigation was far from satisfying him. Still, after a moment's hesitation, he continued his interrogatory.

"What are you doing all alone on this road, José?" he asked him.

"I have come from del Puerto, where I have been engaged as a carpenter. I remained there a month, and as I saved the small sum I wanted, I started yesterday to return to my village."

All this was perfectly probable; the majority of the Hiaqui Indians act in this way; and then what interest could the man have in deceiving him? He was alone and unarmed; the caravan, on the other hand, was numerous, and composed of devoted men. No danger was, therefore, to be apprehended.

"Well, did you earn much money?" the capataz continued.

"Yes," the Indian said triumphantly; "five piastres, and these three besides."

"Why, José, you are a rich man."

The Hiaqui smiled doubtfully

"Yes," he said, "Tiburon has money.

"Is your name Tiburon (shark)?" the capataz said distrustfully. "That is an ugly name."

"Why so? The pale faces gave that name to their red son, and he finds it good, since it comes from them, and he keeps it."

"Is your village far from here?"

"If I had a good horse I should arrive in three days. The village of my tribe is between the Gila and Guetzalli."

"Do you know Guetzalli?"

The Indian shrugged his shoulders disdainfully.

"The red-skins know all the hunting-grounds on the Gila," he said.

At this moment the caravan caught up the two speakers.

"Well, Blas," Don Sylva asked, "who is the man?"

"A Hiaqui Indian. He is returning to his village, after earning a trifle at the Puerto."

"Can he be of service to us?"

"I believe so. His tribe, he says, is encamped near the Gila."

" Ah!" said the count, drawing nearer, "does he belong to the White Horse tribe?"

" Yes," the Indian said.

" In that case I answer for the man," the count said quickly. "Those Indians are very gentle; they are miserable beggars, often starving; and I employ them at the hacienda."

" Listen!" Don Sylva said, tapping the red-skin's shoulder amicably "We are going to Guetzalli."

" Good."

" We want a faithful and devoted guide."

" Tiburon is poor; he has only a poor donkey, which cannot march so quickly as his pale brothers drive their horses."

" Do not trouble yourself about that," the haciendero added. " I will give you such a horse as you never mounted, if you serve us honestly. On arriving at the hacienda, I will add ten piastres to those you already possess. Does that suit you?"

The Indian's eye sparkled with greed at this proposal.

" Where is the horse?" he asked.

" Here," the capataz replied, pointing to a superb stallion led by a peon.

The red-skin looked at it with the eye of a connoisseur.

" Well, do you accept?" the haciendero said.

" Yes."

" Then get off your donkey, and let us start."

" I cannot abandon my donkey; it is a famous brute, which has done me good service."

" That need not trouble you; it can follow with the baggage mules."

The Indian gave a nod of assent, but made no further reply. In a few minutes he was mounted, and the caravan continued its march. The capataz alone

did not appear to place any great confidence in the
guide so singularly met.

"I will watch him," he said in a low voice.

The march went on the whole day without any fresh
incident, and the next day they reached the Rio Gila.
The banks of this river contrast by their fertility with
the desolate aridity of the plains that surround
them. Don Sylva's journey, though recommenced at
the moment when the sun, arrived at its zenith, pours
down its burning beams perpendicularly, was only an
agreeable promenade of a few leagues, beneath the dense
shade of tufted woods which grow with an amount of
sap unknown in our climates.

It was nearly three o'clock when the travellers saw
before them the colony of Guetzalli, founded by the
Count de Lhorailles, and which, although it only had a
few months' existence, had already attained a considerable size. This colony was composed of a hacienda,
round which were grouped the labourers' huts. We
will devote a few words to it.

The hacienda was built on a peninsula nearly three
leagues in circumference, covered with wood and pasture, on which more than four thousand head of cattle
grazed peacefully, returning at night to the parks
adjoining the house, which was surrounded by the
river, forming an *enceinte* of natural fortresses. The
tongue of land, not more than eight yards in width,
attaching it to the main land, was commanded by a
battery of six heavy guns, in its turn surrounded by
a wide, wet ditch.

The house, surrounded by tall embattled walls, bas-
tioned at the angles, was a species of fortress capable of
sustaining a regular siege, with the eight guns mounted
on the bastions which guarded the approaches. It was

composed of a huge main building, one story high, with a terraced roof, having ten windows in the frontage, and flanked on the right and left by two buildings running out at right angles, one of which served as a magazine for grain and maize, while the other was occupied by the capataz and the numerous *employés* of the hacienda.

Wide steps, garnished with a double iron balustrade, curiously worked, and surmounted by a verandah, formed the approach to the count's apartments, which were furnished with that simple and picturesque taste which distinguishes the Spanish farms of America.

Between the house and the outer wall was a vast garden, exquisitely laid out, and so covered with bushes that at four paces' distance it was impossible to see any thing. The space left free behind the farm was reserved for the parks or corrals in which the animals were shut up at night, and a species of large court, in which the *matanza del ganado*, or slaughter of the cattle, was performed once annually.

Nothing could be so picturesque as the appearance of this white house, whose roof could be seen for a long distance, half concealed by the branches which formed a curtain of foliage most refreshing to the eye. From the windows of the first floor the eye surveyed the plain on one side; on the other, the Rio Gilá, which, like a wide silvery ribbon, rolled along with the most capricious windings, and was lost an immense distance off in the blue horizon.

Since the time when the Apaches all but surprised the hacienda, a *mirador* had been built on the roof of the main building, where a sentinel was stationed day and night to watch the neighbourhood, and announce, by means of a bullock's horn, the approach of any stranger to the colony. Besides, a post of six men guarded the isthmus battery, whose guns were ready to thunder at the slightest alarm.

Thus the arrival of the caravan had been signalled when it was still a long distance off; and the count's lieutenant, Martin Leroux, an old African soldier, was standing behind the guns to interrogate the arrivals so soon as they were within hail. Don Sylva was perfectly aware of the regulations established in the hacienda, which were, indeed, common to all the establishments held by white men; for at these frontier posts, where people are exposed to the constant depredations of the Indians, they are obliged to be incessantly on the watch. But the thing the Mexican could not comprehend was that the count's lieutenant, who must have recognised him, did not open the gates immediately, and he made a remark to that effect.

"He would have done wrong," the count replied. The colony of Guetzalli is a fortress, and the regulations must be the same for all: the general welfare depends on their strict and entire observation. Martin recognised me long ago, I am convinced; but he may suppose that I am a prisoner of the Indians, and that, in leaving me apparently free, they intend to surprise the colony. Be assured that my excellent lieutenant will not let us pass till he is quite certain that our European clothes do not cover red skins."

"O yes!" Don Sylva muttered to himself; "that is true. The Europeans foresee everything. They are our masters."

The caravan was now not more than twenty yards from the hacienda.

"I fancy," the count observed, "that if we do not wish to receive a shower of bullets we had better halt."

" What !" Don Sylva said in amazement ; " they would fire?"

" I am certain of it."

The two men checked their horses and waited to be challenged.

" Who goes there ?" a powerful voice shouted in French from behind the battery.

" Well, what do you think of it now?" the count said to the haciendero.

" It is perfectly wonderful," the latter observed.

" Friends," the count answered. " Lhorailles and freedom !"

" All right—open ! " the voice commanded. " They are friends. Would that we often received such visitors ! "

The peons lowered the drawbridge (the only passage by which the hacienda could be entered), the caravan passed over, and the drawbridge was immediately raised after them.

" You will excuse me, captain," Martin Leroux said, respectfully approaching the count, " but, although I recognised you, we live in a country where, I think, too great prudence cannot be exercised."

" You have done your duty, lieutenant, and I can only thank you for it. Have you any news?"

" Not much. A troop of horse I sent out into the plain discovered a deserted fire. I fancy the Indians are prowling round us."

" We will be on our guard."

" Oh ! I keep good watch, especially at present, for the month is drawing on which the Comanches call so audaciously the Mexican moon. I should not be sorry, if they dared to meddle with us, to give them a lesson which would be profitable for the future."

"I share your views entirely. Redouble your vigilance, and all will be well."

"You have no other orders to give me?"

"No."

"Then I will withdraw. You know, captain, that you intrust the internal details to me, and I must be everywhere in turn."

"Go, lieutenant; let me not keep you."

The old soldier saluted his chief, and retired with a friendly signal to the capataz, who followed him with the peons and baggage mules.

The count led his guests to the apartments kept for visitors, and installed them in comfortably-furnished rooms.

"Pray rest yourself, Don Sylva," he said; "you and Dona Anita must be fatigued with your journey. To-morrow, if you permit me, we will talk about our business."

"Whenever you like, my friend."

The count bowed to his guests, and withdrew. Since his meeting with his betrothed he had not exchanged a word with her. In the courtyard he found the Hiaqui Indian smoking, and walking carelessly about. He went up to him.

"Here," he said, "are the ten piastres promised to you."

"Thanks," said the Indian as he took them.

"Now, what are you going to do?"

"Rest myself till to-morrow; then join the men of my tribe."

"Are you in a great hurry to see them?"

"I? Not at all."

"Stay here, then."

"What to do?"

" I will tell you : perhaps I may need you within a few days."

" Shall I be paid? "

" Amply. Does that suit you? "

" Yes."

" Then you will remain ? "

" I will."

The count went away, not noticing the strange expression in the glance the Indian turned on him.

CHAPTER IX.

A MEETING IN THE DESERT.

ABOUT three musket shots' distance from the hacienda, in a thicket of nopals, mastic trees, and mesquites, intermingled with a few mahogany cedars, wild cotton-wood trees, and pines, just an hour before sunset, a horseman dismounted ; hobbled his horse, a magnificent mustang, with flashing eyes and fine chest ; then, after turning an inquiring glance around, probably satisfied with the profound silence and tranquillity pervading at the spot, he made his arrangements for camping.

The man had passed middle life : he was an Indian warrior of great height, dressed in the Comanche costume in its utmost purity. Although he appeared to be sixty years of age, he seemed gifted with great vigour, and no sign of decrepitude could be traced in his muscular limbs and intelligent face : the eagle's feather fixed in the centre of his war-lock allowed him to be recognised as a chief. This man was Eagle-head, the Comanche chief.

After laying his rifle by his side he collected dry wood, and lit a fire ; then he threw several yards of tasajo on the ashes with several maize tortillas ; and all these preparations for a comfortable supper made, he filled his calumet, crouched near the fire, and began smoking with that placid calmness which never deserts the Indians under any circumstances.

Two hours thus passed peacefully, and nothing disturbed the repose the chief was enjoying. Night succeeded day; darkness had invaded the desert, and with it the silence of solitude began to reign in the mysterious depths of the prairie.

The Indian still remained motionless, contenting himself with turning now and then to his horse, which was gaily devouring the climbing peas and the young buds of the trees.

Suddenly Eagle-head looked up, bent forward, and, without otherwise disturbing himself, stretched out his hand to his rifle, while the mustang left off eating, laid back its ears, and neighed noisily. Still the forest appeared as calm as ever. It needed all an Indian's sharp ear to have heard a suspicious rustling through the silence.

At the end of a moment the chief's frowning brows returned to their proper position, he re-assumed his easy posture, and, lifting his two forefingers to his mouth, imitated with rare perfection, for two or three minutes, the harmonious modulations of the centzontle, or Mexican nightingale : the horse had also begun eating again.

Only a few minutes passed ere the cry of the night hawk was twice heard in the direction of the river. Soon after the sound of horses became audible, mingled with the cracking of branches and the rustling of leaves, and two mounted men made their appearance. The chief did not turn to see who they were; he had probably recognised them, and knew that they alone, or at any rate one of them, were to come to him here.

These two horsemen were Don Louis and Belhumeur

They hobbled their horses by the side of the chief's, lay down by the fire, and, on the Indian's silent invitation, vigorously attacked the supper prepared for them They had left the Rancho the previous evening, and ridden without the loss of a moment to join the chief.

The Count de Lhorailles had invited them at the pulqueria to join his party, but Belhumeur had declined the offer. Not knowing for what purpose the Indian chief had appointed to meet him, he did not care to mix up a stranger in his friend's affairs. Still, the three men had parted on excellent terms, and the count pressed Don Louis and the Canadian to pay him a visit at Guetzalli, an offer to which they had replied evasively.

Singular is the effect of sympathy. The impression the count produced on the two adventurers was so unfavourable for him, that the latter, while replying with the utmost politeness, had not thought it wise to give their names, and had employed the greatest reserve, carrying their prudence to such an extent as to leave him ignorant of their nationality, by continuing to converse in Spanish, though at the first word he uttered they recognised him to be a Frenchman.

When they had ended their meal Belhumeur filled his pipe, and put out his hand to take up a coal.

" Wait," the chief said sharply.

This was the first word the Indian uttered ; up to that moment the three men had not interchanged a syllable. Belhumeur looked at him.

" H'm ! " he said, " what is the matter now ? "

" I do not know yet," the chief answered. " I have heard a suspicious rustling in the bushes ; and at a great distance off, to leeward of us, several buffaloes peacefully grazing took to flight without any apparent cause."

"Hum!" the Canadian went on, "that is growing serious. What do you think, Louis?"

"In the desert," the latter replied slowly, "everything has a cause—nothing happens by accident. I believe that we had better be on our guard. Stay!" he added, as he raised his head, and pointed out to his friends several birds that passed rapidly over them. "Have you often seen at this hour a flight of condors soaring in the sky?"

The chief shook his head.

"There is something the matter," he muttered: "the dogs of Apaches are hunting."

"'Tis possible," Belhumeur said.

"Before all," the Frenchman observed, "let us put out the fire: its gleam, slight as it is, might betray us."

His companions followed his advice, and the fire was extinguished in a second.

"My brother, the paleface, is prudent," the chief said courteously. "He knows the desert. I am happy to see him by my side."

Don Louis thanked the chief courteously.

"And now," Belhumeur went on, "we are almost invisible—no visible danger threatens us; so let us hold a council. The chief had the first scent of peril: it is, therefore, his place to tell us what he observed."

The Indian wrapped himself up in his fressada; the three men drew closer, so as to be able to speak in a whisper, and the council commenced.

"Since sunrise this morning," Eagle-head said, "I have been marching in the desert. I was anxious to reach the place of meeting, and proceeded in a straight line to arrive sooner. All along the road I found evident signs of the passage of a numerous band; the tracks were wide and full, like those made by a party of warriors so large that they care not for discovery. These trails continued for a long distance, then suddenly disappeared: it was impossible for me to find them again."

" Deuce, deuce! " the Canadian muttered, " that is awkward."

" At first I did not pay much attention to the trail, but presently I began to feel restless, and that is the reason I have mentioned it to you."

" What reason rendered you restless ? "

" I believe that the expedition whose passage I discovered is directed against the great cabin of the pale-faces at Guetzalli."

" What makes you suppose so ? " Louis asked.

" This. At the hour the alligator leaves the mud of the bank to plunge again into the Gila, the sound of horses I heard a short distance off compelled me, lest I should be discovered, to bury myself in a thicket of mangroves and floripondios. When sheltered from a surprise I looked out. A band of pale-faces passed within bow-shot of me, in the direction of Guetzalli."

" I know who they were," Belhumeur remarked. " What next ? "

" I recognised, in spite of the care he had taken to render himself unrecognisable, the man who served as guide to the party; then I guessed the infernal scheme formed by the Apache dogs."

" Who was it ? "

" A man my brother knows. It is Wah-sho-che-gorah, the Black Bear, the principal chief of the White Crow tribe."

" If you are not mistaken, chief, horrible things will be done ere long. The Black Bear is the implacable enemy of the whites."

" That was the reason I spoke to my brother. But, after all, what does it concern us? In the desert each man has enough to do in taking care of himself, without troubling about others."

The Canadian shook his head.

" Yes, what you say is true," he replied. " We ought, perhaps, to abandon the inhabitants of the hacienda to their fate, and not interfere in matters which may cause us great misery."

" Do you intend to act thus?" the Frenchman asked sharply.

" I do not say so positively," the Canadian replied; " but the case is a difficult one. We shall have to deal with numerous enemies."

" Yes, but the men about to be surprised are your fellow-countrymen."

" It is true; and it is that which renders the affair so awkward. I do not wish to see these unhappy beings scalped. On the other hand, we run the risk, by hurrying rashly into danger, of ourselves being the victims of our devotion."

" Why reflect thus?"

" By Jove! in order to weigh the for and against. There is nothing I detest so much as rushing headlong into an enterprise of which I have not calculated all the consequences beforehand. When I have done so I care for nothing."

Don Louis could not refrain from smiling at this singular reasoning.

" I have my plan," the Canadian went on a moment later. " The night will not pass without our learning something new. Let us draw near the bank of the river. I am greatly mistaken, or we shall soon obtain there the information we require before we make up our minds. Our horses run no risk here: we can leave them; besides, they would only prove an embarrassment to us."

The three men lay down on the ground, and began crawling silently in the direction indicated by Belhumeur.

The night was magnificent, the moon brilliant, and the atmosphere so diaphanous, that objects might have been distinguished for a great distance on an open plain. The three adventurers did not leave their covert; but, on arriving at the skirt of the forest, they hid themselves in an almost inextricable thicket, and waited with that patience so characteristic of the wood-rangers.

The silence which brooded over the desert was so intense that the slightest sounds were perceptible. A leaf falling on the water, a pebble detaching itself from the bank, the slow and continuous murmur of the water running over its gravel bed, the rustling of the owl's wing as it fluttered from branch to branch, were the only distinguishable sounds.

For several hours the three men remained motionless and watchful, eye and ear strained, with the finger on the trigger of the rifle, through fear of a surprize; but nothing had yet happened to corroborate the suspicions of Eagle-head, or the previsions of Belhumeur. Suddenly Louis felt the chief's arm resting gently on his shoulder, as he pointed to the river. The Frenchman rose on his knees and looked.

An almost imperceptible movement agitated the surface of the river, as if an alligator were floating along.

"Oh, oh!" Belhumeur muttered; "I fancy that is what we are expecting."

A black mass soon appeared, floating rather than

swimming on the water, and noiselessly advancing toward the spot where the hunters were in ambush. At the end of a few moments this body, whatever it might be, stopped, and the cry of the prairie dog was heard several times repeated.

At once the howl of the coyote broke forth forcibly so near the three men, that, spite of themselves, they shuddered, and a man hanging by the hands dropped down from an oak tree, scarcely three yards from the spot where they were.

This man wore the Mexican costume.

"Come, chief," he said in a low voice, though not venturing down to the river, "come, we are alone."

The man thus addressed emerged from the water, and clambered up the bank to join the person awaiting him.

"My brother speaks too loudly," he said. "In the desert a man is never alone; the leaves have eyes, the trees ears."

"Bah! what you say, has not common sense. Who on earth would play the spy on us? With the exception of your warriors, who are probably concealed in the neighbourhood, no one can see or hear us."

The Indian shook his head. Now that he was standing only a few spaces from the adventurers, Belhumeur perceived that Eagle-head was not mistaken, and that the man was really the Black Bear. The two men stood for a moment silently gazing at each other. The Mexican was the first to speak.

"You have manœuvred well," he said in an insinuating voice. "I know not how you managed it, but you have succeeded in entering the fort."

"Yes," the Indian replied.

"Now we have only our final arrangements to make,

You are a great chief, in whom I place the utmost confidence. Here is what I promised you. I ought not to pay you till afterwards, but I do not wish the slightest cloud to rise between us."

The Indian silently rejected the purse the other held out to him.

" The Black Bear has reflected," he said coldly.

" On what, may I ask ? "

" A warrior is not a woman to waste his words. What my brother offered the Black Bear, the Apache chief refuses."

" Which means ? "

" That all is broken off."

The Mexican repressed with difficulty a sign of disappointment.

" Then," he said, " you have not warned your warriors ? When I give the order you will not attack the hacienda ? "

" The Black Bear has warned his warriors. He will attack the pale-faces."

" What did you say this moment? I confess that I do not comprehend you, chief."

" Because the pale-face will not comprehend. The Black Bear will attack the hacienda, but on his own account."

" That was agreed between us, I fancy."

" Yes ; but the Black Bear has seen the singing-bird. His hut is empty : he wishes to place in it the young pale virgin."

" Scoundrel ! " the Mexican shouted in his wrath ; " you would betray me in that way ? "

" How have I betrayed the pale-face ? " the Indian replied, still perfectly calm. " He offered me a bargain ; I refused it. I see nothing dishonest in that."

The Mexican bit his lips with rage; he was caught, and could make no reply.

"I will revenge myself," he said, stamping his foot.

"The Black Bear is a powerful chief; he laughs at the croaking of the ravens. The pale-face can do nothing against him."

With a movement swift as thought, the Mexican rushed on the Indian, seized him by the throat, and, drawing his dagger, raised it to strike him. But the Apache carefully watched the actions of his opponent: by a movement no less swift he freed himself from his grasp, and with one bound was out of reach.

"The pale-face has dared to touch a chief," he said in a hoarse voice; "he shall die."

The Mexican shrugged his shoulders, and seized the pistols in his girdle.

It is impossible to say how this scene would have ended, had not a new incident happened to change its features completely. From the same tree in which the Mexican had been hidden a few moments previously, another individual suddenly fell, rushed on the chief, and hurled him to the ground before he could make a gesture to defend himself, so thoroughly was he off his guard.

"By Jove!" Belhumeur muttered with a stifled laugh, "there must be a legion of devils in that tree."

The Mexican and the man who had come so luckily to his help had securely tied the Indian with a reata.

"Now you are in my power, chief," the Mexican said, "and you will be obliged to consent to my terms."

The Apache grinned, and uttered a shrill whistle.

At this signal fifty Indian warriors appeared, as if they had sprung from the ground, and that so suddenly, that the two white men were surrounded in an instant by an impassable circle.

" Deuce ! " Belhumeur said in an aside, " that complicates matters. How will they get out of that ? "

" And we ? " Louis whispered in his ear.

The Canadian replied by that shrug of the shoulders which signifies in all languages, " We must trust in Heaven," and began looking again, interested as he was in the highest degree by the unexpected changes of scene.

" Cucharès ! " the Mexican said to his companion, " hold that scoundrel tight, and at the least suspicious movement kill him like a dog."

" Be calm, Don Martial," the lepero answered, pulling from his vaquera boot a knife, whose sharp blade flashed with a bluish tinge in the moon's rays.

" What decision does the Black Bear come to ? " the Tigrero went on, addressing the chief lying at his feet.

" The life of a chief belongs to thee, dog of the pale-faces : take it if thou darest ! " the Apache replied with a smile of contempt.

" I will not kill you : not because I am afraid, for I know not such a feeling," the Mexican said, " but because I disdain to shed the blood of an enemy who is defenceless, even if he be, like you, an unclean coyote."

" Kill me, I say, if thou canst, but insult me not. Hasten ! for my warriors may lose patience, sacrifice thee to their wrath, and thou mightest die unavenged."

" You are jesting ; you know perfectly well that your warriors will not move an inch so long as I hold you thus. I propose to offer you peace."

" Peace ! " the chief said, and his eyes flashed. " On what conditions ? "

" Two only. Cucharès, unfasten the reata, but watch him closely."

The lepero obeyed.

" Thanks," the chief said as he rose to his knees. " Speak ; I am listening—my ears are open. What are these conditions? "

" First, my comrade and myself will be free to retire whither we please."

" Good, and next ? "

" Next, you will pledge yourself to remain with your warriors, and not return to the hacienda in the disguise you have assumed for the next twenty-four hours."

" Is that all ? "

" It is all."

" Listen to me in your turn, then, pale-face. I accept your conditions, but I must tell you mine."

" Speak."

" I will not re-enter the hacienda save with the eagle feather in my war-tuft, at the head of my warriors, and that before the sun has thrice set behind the lofty peaks of the mountains of the day."

" You are boasting, Apache ; it is impossible for you to enter the hacienda save by treachery."

" We shall see ; " and smiling with a sinister air, he added, " The singing-bird will go into the hut of an Apache chief to cook his game."

The Mexican shrugged his shoulders contemptuously.

" Try to take the hacienda and carry off the maiden," he said.

" I will try. Your hand."

" Here it is."

The chief turned to his warriors, holding the Tigrero's hand clasped in his own.

"Brothers!" he said in a loud voice, and with an accent of supreme majesty, "this pale-face is the friend of the Black Bear—let no one molest him."

The warriors bowed respectfully, and fell back to the right and left, to leave a passage for the two white men.

"Farewell!" the Black Bear said, saluting his enemy. "In twenty-four hours I shall be on your trail."

"You are mistaken, dog of an Apache," Don Martial replied disdainfully; "I shall be on yours."

"Good! we are, then, certain of meeting," the Black Bear said.

And he retired with a slow and firm step, followed by his warriors, whose footfalls soon died away in the depths of the forest.

"On my faith, Don Martial," the lepero said, "I believe that you were wrong to let that Indian dog escape so easily."

The Tigrero shrugged his shoulders.

"Were we not obliged to get out of the wasp's nest into which we had thrust our heads?" he said. "Bah! it is only put off for a time. Let us go and find our horses."

"One moment, if you will grant it me," Belhumeur said, leaving his hiding-place, and advancing politely with his two comrades.

"What's this?" Cucharès said, pulling out his knife again, while Don Martial coolly cocked his pistols.

"This? Caballero," Belhumeur said quietly, "I fancy you can see plainly enough."

"I see three men."

"Indeed, you are not at all mistaken. Three men who have been unseen witnesses of the scene you ended so bravely—three men who held themselves ready to come to your aid had it been necessary, and who now offer to make common cause with you, to prevent the plunder of the hacienda by the Apaches. Does that suit you?"

"That depends," the Tigrero said. "I must know first what interest urges you to act in this manner."

"That of being agreeable to you in the first place," Belhumeur replied politely, "and next, the desire to save the scalps of the poor wretches menaced by those infernal red-skins."

"In that case I heartily accept your offer."

"Be good enough, then, to follow us to our camping ground, that we may discuss the plan of the campaign."

So soon as Cucharès noticed that the men who presented themselves so strangely were really friends, he returned his knife to his boot, and went in search of the horses, which had been left a short distance off. He arrived at this moment, leading the two horses, and the five men proceeded together to the camping-ground.

"Take care," Belhumeur said to Don Martial; "you have made yourself an implacable enemy this night. If you do not make haste to kill him, one day or another the Black Bear will kill you. The Apaches never pardon an insult."

"I know it; so I shall take my precautions, you may be sure."

"That is your concern. Perhaps it would have been better to get rid of him, at the risk of what might have happened afterwards."

"How could I imagine I had friends so near me? Oh, had I but known it!"

"Well, it is of no use crying over spilt milk."

"Do you believe that he will keep scrupulously the conditions he accepted?"

" You do not know the Black Bear; he is a man of noble sentiments, and has a way of his own for understanding the point of honour. You saw that during your entire discussion he disdained to play any trickery; his words were always frank."

" They were."

" Be certain, then, that he will keep his promise."

The conversation was interrupted. Don Martial had suddenly become pensive. The Apache's menaces gave him a good deal to think about. The camp was reached, and Eagle-head immediately set to work rekindling the fire.

" What are you about?" Belhumeur observed to him. " You will reveal our presence."

" No," the Indian said, shaking his head. " The Black Bear has retired with his warriors : they are far away at present; so we need not take useless precautions."

The fire soon crackled again. The five men crouched round it joyfully, lit their pipes, and began smoking.

" I don't care," the Canadian presently said. " Had it not been for the extraordinary coolness you displayed I do not know how you would have escaped."

" Let us now see how best to foil the plans of these demons," the Mexican said.

" It is very simple," Louis interposed. " One of us will proceed to-morrow to the hacienda, to warn the owner of what has passed this night. He will be on his guard, and all will be right."

" Yes, I believe those are the best means, and we will employ them."

" Five men are as nothing against five hundred," Eagle-head observed ; " we must warn the pale-faces."

" That is assuredly the plan we must follow, the

Tigrero remarked; "but which of us will consent to go to the hacienda? Neither my comrade nor myself can do so."

"I fancy there is some love story hidden under all this," the Canadian observed cunningly. "I can understand that you would find a difficulty in——."

"What need of further discussion?" Louis interrupted. "With to-morrow's dawn I will go to the hacienda; I undertake to explain to the owner all the dangers that menace him in their fullest details."

"That is agreed on, then, and all is settled," Belhumeur said.

"Then, so soon as our horses have rested, my comrade and myself will return to Guaymas."

"No, you will not, if you please," the Frenchman objected. "I fancy it is proper that you should know the result of the mission I undertake, for it concerns you even more than us. I suspect——"

The Mexican repressed a lively movement of annoyance.

"You are right," he replied; "I did not think of that. I will therefore await your return."

The hunters interchanged a few more remarks, then wrapped themselves in their blankets, lay down on the ground, and speedily fell asleep. The profoundest silence fell on the clearing, which but was dimly lighted by the reddish rays of the expiring fire. The adventurers had been asleep for about two hours, when the branches of a shrub were gently parted, and a man made his appearance.

He stopped for a moment, seemed to be listening, then crawled without the slightest sound toward the spot where the Tigrero was reposing. It would have been easy to recognise the Black Bear by the light of the fire. The Apache chief plucked his scalping-knife from his girdle, and laid it gently on the Tigrero's chest; then casting a parting glance around, to convince himself that the five men still slept, he retired with the same precautions, and soon disappeared in the scrub, which closed upon him.

CHAPTER X.

BEFORE THE ATTACK.

At the first cry of the maukawis—that is to say, at sunrise—the adventurers awoke.

The night had been calm. They had slept with nothing to disturb their rest. Iced, however, by the abundant dew which had filtered through their blankets during their sleep, they hurriedly rose to restore the circulation of their blood and warm their stiffened limbs.

At the first movement Don Martial made a knife fell down on the ground. The Mexican picked it up, and uttered a cry of amazement and almost of terror as he showed it to his companions. The arm so unexpectedly found was a scalping-knife, whose blade was still stained with large bloody spots.

" What is the meaning of this ?" he asked, brandishing the knife angrily.

Eagle-head seized it, and examined it carefully.

" Wah !" he said in surprise, " the Black Bear has been with us during our sleep."

The hunters could not refrain from a movement of alarm.

" It is impossible," Belhumeur observed.

The Indian shook his head as he displayed the weapon.

" This," he continued, " is the Apache chief's scalping-knife; the *totem* of the tribe is engraved on the hilt."

" 'Tis true."

" The Black Bear is a renowned chief. His heart is large enough to contain a world. Obliged to fulfil the engagements he has made, he wished to prove to his enemy that he was master of his life, and that he would take it whenever he thought proper. That is the meaning of this knife placed on the chest of the *Yori* during his sleep."

The adventurers were confounded by so much bold-ness. They shuddered at the thought that they had been at the mercy of the chief, who disdained to kill them, and contented himself with defying them. The Mexican especially felt a shudder in spite of his courage. The Canadian was the first to recover his coolness.

" Canario!" he exclaimed, " this Apache dog did right to warn us. Now we will be on our guard."

" Hum!" Cucharès said, passing his hands through his thick and matted hair, " I have not the least desire to be scalped."

" Bah!" Belhumeur said, " people sometimes recover."

" That is possible; but I don't care to make the attempt."

" And now that day has quite broken," Louis ob-served, " I fancy the time has arrived for me to go to the hacienda. What do you say, gentle-men?"

" We have not a moment to lose, if we wish to foil the enemy's plans," Don Martial said in support of his suggestion.

" The more so as we have to take certain measures

which it would be as well to determine as soon as possible," Belhumeur remarked.

The Indian and the lepero contented themselves by giving their assent through a nod.

"Now let us arrange a meeting-place," Louis went on. "You cannot wait for me here, as the Indians know where to find you."

"Yes," Belhumeur replied thoughtfully, "but I do not know the country where we now are, and I should be quite troubled to choose a fitting spot."

"I know one," Eagle-head said. "I will lead you to it; our pale brother will join us again there."

"Very good, but for that purpose I must know the spot."

"My brother need not trouble himself about that. When he leaves the great cabin I shall be near him."

"Very good—all right. Good-by, till we meet again."

Louis saddled his horse, and started at a gallop in the direction of the hacienda, which was about three musket shots from the camping-place.

The Count de Lhorailles was walking about anxiously in the hall of the main body of the building. In spite of himself his meeting with the Mexican occupied his mind. He wished to have a frank explanation with Dona Anita in her father's presence, which should dissipate his doubts, or at least give him the key of the mystery that surrounded the affair.

Another circumstance also dulled his humour, and redoubled his alarms. At daybreak Diégo Léon, one of his lieutenants, announced to him that the Indian guide brought home with them the previous day had disappeared during the night, and left no trace. The position was becoming serious. The Mexican moon was approaching.   That guide was evidently an Indian spy, ordered to inquire into the strength of the hacienda, and the means of surprising it.   The Apaches and Comanches could not be far off : perhaps they were already on the watch in the tall grass of the prairie, awaiting the favourable moment to rush on their implacable foes.

The count did not conceal from himself that if the position was difficult, he was the main cause of it.   Invested by the government with an important command, especially charged with the protection of the frontier against Indian invasions, he had not yet made a move, and had in no way tried to fulfil the commission he had not merely accepted but solicited.   The Mexican moon commenced in a month ; before that period he must strike a decisive blow, which would inspire the Indians with a wholesome terror, prevent them combining, and thus foil their plans.

The count had been reflecting for a long time, forgetting in his anxiety the guests he had brought to his house, and after whom he had not yet asked, when his old lieutenant appeared before him.

" What do you want, Martin ? " he asked.

" Excuse me for disturbing you, captain. Diégo Léon, who is on guard at the isthmus battery with eight men, has just sent to tell me that a horseman wishes to see you on a serious matter."

" What sort of man is he ? "

" A white man, well dressed, and mounted on an excellent horse."

" Hem ! did he say nothing further ? "

" Pardon me, he added this : " You will say to the man who commands you that I am one of the men he met at the Rancho of San José."

The count's face grew suddenly serene.

"Let him come in," he said; "'tis a friend."

The lieutenant withdrew. So soon as he was alone the count recommenced his walk.

"What can this man want of me?" he muttered. "When I asked his friend and himself to accompany me here they both refused. What reason can have caused such a sudden change in their plans? Bah! what is the use of addling one's brains?" he added, on hearing a horse's footfall re-echoing in the inner *patio*. "I shall soon know."

Almost immediately Don Louis appeared, led by the lieutenant, who, on a sign from the count, at once disappeared.

"What happy accident," the count said graciously, "procures me the honour of a visit I was so far from expecting?"

Don Louis politely returned the salutation, and replied,

"It is no happy accident that brings me. God grant that I may not be the harbinger of misfortune!"

These words made the count frown.

"What do you mean, senor?" he asked in anxiety. "I do not understand you."

"You will soon do so. But speak French, if you have no objection; we shall understand each other more easily," he said, giving up the Spanish which he had hitherto employed.

"What!" the count exclaimed in surprise, "you speak French?"

"Yes," Louis said, "for I have the honour of being your fellow-countryman, although," he added with a suppressed sigh, "I have quitted our country for more than ten years. It is always a great pleasure to me to be able to speak my own language."

K

The expression of the count's face completely changed on hearing these words.

"Oh!" he continued with effusion, "permit me to press your hand, sir. Two Frenchmen who meet in this distant land are brothers; let us momentarily forget the spot where we are, and talk about France—that dear country from which we are so remote, and which we love so much."

"Alas, sir!" Louis replied, with suppressed emotion, "I should be happy to forget for a few minutes what surrounds us, to summon up the recollections of our common country. Unfortunately the moment is a grave one; great dangers threaten you, and the time we would thus lose might produce a fearful catastrophe."

"You startle me, sir. What is happening? What have you so terrible to announce to me?"

"Did I not tell you that I was a messenger of evil tidings?"

"No matter. When told by you they will be welcome. In the situation in which I am placed in this desert, must I not ever expect misfortune?"

"I hope to be able to help you in warding off the danger that now hangs over you."

"Thanks for your fraternal conduct. Now speak. I am listening to you. Whatever you may tell me, I shall have the courage to hear it."

Don Louis, without revealing to the count his meeting with the Tigrero, as had been agreed on, told him how he had overheard a conversation between his guide and several Apache warriors ambushed in the vicinity of the hacienda, and the plan they had formed to surprise the colony.

"And now, sir," he added, "it is for you to judge of the gravity of this news and the arrangements you will have to make, in order to foil the plans of the Indians."

" I thank you, sir. When my lieutenant told me, a few moments prior to your arrival, of the disappearance of the guide, I immediately saw that I had to do with a spy. What you now report to me converts my suspicions into certainty. As you say, there is not a moment to lose, and I will at once think over the necessary arrangements."

He walked to a table and struck a bell sharply. A peon entered,

" The first lieutenant," he said. In a few minutes the latter arrived.

" Lieutenant," the count said to him, " take twenty men with you, and scour the country for three leagues round. I have just learned that Indians are concealed near here."

The old soldier bowed in reply, and prepared to obey.

" An instant," Louis exclaimed, signing him to stop, ' one word more."

" Eh ? " Martin. Leroux said, turning round in amazement, " you are talking French now."

" As you hear," Louis answered with a smile.

" You wished to make a remark," the count asked.

" I have lived in America a very long time. My home has been the desert, and I know the Indians, whom I have learned to rival in craft. If you allow me I will give you some advice, which, I fancy, may be useful to you under present circumstances."

" By Jove ! " the count exclaimed ; " pray speak, my dear countryman. Your advice will be very advantageous to us, I feel assured."

At this moment Don Sylva entered the room.

" Ah ! " the count continued, " come hither, my

friend. We have great need of you. Your knowledge of Indian habits will prove most useful to us."

"What has happened?" the haciendero asked as he bowed courteously to all present.

"We are threatened with an attack from the Apaches."

"Oh, oh! that is serious, my friend. What do you propose doing?"

"I do not know yet. I had given Don Martin orders to scour the neighbourhood; but this gentleman appears to be of a different opinion."

"The caballero is right," the Mexican answered, bowing to Don Louis; "but, in the first place, are you certain about this attack?"

"This gentleman came expressly to warn me."

"Then there can be no further doubt. We must make the necessary arrangements as quickly as possible. What is the caballero's opinion?"

"He was about to give it at the moment you came in."

"Then pray do not let me disturb your conference Speak, sir."

Don Louis bowed and took the word.

"Caballero!" he began, turning to Don Sylva, "what I am about to say is addressed principally to the French senores, who, accustomed to European warfare and the white mode of fighting, are, I am convinced, ignorant of Indian tactics."

"'Tis true," the count observed.

"Bah!" Leroux said, twirling his long moustaches with great self-sufficiency, "we will learn them."

"Take care you do not do so at your own expense," Don Louis continued. "Indian war is entirely one of stratagems and ambushes. The enemy who attacks you never forms in line; he remains constantly concealed, employing all means to conquer, but principally treachery. Five hundred Apache warriors, commanded by an intrepid chief, would defeat in the prairie your best soldiers, whom they would decimate, while not giving a chance for retaliation."

"Oh, oh!" the count muttered, "is that their only way of fighting?"

"The only one," the haciendero said in confirmation.

"Hum!" Leroux remarked, "I fancy it is very like the war in Africa."

"Not so much as you suppose. The Arabs let themselves be seen, while the Apaches, I repeat to you, only show themselves in the utmost extremity."

"Then my plan of pushing forward a reconnoissance——"

"Is impracticable for two reasons: either your horsemen, though surrounded by enemies, will not discover one of them, or they will be attracted into an ambush, where, in spite of prodigies of valour, they will perish to the last man."

"All that this gentleman says is most perfectly true: it is easy to see that he has a great experience of Indian warfare, and has often measured himself with the *Indios bravos*."

"That experience cost my happiness. All those I loved were massacred by these ferocious enemies," Don Louis replied sorrowfully. "Fear the same fate if you do not display the greatest prudence. I know how repugnant it is to the chivalrous character of our nation to follow such a course; but in my opinion it is the only one that offers any chances of salvation."

"We have here several women, children, and your

daughter before all, Don Sylva. We must absolutely shelter her from all danger; if possible, spare her the slightest alarm. I, therefore, accept this gentleman's views, and am determined to act with the greatest circumspection."

" I thank you for my daughter and myself."

" And now, sir, as we are already indebted to you for such good advice, complete your task. In my place, what would you do?"

" My advice is as follows," Louis answered seriously. " The Apaches will attack you for certain reasons I know, and which it is unnecessary to tell you. They make a point of honour of the success of that attack. Hence intrench yourselves here as well as you can. You have a considerable garrison composed of tried men; consequently, nearly all the chances are in your favour."

" I have one hundred and seventy resolute Frenchmen, who have all been soldiers."

" Behind good walls, and well armed, they are more than you want."

" Without counting forty peons, accustomed to pursuing the Indians, and whom I brought with me," Don Sylva remarked.

" Are those men here at this moment?" Louis asked sharply.

" Yes, sir."

" Oh! that simplifies the question materially. If you will believe me, the Indians have now everything to fear instead of you."

" Explain."

" It is evident that you will be attacked from the river. Perhaps, in order to divide your forces, the Indians will make a feigned attack from the side of the isthmus; but that point is too strongly defended for them to attempt to carry it. I repeat, then, all the enemy's efforts will be directed on the side of the river."

"I would call your attention to the fact, sir," the lieutenant said, "that at this moment the river is rendered unnavigable by thousands of trees torn from the mountains by the storms, and which it bears along with it."

"I know not whether the river is navigable or not," Don Louis replied firmly, "but of one thing I am certain, that the Apaches will attack you on that side."

"In any case, and not to be taken by surprise, two of the guns will be moved from the isthmus battery, leaving four there, which are more than sufficient, and laid so as to enfilade the river, care being taken to mask them. You will also, Leroux, mount a culverin on the platform of the mirador, whence we shall command the course of the Gila. Go and have these orders executed at once."

The old soldier went out without any reply, in order to carry out the commands of his chief.

"You see, gentlemen," the count then said, "that I hasten to profit by the counsels you are good enough to give me. I recognise my utter inexperience of this Indian warfare, and I repeat that I am happy at being so well supported."

"This gentleman has foreseen everything," the haciendero said; "like him, I believe that the house is most exposed on the river front."

"A last word," Don Louis continued.

"Speak, speak, sir."

"Did you not say, caballero, that you brought with you forty peons,. accustomed to Indian warfare, and that they were still here?"

"Yes, I said so, and it is perfectly true."

"Very good. I believe—and be good enough to take it as a simple observation, caballero—I say I believe that it would be a master-stroke, which would insure you the victory, to place your enemies between two fires."

"Indeed it would," the count exclaimed; "but how to do it? You yourself said, only a moment ago, that it would be the height of imprudence to send out a scouting party."

"I said, and I repeat it, the grass and woods are at this moment filled with eyes fixed on the hacienda, who will let no one pass out unnoticed."

"Well?"

"Did I not also tell you that this war was one of stratagems and ambushes?"

"You did; but I do not understand, I confess, what you are driving at."

"It is, however, excessively simple: you will understand me in two words."

"I much desire it."

"Senor caballero," Don Louis went on, turning to Don Sylva, "do you intend to remain here?"

"Yes; for certain private reasons I must remain some time here."

"I have no intention, be assured, senor, to interfere in your private affairs. So you remain here?"

"Yes."

"Very good. Have you among your peons a devoted man on whom you can count as on yourself?"

"Cascaras! I should think so. I have Blas Vasquez."

"Would you be good enough to tell me who this Blas is, as I have not the honour of his acquaintance?" -

"He is my capataz, and I can trust to him as to myself in matters of danger."

"Excellent! All is going on famously, then."

"I really cannot make you out," the count said.

"You shall see," said Louis.

"I have been trying to do so for the last half hour."

"Your capataz, to whom you will give your instructions, will put himself at the head of his peons within an hour, and ostensibly take the road to Guaymas; but, so soon as he has gone two or three leagues to a point we shall settle on, he will halt. The rest will be the business of myself and friends."

"Oh! I understand your plan now. The peons hidden by you will attack the Indians in the rear so soon as the action has commenced between them and us."

"That is it."

"But the Apaches? Do you believe they will allow a troop of white men to retire without harassing them?"

"The Indians are too shrewd to oppose them. What good would it do them to attack a body of men who have no baggage? The fight would not profit them, but cause their position to be discovered. No, no, be easy, caballero, they will not stir: they have too great an interest in remaining invisible."

"And what do you intend to do?"

"The Indians certainly saw me come in this direction; they know I am here. If I went out with them it would betray all. I shall go away alone as I came, and that immediately."

"The plan is so simple and well arranged that it must succeed. Receive our thanks, sir, and be kind enough to tell us your name, that we may know the man to whom we are indebted for so great a service."

" To what end, sir ? "

" I join my entreaties, caballero, to those of my
friend, Don Gaëtano, in order to induce you to reveal
the name of a man whose memory will be eternally engraved on our hearts."

Don Louis hesitated, though unable to account to
himself for the reason that made him do so.   He felt a
repugnance to give up his incognito as respected the
count.   The two men, however, pressed him so politely,
that having no serious reason to offer for the main-
tenance of his incognito, he allowed himself to be
vanquished by their entreaties, and consented to give
his name.

" Caballeros," he at length said, " I am the Count
Louis Edward Maxime de Prébois Crancé."

" We are friends, I trust," De Lhorailles said, holding
out his hand to him.

" What I have done is a proof of it, I think, sir," the
other replied with a bow, but not taking the offered
hand.

" I thank you," the count went on, without appearing to notice Louis' repugnance.   " Do you intend to
leave us soon ? "

" I must leave you to the urgent business you have
on hand.   If you will allow me, I will take my leave
at once."

" Not before breakfasting, at least ? "

" You will excuse me, but time presses.   I have
friends I have now left for some hours, and who must
be alarmed by my lengthened absence."

" As they know you are at my house, that is impossible, sir." the count said, somewhat piqued.

" They do not know that I arrived here without accident."

" That is different; then I will not delay you. Once again I thank you, sir."

" I have acted in accordance with my conscience; you owe me no thanks."

The three men quitted the hall, and proceeded towards the isthmus battery, talking of indifferent matters. About half way they met Don Blas, the capataz. Don Sylva made him a sign to join them, and when he was near them explained to him in two words the events that were preparing, and the part he would have to play.

" Voto à Brios ! " the capataz exclaimed joyously. " I thank you, Don Sylva, for this good news. We shall have a row at last, then, with those Apache dogs ! Caraï ! they 'll see some fun, I swear."

" I trust entirely to you, Blas."

" But at what place must I await this caballero ? "

" That is true : we have not fixed the place of meeting."

" About three leagues from here, on the Guaymas road, at a place where the road makes a bend, there is an isolated hill called, I think, *El Pan de Azucar :* you can ambush there without any fear of discovery. I will join you at that spot with my friends."

" That is agreed. At about what hour ? "

" I cannot say for certain : that must depend on circumstances."

A few minutes later Don Louis was riding back to the prairie, while the Count de Lhorailles and the two Mexicans, made preparations for an active defence of the colony.

" It is strange," Don Louis muttered to himself as he galloped on, " that this man who is my countryman,

and for whom I shall risk my life ere long, inspires me
with no sympathy."

Suddenly his horse shied. Roughly startled from his
reverie, the Frenchman looked up.

Eagle-head stood before him.

CHAPTER XI.

THE MEXICAN MOON.

After his visit to the hunters the Black Bear set out,
at the head of his warriors, to proceed to a neighbouring
island, known by the name of Choke-Heckel, which was
one of the advanced Apache posts on the Mexican frontier.
He reached the isle at daybreak. At this spot the Gila
attains its greatest width: each of the arms formed by the
island is nearly two miles wide. The island which rises
in the middle of the water, like a basket of flowers, is
about two miles long by half a mile wide, and is one
immense bouquet, exhaling the sweetest perfumes, and
the melodious songs of the birds which congregate in
incalculable numbers on all the branches of the trees
by which it is covered.

Illumined on this day by the splendid beams of a
flashing sun, the place had a strange and unusual appearance which had a powerful effect on the imagination.
As far as the eye could reach over the island and the two
banks of the Gila could be seen tents of buffalo hide,
or huts of branches leaned against each other, and whose
strange colours wearied the sight. Numerous canoe.
made of horse-skins sewed together, and mostly round,
or else hollowed out of trunks of trees, traversed the
river in every direction. The warriors dismounted and
set their horses free, which immediately proceeded to
join a number of others.

The chief went towards the huts before which feather flags and the scalps of renowned warriors fluttered in the breeze, passing through the women who were preparing the morning meal. But the Black Bear had been recognised immediately on his arrival, and all got out of his way with respectful bows. A thing no European could credit is the respect all Indians, without exception, pay to their chiefs. Among those who have kept up the manners of their forefathers, and, disdaining European civilisation, have continued to wander about the prairies as free men, this respect is changed into fanaticism, almost into adoration.

The gold fillet adorned with two buffalo horns, placed on the Black Bear's brow, caused him to be recognised by all, and the liveliest joy was evinced on his passage. He at length reached the river's bank. On arriving there he made a sign to a man fishing a short distance off in a canoe; the latter hastened up, and the chief passed over to the island. A hut of branches had been prepared for him. It is probable that invisible sentinels were watching for his arrival, for the moment he set foot on land, a chief called the Little Panther presented himself before him.

" The great chief is welcome among his brothers," he said, bowing courteously before the Black Bear. " Has my father had a good journey? "

" I have had a good journey, I thank my brother."

" If my father consents I will lead him to the *jacal* built to receive him."

" Let us go," the chief said.

The Little Panther bowed a second time, and guided the chief along a path formed through the shrubs. They soon arrived at a jacal, which, in the mind of the Indians, offered the ideal of what was comfortable,

through its size, the brilliancy of the colours with which
it was painted, and its cleanliness.

" My father is at home," the Little Panther said,
respectfully raising the *fressada* (blanket) which closed
the jacal, and falling back to let the Black Bear pass.
The latter entered.

" My brother will follow me," he said.

The Little Panther walked in behind him, and let the
curtain fall. This abode did not in any way differ
from that of the other Indians. A fire burned in the
centre. The Black Bear made a sign to the other
chief to sit down on a buffalo skull. He then chose one
for himself, and sat down near the fire. After
a moment's silence, employed by the two chiefs
in smoking gravely, the Black Bear addressed the
Little Panther :—

" Are the chiefs of all the tribes of our nation collected on the island as I ordered ? "

" They are."

" When will they come to my jacal ? "

" That depends on my father. They await his good
pleasure."

The Black Bear began smoking again silently. A
long period was thus spent.

" Nothing new has happened during my absence ? "
the Black Bear asked, shaking the ash out of his
calumet on his thumb.

" Three chiefs of the prairie Comanches have arrived,
sent by their nation to treat with the Apaches."

" Wah ! " the chief said. " Are they renowned
warriors ? "

" They have many wolfs' tails on their moccasins.
They must be valiant."

The Black Bear nodded his head in affirmation.

"One of them, it is said, is the Jester," the Little Panther continued.

"Is my brother certain of what he says?" the chief asked sharply.

"The Comanche warriors refused to give their names when they learned the absence of my father. They answered it was well, and that they would await his return."

"Good! they are chiefs. Where are they?"

"They have lighted a fire, round which they are camping."

"Time is precious. My brother will warn the Apache chiefs that I await them at the council fire."

The Little Panther rose without replying, and quitted the jacal.

For about an hour the Indian chief remained alone buried in thought : at the end of that time a sound of several approaching men could be heard outside. The curtain was raised by the Little Panther, who walked in.

"Well?" the Black Bear asked.

"The chiefs are waiting."

"Let them come in."

The chiefs made their appearance. They were ten in number ; each had put on his best ornaments, and all wore their war paint. They entered silently, and ranged themselves silently round the fire, after silently saluting the great chief, and kissing the hem of his robe.

As soon as all the chiefs had assembled in the interior of the *toldo* a troop of Apache warriors drew up outside, to keep off the curious, and insure the secrecy of the deliberations. The Black Bear, in spite of his self-mastery, could not refrain from a movement of joy at the sight of all these men, who were entirely devoted to him, and by whose help he felt certain of accomplishing his projects.

" My brothers are welcome," he said, inviting **them** by a sign to take seats on the buffalo skulls ranged round the fire. "I was awaiting them impatiently."

The chiefs bowed and sat down. Then the pipe-bearer entered and presented the calumet to each warrior, who drew two or three puffs of tobacco. When this ceremony was over, and the pipe-bearer had departed, the deliberation began.

" Before all," said the Black Bear, " I must give you an account of my mission. The Black Bear has completely fulfilled it ; he has entered the hut of the white men ; he has thoroughly examined it ; he knows the number of pale-faces that defend it ; and when the hour arrives for him to lead his warriors there the Black Bear will know how to find the road again."

The chiefs bowed with satisfaction.

" This great cabin of the whites," the Black Bear continued, " is the only serious obstacle we shall find on our road in the new expedition we are undertaking."

" The Yoris are dogs without courage. The Apaches will give them petticoats, and make them prepare their game," the Little Panther said with a grin.

The Black Bear shook his head.

" The pale-faces of the great cabin of Guetzalli are not Yoris," he said. " A chief has seen them—they are men. Nearly all of them have blue eyes, and hair of the colour of ripe maize ; they seem very brave—my brothers must be prudent."

" Does not my father know who these men are ? " a chief inquired.

" The Black Bear does not know. He was told down there, near the great Salt Lake, that they inhabited a country very far from here, towards the rising sun : that is all."

"These men have no trees, nor fruit, nor buffaloes in their own country, that they come to steal ours."

"The pale-faces are insatiable," the Black Bear replied. "They forget that the Great Spirit has only given them, like other men, one mouth and two hands. All they see they covet. The Wacondah, who loves his red sons, let them be born in a rich country, and has covered them with his gifts. The pale-faces are jealous, and seek continually to rob and dispossess them ; but the Apaches are brave warriors : they can defend their hunting-grounds, and prevent them being trampled by these vagabonds, who have come from the other side of the Great Salt Lake on the floating cabins of the *Great Medicine*."

The chiefs warmly applauded this harangue, which expressed so well the sentiments that affected them, and the animosity with which they were animated against the white race—that conquering and invading race, which constantly drives them further into the desert, not even leaving them the requisite space to breathe and live quietly after their fashion.

"The great nation of the Comanches of the Lakes, that which is called the Queen of the Prairies, has deputed to our nation three renowned warriors. I know not the object of this embassy, which, however, must be peaceful. Does it please you, chiefs of my nation, to receive them, and admit them to smoke the calumet of peace round our council fire ? "

"My father is a very wise warrior," the Little Panther replied : " he can, when he likes, divine the most hidden thoughts in the heart of his enemies. What he does will be well done. The chiefs of his nation will be always happy to regulate their conduct by the counsels he may deign to give them."

L

The Black Bear threw a glance round the assembly, as if to assure himself that the Little Panther had truly expressed the general will. The members of the council silently bowed their heads in acquiescence. The chief smiled proudly on seeing himself so appreciated by his companions, and addressing the Little Panther, said,—

"Let my brothers, the Comanche chiefs, be introduced."

These words were pronounced with a majesty equal to that of an European king sitting in parliament.

The Little Panther went out to execute the order he had received. During his absence, which was rather long, not a word was exchanged between the chiefs seated on buffalo skulls, with their elbows on their knees, and their chins on the palm of their hand; they remained motionless and silent, apparently plunged into deep thought.

The Little Panther at length returned, preceding the Comanche warriors. On their entry the Apache chiefs rose and saluted them ceremoniously. The Comanches returned the salutation with no less courtesy, but without any other response, and waited till they were addressed.

The Comanche warriors were young and finely built; they had a martial bearing, a free glance, and thoughtful brow. Dressed in their national costume, with heads proudly upraised, and hands stemmed in their sides, they had something noble and loyal about them which aroused sympathy. One of them specially, the youngest of the three—he was hardly five-and-twenty—must be a superior man, to judge by appearances: the stern lines of his countenance, the brilliancy of his glance, the elegance and majesty of his bearing, caused him to be recognised at the first glance as a chosen man.

His name was the Jester; and, as might be guessed from the tuft of condor feathers passed through his war-lock, he was one of the principal chiefs of the nation.

The Apache chiefs bent on the new arrivals, while not appearing to notice them, that profoundly inquisitive glance possessed to so eminent a degree by the Indians. The Comanches, though they might guess the power of the glances fixed on them, did not make a sign, nor allow a movement to escape them, indicating that they knew themselves to be the object of attention to all present.

Machiavel, author of the *Prince* though he was, com-pared with the red-skins, was only a child in matters of policy. These poor savages, as they are called by those who do not know them, are the cleverest and most cunning diplomatists in existence.

After an instant's delay the Black Bear took a step toward the Comanche chiefs, bowed to them, and holding out his right-hand palm upwards, said,——

" I am happy to receive beneath my cabin, in the midst of my people, my brothers, the Comanches of the Lakes. They will take their place at the council fire, and smoke with their brothers the calumet of peace."

" Be it so, " the Jester replied in a stern voice. " Are we not all children of Wacondah ? "

And, without adding another word, he took his seat with the other chiefs at the council fire, side by side with the Apaches. The conversation was again broken off, for every one was smoking. At length, when the calumet bowls contained only ashes, the Black Bear turned with a courteous smile to the Jester.

" My brothers, the Comanches of the Lakes are

doubtlessly hunting the buffalo not far from here, and then the thought occurred to them to visit their Apache brothers.   I thank them for it."

The Jester bowed.

" The Comanches of the Lakes are far away chasing the antelopes on the Del Nato.   The Jester, and a few devoted warriors of his tribe who accompany him, are alone encamped on the hunting-grounds."

" The Jester is a renowned chief on the prairie," the Apache graciously remarked. " The Black Bear is happy to have seen him.   So great a warrior as my brother does not act thus without some plausible motive."

" The Black Bear has guessed it.   The Jester has come to renew with his Apache brothers the narrow bonds of a loyal friendship.   Why, instead of disputing a territory to which we have equal claims, should we not divide it between us ?   Should the red men destroy each other ?   Would it not be better to bury the war-hatchet by the council fire at such a depth that, when an Apache met a Comanche, he would only see in him a well-beloved brother ?   The pale-faces, who each moon invade our possessions more and more, carry on a furious war with us ; then why should we help them by our intestine dissensions ?"

The Black Bear rose, and, stretching his arm out with authority, said,—

" My brother, the Jester, is right.   Only one sentiments hould henceforth guide us—patriotism !   Let us lay aside all our paltry enmities, to think but of one thing—liberty !   The pale-faces are perfectly ignorant of our plans.   During the few days I passed at Guaymas I was able to convince myself of that : thus our sudden invasion will be to them a thunderbolt, which will ice them with terror. They will be more than half conquered by our approach."

There was a solemn silence. The Jester then turned a calm and proud glance round the meeting, and exclaimed,—

" The Mexican moon will begin in twenty-four hours. Red-skin warriors! shall we allow it to pass away without attempting one of those daring strokes which we usually perform at this period of the year? There is one establishment above all, over which we should rush like a whirlwind: that establishment founded by pale-faces, other than the Yoris, is for us a permanent menace. I will not deal craftily with you. Apache chiefs! I come to offer you frankly, if you will attack Guetzalli, the support of four hundred Comanche warriors, at whose head I will place myself."

At this proposition a quiver of pleasure ran through the meeting.

" I joyfully accept my brother's proposal," the Black Bear said. "I have nearly the same number of warriors: our two bands will be strong enough, I hope, to utterly destroy the establishment of the pale-faces. To-morrow, at the rising of the moon, we will set out "

The chiefs retired, and the Black Bear and the Jester were left alone. These two chiefs enjoyed an equal reputation, and both were adored by their countrymen. Hence they examined each other curiously, for up to that moment they had always been enemies, and never had the chance of meeting save with weapons in their hands.

" I thank my brother for his cordial offer," the Black Bear was the first to say. " Under present circumstances his help will be very advantageous for us; but once the victory is decided, the spoil will be equally shared between the two nations."

The Jester bowed.

" What plan has my brother formed ? " he asked.

" A very simple one.   The Comanches are terrible horsemen : with my brother at their head, they must be invincible.   So soon as the moon shines in the heavens the Jester will set out with his warriors, and proceed toward Guetzalli, being careful to fire the prairie in front of his detachment, in order to raise a curtain of smoke which will conceal his movements and prevent his warriors being counted.   If, as is not probable, the pale-faces have placed vedettes before their great lodge to announce the arrival of the expedition, my brother will seize and kill them at once, to prevent them giving any alarm.   In this expedition, as in all those that have preceded it, everything belonging to the pale-faces— lodges, jacals, houses—will be burnt ; the beasts carried off and sent to the rear.   On arriving in front of Guetzalli my brother will hide himself as well as he can, and await the signal I will give him to attack the pale-faces."

" Good! My brother is a prudent chief.   He will suc- ceed.   I will do exactly as he has told me ; and he, what will he do while I am executing this portion of the general plan ? "

A strange smile played on the Black Bear's lips.

" He will see," he said, laying his hand on the Comanche's shoulder.   " Let him act as a chief, and I promise him a glorious victory."

" Good!" the Comanche made answer.   " My brother is the first of his nation ; he knows how he should be- have ; the Apaches are not women.   I go to rejoin my warriors."

" 'Tis well ; my brother has understood.   To-morrow at the rising of the moon."

The Jester bowed, and the two chiefs separated, apparently the best friends in the world. A few minutes later the greatest animation prevailed in the Apache camp; the women struck the tents and loaded the mules, the children lassoed and saddled the horses, and all preparations were made for a hurried departure.

CHAPTER XII.

A WOMAN'S STRATAGEM.

THE next day at the rising of the moon, as had been agreed, the Jester ordered his detachment to set out. Presently a party of horsemen who had hurried onwards threw lighted torches amid the shrubs, and in a few minutes an immense curtain of flames rose to the sky, and completely veiled the horizon. The Comanches carried out the orders of the Apache chief with such rapidity and intelligence, that in less than half an hour all was consumed.

The Black Bear, concealed in the island with his war party, had not made a move. The traces left by the Comanches were, alas! very visible, for the country only that morning so lovely, rich, and luxuriant, was at present gloomy and desolate. There was no verdure, no flowers, no birds hidden beneath the frondage, and twittering as if to outrival each other.

The Indians' plan would have met with perfect success through the arrangement of the campaigners, and the Guetzalli colonists would have been surprised, had other men than Belhumeur and his friends been on the route of the Indian army.

The Canadian was watching. At the first smoke that arose in the distance he understood the intention of the red-skins, and without losing a moment he sent off Eagle-head to the colony to inform the count of what was taking place. Still, behind the fire, the Comanches were arriving at full speed, destroying and trampling beneath their horses' hoofs what the flames might have spared.

Night had completely set in when the Jester arrived in sight of the colony. Supposing that, through the rapidity of his march, the white men would not have had time to place themselves on the defensive, he ambushed a portion of his men, placed himself at the head of the rest, and crawled with all the precautions employed in such cases toward the isthmus battery.

No one appeared : the glacis and entrenchments seemed abandoned. The Jester uttered his war-cry, rose suddenly, and bounding forward like a jaguar, crossed the entrenchment, followed by his warriors. But, at the moment when the Comanches prepared to leap into the interior, a fearful discharge at point-blank range levelled more than one-half of the Indian detachment, while the survivors took to flight.

The Comanches had one great disadvantage—they possessed no fire-arms. The musketry decimated them, and they could only reply by firing their arrows, or by hurling their javelins. Noticing, therefore, though too late for himself, that the French were on their guard, the Jester, desperate at the check he had experienced, and his serious losses, was unwilling to further weaken the confidence of his warriors by useless tentatives. He concealed his detachment under cover of the virgin forest, and resolved to wait for the Black Bear's signal ere he made a move.

Don Louis had followed Eagle-head. The Indian, after several turnings, led him almost opposite the isthmus battery to the entrance of a dense thicket of cactus, aloes, and floripondios.

" My brother can dismount," he said to the French-man ; " we have arrived."

" Arrived where ? " Louis asked, looking around him in vain.

Without replying the chief took the horse, and led it away. Louis during the interval looked all around him ; but his researches had no result.

" Well," Eagle-head asked on his return, " has my brother found it ? "

" On my faith, no, chief. I give it up."

The Indian smiled.

" The pale-faces have the eyes of moles," he said.

" It is possible ; at any rate, I should feel obliged by your lending me yours."

" Good ! My brother shall see."

Eagle-head glided along the ground, and Louis imitated him : in this way they entered the thicket. After about a quarter of an hour of this exercise, which was more than fatiguing, the Indian stopped.

" Let my brother look," he said.

They were in a small clearing, formed in the midst of an inextricable medley of branches and shrubs, com-pleted by a profusion of leaves so artistically interlaced, that without deep observation it would be impossible to suspect the existence of this hiding-place. Belhumeur and the two Mexicans were philosophically smoking while awaiting the return of the envoy.

" You are welcome," the Canadian said, so soon as he caught sight of him. " How do you like our camp ? Charming, is it not ? Eagle-head discovered it. Those devils of Indians have a peculiar talent for forming an ambuscade. We are as safe here as in Quebec Cathedral."

During this flood of words, to which he only responded

by a hearty pressure of the hand, Louis had comfortably seated himself by the side of his companions, and began to do honour, with excellent appetite, to the provisions they had put aside for him.

"But where are the horses?" he asked.

"Here, two paces from us; not to be found by any one save ourselves."

"Very good. Shall we be able to get them so soon as we want them?"

"Pardieu!"

"The fact is we shall probably need them soon."

"Ah, ah! but," he added, checking himself, "I am chattering, and not noticing that you must be probably savagely hungry. Finish your meal, and we will talk afterwards."

"Oh! I can answer very well while eating."

"Wo! No, everything has its proper time. Finish your breakfast: we will listen to you afterwards."

When Louis had finished eating he described fully the way in which he had carried out his mission.

"All that is very good," Belhumeur said when he had ended his report. "I believe that we can henceforth feel assured about the safety of our countrymen, especially with the help of the forty peons, who will take the enemy between two fires."

"Yes, but where shall they be concealed?"

"Leave that to Eagle-head. The chief knows this country thoroughly; he has hunted in it for a long time. I am certain he will find a suitable place for the Mexicans. What do you say, chief?"

"It is easy to hide one's self in the prairie," the chief answered laconically.

"Yes," Don Martial remarked, "but there is one thing you forget."

"What?"

"I live on the frontier, and have long been accustomed to Indian tactics. The Apaches will arrive, preceded by a curtain of smoke; the plain will soon be only one vast sheet of flame, in the midst of which we shall struggle in vain, and which will end by swallowing us up, if we do not take the proper precautions."

"That is true: it is a serious matter. Unfortunately, I only see one way of escaping from the danger, and that we cannot employ."

"What is it?"

"By Jove! making off."

"I know another," Eagle-head observed.

"You, chief? Then you will tell us of it."

"Let the pale-faces listen. The Rio Gila, like all other large rivers, brings down with it dead trees, at times in such quantities that at certain spots they completely block up the passage; in time these trees press against each other, and their branches become entwined; then grass grows, to cement them more firmly together; the sand and earth are piled up gradually on these immense rafts, which at a distance resemble islands, until a storm comes as a flood, which breaks up the raft, and bears it away."

"Yes, I know that. I have seen frequent instances of it, chief," Belhumeur said. "These rafts at last grow to look so like islands that the man most accustomed to desert life and the grand spectacles of nature is frequently deceived by them. I understand all the advantages your idea possesses for us; but, unhappily, I do not see how it will be possible for us to carry it out."

"In the simplest way. The Indian's eye is good; he sees everything within two bow-shots of him. Above the great lodge of the pale-faces, did not my brother notice an islet about fifty yards almost from the bank?"

"What you say is quite correct," Belhumeur exclaimed; "I can call the island to mind now."

"From the position it occupies there will be nothing to apprehend from fire," Louis remarked. "If it is large enough to hold us all it will be extremely useful as an advanced post."

"We have not a moment to lose: we must take possession of it at once, and when we are certain that it offers all we want we will lead the peons to it."

"Let us start, then, without further delay," the Tigrero said as he rose.

The others imitated him, and the five men left the clearing. After fetching their horses they proceeded toward the island under the guidance of Eagle-head.

The Indian chief had not deceived them. With that infallible glance his countrymen possess, he had at once formed a correct opinion of the spot he so cleverly selected. There was another consideration highly advantageous for the adventurers—a thick line of mangroves bordered the river's edge, and advanced sufficiently far into the stream to diminish the distance separating the isle from the mainland, while forming a natural defence for men concealed in the tall grass; for it was perfectly impossible that the Indians could hide themselves in the mangroves to harass their enemies, who, on the other hand, could do them considerable mischief.

This islet (we will retain the name, though it was really only a raft) was covered with a close, strong herbage, about two yards in height, in the midst of which men and horses completely disappeared. When the reconnoissance was ended. Belhumeur and the two

Mexicans installed themselves in the centre, while Louis and Eagle-head returned to the bank to go and meet the capataz and his people.

Don Martial did not care to accompany them. So near the colony he was afraid of being recognised by Don Sylva, and preferred to maintain, as long as he could, an incognito necessary for the ulterior success of his plans. Louis, after making him the offer to accompany them, pressed him no further, and appeared to accept his refusal without any discussion. The truth was, that the count felt, without being able to explain it, a species of repulsion for this man, whose cautious manner and continual hesitation had ill disposed him in his favour.

Eagle-head and Louis, certain that the Black Bear had really retired with his detachment, and left no spies on the prairie, thought it unnecessary to let the Mexicans take a long and wearisome ride before leading them to the hiding-place ; consequently, they hid themselves in the shrubs at the end of the isthmus to watch their exit, and lead them straight to the spot.

In the mean while the news Don Louis had carried to the colony had turned everything topsy-turvy. Although, since the first foundation of the hacienda, the Indians had constantly tried to harass the French, the various attempts they made had been unimportant, and this was really the first time they would have a serious contest with their ferocious enemies.

The Count de Lhorailles had with him about two hundred Dauph'yeers, who had come from Valparaiso, Guyaquil, Callao, and the other Pacific ports, which are always crowded with adventurers of every description. These worthy people were a singular mixture of all the nationalities peopling the two hemispheres, although the French supplied the largest factor. Half bandits, half soldiers, these men put the utmost faith in the chief they had freely chosen.

The news of the attack premeditated by the Apaches was received by the garrison with shouts of joy and enthusiasm. It was an amusement for these adventurers to exchange shots, or rub the rust off a little, as they naïvely said in their picturesque language. They desired before all to prove to the Apaches the difference existing between the Creole colonists, whom they have been in the habit of killing and plundering from time immemorial, and Europeans whom they did not yet know.

The count, therefore, had no need to recommend firmness to them; he was, on the contrary, obliged to repress their ardour, and beg them to be prudent, by promising that they should soon have an opportunity of meeting the red-skins in the open field.

As soon as the defensive preparations were made the count left the details to his two lieutenants, two old soldiers, on whom he believed he could count; then he thought of Blas Vasquez and his peons. In the probable event that the Indians had left spies round the colony, they must be persuaded that this band had really retired. For that purpose several mules were laden with provisions, as if for a long journey; then the capataz, well instructed, put himself at the head of the squadron, and left the colony, rifle on thigh.

The count, Don Sylva, and the other inhabitants followed the party with an interest easy to comprehend, ready to help them if attacked. But nothing stirred in the prairie; the calm and silence continued to prevail, and the Mexicans soon disappeared in the tall grass.

"I cannot at all understand the Indian tactics," Don Sylva muttered thoughtfully. "As they have allowed that party to pass so quietly, they must be planning some trick which offers a good prospect of success."

"We shall soon know what we have to expect," the count replied; "besides, we are ready to receive them. I am only sorry that Dona Anita should be here; not that she runs the slightest risk, but the sound of the contest may terrify her."

"No, senor conde," the lady said, who came from the house at the moment; "fear nothing of that nature for me. I am a true Mexican, and not one of your European dames, whom the slightest thing causes to faint. Often, in circumstances graver than these, I have heard the Apache war-yell echo in my ears, without, however, feeling that intense alarm you seem to apprehend from me to-day."

After uttering these words with that haughty and profoundly contemptuous accent women know so well to employ to a man they do not love, Dona Anita passed before the count without deigning him a glance, and took her father's arm.

The Frenchman made no reply: he bit his lips till they bled, and bowed as if he did not understand the epigram launched at him. He intended to have an explanation with his betrothed at a later date; for though he did not love her, as often happens in such cases, he did not pardon her being loved by another, and especially for regarding him with indifference; but the events which had hurried on with such rapidity during the last two days had hitherto prevented him asking this important interview of the dona.

The haciendero's daughter was an Andalusian from head to foot, all fire and passion, only obeying the pre-

cipitate movements of her heart.   Loving with all the
strength of her soul, safeguarded by her love for Don
Martial, she had judged the Count de Lhorailles coolly,
and guessed the speculator under the garb of the gentleman ; hence she made up her mind at once to render it
an impossibility ever to become his wife. To commence
an overt struggle with her father—she knew, too well to
risk it, the old Spanish blood that boiled in his veins.
A woman's strength is her apparent weakness ;   her
means of defence, stratagem.   As much Indian as
she   was   Spaniard,   Anita   chose   stratagem,   that
terrible woman's weapon, which often renders her so
dangerous.

Blas Vasquez, the capataz, had seen the birth of
Dona Anita : his wife had been her nurse—that is, he
was devoted to the young girl, and on a sign from her
he would have pledged his soul to the demon.

When Don Louis visited the hacienda the young
lady was considerably curious as to the motive of his
arrival. After the Frenchman's departure she asked
coolly for information from the capataz, who saw no
harm in giving it to her, the more so because every
one in the colony would soon know the news the count
brought.   The only thing no one could know, and
which Dona Anita guessed with that heart instinct
which never deceives, was the presence of the Tigrero
among the hunters ambushed in the vicinity of the
hacienda.

On leaving her at Guaymas, Don Martial had said
that he would constantly watch over her, and save her
from the fate with which she was menaced. After
that, it was plain that he must have followed her.
Had he done so (which she did not for a moment
doubt), he must certainly be among the brave men who

at that moment were devoting themselves to save her, while seeking to protect the colony.

The logic of the heart is the only species that is positive and never deceives. We have seen that Dona Anita, enlightened by passion, reasoned justly. When the girl had drawn from the capataz all the information she desired,—

"Don Blas," she said to him, "it is probable that if the colony is attacked, after the services you will be able to render, and when my father and Don Gaëtano no longer want you and your men, that you will receive orders to return to Guaymas."

"'Tis probable, certainly, senora," the worthy man answered.

"In that case you will have no objection to do me a service?" she went on, looking at him with her most fascinating smile.

"You know, senorita, that I would throw myself into the fire for you."

"I do not wish to put your friendship to such a rude trial, my good Blas; still I thank you for your kindly feeling."

"What can I do to oblige you?"

"Oh! a very easy matter. You know," she said lightly, "that for a very long time I have wished to have two jaguar skins as a carpet for my bedroom?"

"No," he replied simply; "I was not aware of it."

"Ah! well, I tell it you now, so you know it."

"I shall not forget it, senorita, you may be sure."

"Thanks; but that is not exactly what I want."

"What?"

"That you should get the skins for me."

"Oh! so soon as I am my own master again you can depend on me."

M

"I do not wish you to expose your life to satisfy a whim."

"Oh, senorita !" he said reproachfully.

"No ; I have a way to procure them more easily."

"Ah ! Very good. Let us see."

"A renowned Tigrero arrived at Guaymas a few days back."

"Don Martial Asuzena?" he quickly interrupted her.

"Do you know him ?"

"Who does not know the Tigrero ? "

"Well, I heard that he has brought back from his last hunt on the western prairies some magnificent jaguar skins, which, I have no doubt, he would be willing to sell at a fair price."

"I am certain of it."

"Here," she said, drawing a small, carefully-sealed note from her bosom, "is a letter you will give that man. I describe in it the way in which I should like to have the skins prepared, and the price I am willing to give. Here is the money," she added, as she handed him a purse ; "you will arrange the matter for me."

"There was no occasion to write," the capataz remarked.

"Pardon me, my friend, you have so many things to think of, that a trifle like this might easily slip your memory."

"Well, that is possible ; so perhaps you have acted wisely."

"Well, then, it is agreed—you will perform my commission ? "

"Can you doubt it ? "

"No, my friend. But stay, one word more. Do not say anything to my father. You know how kind he is; he would want to make me a present of them, and I wish to pay for the skins out of my own purse."

The capataz began laughing at the joke. The worthy man was delighted at sharing a secret, however slight it might be, with his darling child, as he called his young mistress.

"It is settled," he said; "I will be dumb."

The girl gave him a friendly nod and withdrew. What was the meaning of the note? Why did she write it? We shall soon learn.

The day passed at the hacienda without further incidents. The count made several attempts to have a conversation with the dona, which she constantly sought to avoid.

Blas Vasquez, on quitting the colony, struck the Guaymas road, and made his troop go at a sharp trot, through fear of a surprise. He had scarce lost sight of the colony, and entered the tall grass, when two men, leaping into the middle of the path, checked their horses about twenty paces ahead of him. One of them was an Indian; the other the capataz recognised at a glance as the man who had come to the hacienda that morning. Vasquez commanded his men to halt, and advancing alone to meet the stranger, said,—

"By what accident do I meet you here, Senor Francès? You are still far from the meeting-place you indicated yourself."

"We are so," was the reply; "but as we found no Apache trail in the prairie we thought it useless to give you a long journey. I have been sent to conduct you to the ambush we have chosen."

"You did right. Have we far to go?"

"No, hardly a quarter of an hour's ride. We are going to that islet, which you can see by standing in your stirrups," he added, stretching out his arm in the direction of the river.

" Eh ?" the capataz said. " The spot is well chosen : we can command the river from there."

"That is the reason why we selected it."

" Be good enough, then, to serve as our guide, Senor Francès : we will follow you."

The detachment set out again. As Don Louis had stated, within a quarter of an hour the capataz and the peons were encamped on the islet with the five adventurers, so well masked by grass and mangroves, that it was impossible to see them from either bank of the river.

So soon as the capataz had performed his duties as head of the detachment, he sat down at the bivouac fire by the side of his new friends, to whom Don Louis presented him. The first person Blas perceived was Don Martial, the Tigrero. At the sight of him he could hardly refrain from a movement of surprise.

" *Caspita !* " he exclaimed, with a loud laugh ; " the meeting is curious."

" Why so ? " the Mexican asked, rather annoyed by this recognition, which he had not expected, for he did not think the capataz knew him.

" Are you not Don Martial Asuzena ? "

" Yes," he replied, more and more restless.

" My faith ! I should have found it difficult to meet you at Guaymas ; but I did not expect to find you here."

" Explain yourself, I beg. I cannot understand you at all."

" My young mistress gave me a message for you."

" What do you say ? " the Tigrero exclaimed, his heart beginning to palpitate.

" What I say, nothing else. Dona Anita wishes to buy two jaguar skins of you, it appears."

" Of me ? "

" Yes."

Don Martial regarded him with such an air of amazement that the capataz began again laughing heartily. This laughter aroused the young man; made him conjecture there was some mystery in the affair; and that if he continued to look so astonished, he would arouse suspicions in the worthy man, who probably did not know the word of the riddle.

" 'Tis true," he said, as if trying to remember something, " I fancy I can call to mind some time back——"

" Then," the capataz interrupted him, " it's all right; besides, I was asked to hand you a letter so soon as I met you."

" A letter from whom ? "

" Why, from my mistress, I suppose."

" From Dona Anita ? "

" Who else ? "

" Give it me quickly," the Tigrero exclaimed in great agitation.

The capataz handed it to him. Don Martial tore it from his hands, broke the seal with trembling fingers, and devoured it with his eyes. When he had finished reading it he concealed it in his bosom.

" Well," the capataz asked him, " what does my mistress say ? "

" Only what you told me yourself," the Tigrero replied, in anything but a firm voice.

Blas Vasquez shook his head.

" Hem ! that man is certainly hiding something from me," he muttered. " Can Dona Anita have deceived me ? "

In the mean while the Tigrero walked about in agitation, apparently revolving some important project. At length he approached Belhumeur, who was smoking silently, and, leaning over his ear, uttered a few words in a low voice, to which the Canadian answered with a nod of assent. A flash of joy illumined the Tigrero's gloomy face as he made a sign to Cucharès to follow him, and quitted the bivouac a few minutes later. Don Martial and the lepero, both mounted, swam across the space separating them from the main land. The capataz perceived them at the moment they landed, and uttered a cry of astonishment.

" Why," he exclaimed, " the Tigrero is leaving us. Where can he be going ?"

Belhumeur regarded the Mexican with his bitter-sweet look, and replied, with a jesting accent,—

" Who knows ? Perhaps he is going to carry the answer to the letter you gave him."

" That is not impossible," the capataz remarked thoughtfully, little suspecting that he spoke the exact truth.

At this moment the sun set in floods of purple and gold far away in the horizon behind the snow-clad peaks of the lofty mountains of the Sierra Madre, and night soon stretched her black cere-cloth over the earth.

CHAPTER XIII.

A NIGHT JOURNEY.

EVENTS have so multiplied during the course of this night that, to keep headway with the incidents, we are compelled to pass incessantly from one person to the other.

Don Martial was rich—very rich—eager for excitement, and endowed with warlike instincts. He had only embraced the profession of *Tigrero* in order to have a plausible excuse for his constant travels in the desert, which he had passed his whole life in traversing in every direction.

The Tigreros are generally wood-rangers or old hunters, who, for a certain salary and a premium on each hide, engage with a haciendero to kill the wild beasts that decimate his herds. What others did for money he performed simply for pleasure: hence he was greatly liked on the frontiers, and especially welcomed by all the hacienderos, who found in him not only the clever and daring hunter, but also the boon companion and the caballero.

Don Martial saw Dona Anita for the first time when the chances of his adventurous life had led him to a hacienda belonging to Don Sylva, where, within the space of a month, he killed some dozen wild beasts. As the Tigrero constantly watched the young girl, whom he could not see without falling madly in love with, it happened that one day, when Anita's horse ran away, he was near enough to save her at the peril of his own life. It was through this event that the girl first noticed and spoke to him. We know the rest.

Cucharès was not at all pleased with the sudden departure from the island. He inwardly cursed the folly which made him attach himself to a man like him he now followed, who might expose him at any moment to the chances of getting an arrow through his body, without any profit or available excuse. Still Cucharès was not the man to feel long angry with the Tigrero. He knew that grave reasons alone could have induced him to leave a shelter at that hour of the night, resign the aid of the hunters, and go wandering about the desert without any apparent object. He burned to know the reasons; but he knew that Don Martial was no great talker, and had a great objection to having his secrets spied out; and as, in spite of all his bounce, he entertained a great respect for the Tigrero, mingled with a decent amount of fear, he deferred to a more favourable moment the numerous questions he longed to ask him.

The two men, then, marched on side by side silently, allowing the reins to hang on their horses' heads, and each indulging in his own reflections. Still Cucharès remarked that Don Martial, instead of seeking the cover of the forest, obstinately followed the river bank, and kept his horse as close to it as possible.

The darkness grew rapidly denser around them; distant objects began to be lost in the masses of shadow on the horizon, and they soon found themselves in complete obscurity. For some time the lepero tried, by coughing or uttering exclamations, to attract his comrade's attention, though unsuccessfully; but when he saw that the night had completely set in, while the Tigrero marched on without appearing to notice the fact, he at length mustered up courage to address him.

" Don Martial," he said.

" Well," the latter replied carelessly.

" Do you not think it is time for us to stop a little ? "

" What for ? "

" What for ? " the lepero replied, with a bound of surprise.

" Yes ; we have not arrived yet."

" Then we are going somewhere ? "

" Why else should we have left our friends ? "

" That 's true. Where are we going, though ? That is what I should like to know."

" You will soon do so."

" I confess that I should be glad of it."

There was again silence, during which they continued to advance. They had left the hill of Guetzalli about two musket-shots behind them, and reached a sort of creek, which, through the windings of the river, was almost parallel with the back of the hacienda, whose gloomy and imposing mass rose before them, and cast its shadow over them. Don Martial stopped.

" We have arrived," he said.

"At last!" the lepero muttered with a sigh of satisfaction.

"I mean to say," the Tigrero went on, "that the easiest part of our expedition is ended."

" We are making an expedition, then ? "

" By Jove ! do you fancy, then, my good fellow, that I am marching along the banks of the Gila merely for amusement ? "

" That surprised me, too."

" Now our expedition will commence in reality "

" Good ! "

" I must warn you, however, that it is rather dangerous ; however, I counted on you."

" Thanks," Cucharès answered, making a grimace which had some pretensions to resemble a smile. The truth is, the lepero would have preferred that his friend had not given him this proof of confidence. Don Martial continued,—

" We are going there ; " and he extended his arm in the direction of the river.

" Where then ? to the hacienda? "

" Yes."

" You wish us to be cut to pieces."

" How so ? "

" Do you believe we shall reach the hacienda without being discovered ? "

"We will try it at any rate."

"Yes; and as we shall not succeed, those demons of Frenchmen, who are on the watch, will take us for savages, and be safe to shoot us."

"It is a risk to run."

"Thanks! I prefer remaining here, for I confess I am not yet mad enough to put myself in the wolf's jaws for mere sport. Go where you please, but I stay here."

The Tigrero could not suppress a smile.

"The danger is not so great as you suppose," he said. "We are expected at the hacienda by some one, who will doubtlessly have moved the sentinels from the spot where we shall land."

"That is possible, but I do not care to try the experiment, for a bullet never pardons; besides, those Frenchmen are tremendous marksmen."

The Tigrero made no reply; he did not seem even to have heard his companion's remark. His mind was elsewhere. With his body bent forward, he was listening. During the last few minutes the desert had assumed a singular appearance. It woke up. All sorts of noises were heard from the depths of the thickets and clearings. Animals of every description rushed from the covert, and madly passed the two men without noticing them. The birds, startled from their first sleep, rose uttering shrill cries, and circled in the air. In the river might be seen the outlines of wild beasts swimming vigorously to reach the other bank. In a word, something extraordinary was taking place.

At intervals dry crackling sounds and hoarse murmurs, like those of rising water, broke the silence, and became with each moment more intense. On the extreme verge of the horizon a large band of bright red, growing wider from minute to minute, spread over the scene a purple and gold glare, which gave it a fantastic appearance. Already, on two different occasions, enormous clouds of smoke spangled with sparks had whirled over the heads of the two men.

" Halloh ! what is happening now ? " the lepero suddenly exclaimed. " Look at our horses, Don Martial."

In fact, the noble beasts, with neck outstretched and ears laid back, were breathing heavily, stamping on the ground, and trying to escape from their riders.

" *Caspita !* " the Tigrero said calmly, " they smell the fire, that is all."

" What fire ? Do you think the prairie is on fire ? "

" Of course. You can see it as well as I if you like."

" Hem ! what is the meaning of that ? "

" Not much. It is one of the ordinary Indian tricks. We are in the Comanche moon : are you not aware of that ? "

" I beg your pardon, I am not a wood-ranger. I confess to you that all this alarms me greatly, and that I would willingly give a trifle to be out of it."

" You are a child," Don Martial answered him laughingly. " It is evident that the Indians have fired the prairie to conceal their numbers : they are coming up behind the fire. You will soon hear their war-cry sounding amid the clouds of smoke and fire which are approaching, and will soon surround us. By remaining here you run three risks—of being roasted, scalped, or killed : three most unpleasant things, I grant, and which I do not think will suit you. You had better come with me. If you are killed, well, what then ? It is a risk to run. Come, dismount ; the fire is gaining on us : soon we shall not have the chance. What will you do ? "

" I will follow you," the lepero replied in a mournful

voice. "I must. I was mad—deuce take me!—to leave
Guaymas, where I was so happy—where I lived without
working—to come and thrust my head into such
wasps' nests. I assure you that if I escape he will be
a sharp fellow who catches me here a second time."

"Bah, bah! people always say that. Make haste;
we have no time to lose."

In fact, the desert for a distance of several leagues
burned like the crater of an immense volcano; the
flames undulated and shot along like the waves of the
sea, twisting and felling the largest trees like wisps of
straw. From the thick curtain of copper-coloured
smoke which preceded the flames there escaped, at each
moment, bands of coyotes, buffaloes, and jaguars, which,
maddened with terror, rushed into the river, uttering
yells and deafening cries.

Don Martial and the lepero entered the water; and
their noble animals, impelled by their instinct, hurried
in the direction of the other bank.

This part of the desert formed a strange contrast to
that which the men were leaving. The latter appeared
an immense furnace, from which issued vague rumours,
cries of distress, agony, and terror; a sea of fire, with
its billows and majestic waves, whose devouring activity
swallowed up everything on their passage, crossing
valleys, escalading mountains, and reducing to impalpable ashes the products of the vegetable and animal
kingdoms.

The Gila, at this period of the year swollen by the
rains which fall in the sierra, had a width double of
what it was in the summer. At that period its current
becomes strong, and frequently dangerous through its
rapidity; but, at the moment our adventurers crossed
it, the numerous animals which sought to cross it simul-

taneously in a dense body had so broken its force, that they reached the other bank in a comparatively short period.

"Eh!" Cucharès observed at the moment the horses struck land and began ascending the bank, "did you not tell me, Don Martial, that we were going to the hacienda? We are not taking the road, I fancy."

"You fancy wrong, comrade. Remember this—in the desert a man must always appear to turn his back on the object he wishes to reach, or he will never arrive."

"Which means?"

"That we are going to hobble our horses under this tuft of mesquites and cedar-wood trees, where they will be in perfect safety, and then go straight to the hacienda."

The Tigrero immediately dismounted, led his horse under the shelter of the great trees, took off its bridle in order that it might graze, hobbled it carefully, and returned to the bank.

Cucharès, with that resolution of despair which, under certain circumstances, bears a striking resemblance to courage, imitated his companion's movements point for point. The worthy lepero had at length formed an heroic resolve. Persuaded that he was lost, he yielded himself to the guidance of his lucky or unlucky star with that half-timid fanaticism which can only be compared with that found among the Easterns.

As we have said, this side of the river was plunged in shade and silence, and the adventurers were temporarily protected from any danger.

"Stay," the lepero again remarked; "it is a good distance from this place to the hacienda; I can never swim it."

"Patience. We shall find, I am certain, if we take

the trouble to look, means to shorten it. Ah, look!"
he said, a moment later. "What did I say to you?"

The Tigrero pointed out to the lepero a small canoe
fastened to a stake in a small creek.

"The colonists often come here to fish," he continued;
"they have several canoes concealed like this at various
spots. We will take this one, and in a few moments
we shall reach our destination. Do you know how to
manage a paddle?"

"Yes, when I am not afraid."

Don Martial looked at him for a few seconds, then
laying his hand roughly on his shoulder, said in a sharp
voice,—

"Listen, Cucharès, my friend. I have no time to
discuss the matter with you; I have extremely serious
reasons for acting as I am now doing. I want on your
part hearty co-operation, so take warning in time.
You know me: at the first suspicious movement I will
blow out your brains as I would a coyote's. Now help
me to launch the canoe and start."

The lepero understood—he resigned himself. In a
few minutes the canoe was ready, and the two men in
it. The passage they had to make to reach the back of
the hacienda was not long, but bristled with dangers.
In the first place, through the strength of the current
which bore with it a large quantity of dead trees, most
of them still having their branches, and which, floating
half submerged in the water, threatened at each pull to
pierce the frail boat. Next, the animals which continued to shun the fire, traversed the river in compact
bands; and if the canoe were entangled in one of those
manadas mad with terror, it must be crushed with its
passengers. The lightest danger the adventurers ran
was the receipt of a bullet from the sentinels hidden in

the bushes which defended the approach to the colony on the river side. But this danger was as nothing compared with the others to which we have alluded. There was every reason for assuming that the French, aroused by the flames, would direct all their attention to the land side. Besides, Don Martial believed he had nothing to fear from the sentries, who would probably have been withdrawn.

At a signal from Don Martial, Cucharès took up the paddles, and they started. The fire was rapidly retiring in a western direction while continuing its ravages. The canoe advanced slowly and cautiously through the innumerable objects which each moment checked its progress.

Cucharès, pale as a corpse, with hair standing on end, and eyes enlarged by terror, rowed on frenziedly, while recommending his soul fervently to all the numberless saints of the Spanish calendar, for he was more than ever convinced that he would never emerge in safety from the enterprise on which he had so foolishly entered.

In fact, the position was a grave one, and it required all the resolution with which the Tigrero was endowed, as well as the excitement caused by the object he hoped to attain, to keep him from sharing the terror which had seized on his comrade. The further they advanced the greater the obstacles grew. Obliged to make continued turns, in consequence of the trees that barred their passage, they only turned on their own axis, as it were, forced to pass the same spot a dozen times, and watch on all sides at once, not to be sunk by the objects, either visible or invisible, which incessantly rose before them.

For about two hours they continued this wearying navigation ; but they insensibly approached the hacienda, whose sombre mass stood out from the star-lit sky. Suddenly a terrible cry, raised by a considerable number of voices, filled the air, and a discharge of artillery and musketry roared like thunder.

"Holy Virgin!" Cucharès exclaimed, letting go the paddles and clasping his hands, "we are lost!"

"On the contrary," the Tigrero said, "we are saved. The Indians are attacking the colony; all the French are at the entrenchments, and no one will dream of watching us. Bold, my good boy! One more good pull, and all will be over,"

"May God hear you!" the lepero muttered, beginning to paddle again with a trembling hand.

"Ah! the attack is serious, it appears. All the better. The harder they fight over there, the less attention will be paid to us. Let us get on."

The two adventurers, hidden in the shade, paddled on silently, and gradually approached the hacienda. Don Martial looked searchingly around: all was silent in this part of the river, which was half a pistol-shot distant from the buildings. There was no reason for supposing that they had been seen. The Tigrero bent over his companion.

"That will do," he whispered; "we have arrived."

"What! arrived?" the lepero repeated with a frightened air. "We are still a long way off."

"No; at the spot where we now are, whatever may happen, you have nothing to fear. Remain in the canoe, fasten it to one of the stumps that surround you, and wait for me."

"What! are you going away?"

"Yes; I shall leave you for an hour or two. Keep a good watch. If you notice anything new you will imitate the cry of the water-hen twice: you understand?"

" Perfectly; but if a serious danger threatened us what ought I to do? "

The Tigrero reflected for an instant.

" What danger can threaten you here?" he said.

" I do not know; but the Indians are fiends incarnate : with them you must be prepared for anything."

" You are right. Well, in case of any serious danger threatening us—but only in that case, you understand—after giving your signal, you will put across to that point. Mangroves grow there, under the shelter of which you will be perfectly safe, and I will join you immediately."

" Very good; but how shall I know where to find you? '

" I will imitate twice the bark of the prairie dog. Now, be prudent."

" You may be sure of that."

The Tigrero took off all the articles of clothing that might embarrass him, such as his zarapè and botas vaqueras, only keeping on his trousers and vest, put his knife in his belt, made up his pistols, rifle, and cartouche-box in a packet, and imitated the song of the *maukawès*. Presently a similar sound rose from the bank. The Tigrero then held his weapons over his head, and glided gently into the water. The lepero soon perceived him swimming silently and vigorously in the direction of the hacienda; but the Tigrero was gradually lost in the distance.

So soon as he was alone Cucharès began to inspect his weapons carefully, changing the caps so as to be ready for anything, and run no risk of being taken unawares; then, reassured by the calmness that prevailed around, he lay down in the bottom of the canoe in spite of the Tigrero's recommendations, and got ready for a nap.

The noise of the combat had gradually died away—neither shouts nor shots could be heard. The Indians, repulsed by the colonists, had given up their attack. The flames of the fire became less and less bright. The desert seemed to have fallen back into its ordinary silence and solitude.

The lepero, lying on his back at the bottom of the canoe, gazed at the brilliant stars glistening in the azure sky. Gently cradled by the rippling, his eyes closed. At length he reached that point which is neither sleeping nor waking, and would probably soon have fallen asleep. At the moment, however, when he was going to yield to his feelings, he cast a parting sleepy glance over the river. He shuddered, repressed with difficulty a cry of terror, and started up so violently that he almost upset the canoe.

Cucnarès had had a fearful vision : he rubbed his eyes vigorously to assure himself that he was really awake, and looked again. What he had taken for a vision was only too real ; he had seen correctly.

We have said that the river carried with it a large number of stumps and dead trees still laden with their branches. During the last hour an enormous quantity of these trees had collected round the canoe, the lepero being quite unable to account for the fact, the more so because these trees, which by the natural law should have followed the current and descended with it, cut it in every direction, and, instead of keeping to the centre of the river, drew constantly nearer to the bank on which stood the hacienda.

More extraordinary still, the progress of this floating wood was so carefully regulated that all converged on one point—the extremity of the isthmus at the back of the hacienda. Another alarming fact was, that Cucharès saw eyes flashing and frightful faces peering out from amidst this raft of interlaced branches, stumps, and trees.

There was no room for doubt: each tree carried at least one Apache. The Indians, having failed in their attempt on one side, hoped to surprise the colony from the river, and were swimming up concealed by the trees, in the midst of which they had collected. The lepero's position was perplexing. Up to this moment the Indians, busied with their plans, had paid no attention to the canoe; or, if they had noticed it, thought that it belonged to one of their party; but the error might be detected at any moment, and the lepero knew that, in such a case, he would be hopelessly lost.

Already, more than once, hands had been laid for a few seconds on the sides of the frail boat; but, by some providential chance, the owners of those hands had not thought of looking into the interior of the canoe.

All these reflections, and many others, Cucharès indulged in while lying apparently most comfortably at the bottom of the canoe, gently balanced by the ripple, and watching the brilliant stars defile above his head. With his features distorted by terror, his face blanched, and holding a pistol butt convulsively clutched in either hand, while mentally recommending himself to his patron saint, he awaited the catastrophe which every passing minute rendered more imminent.

He had not long to wait.

CHAPTER XIV.

AN INDIAN TRICK.

AMONG the indomitable nations that wander about the deserts contained in the delta formed by the Rio Gila, the Rio del Norte, and the Colorado, two claim sovereignty over the rest. They are the Apaches and Comanches. Irreconcilable enemies, incessantly at war with each other, these two nations were now allied by a common hatred of the white men, and all that belongs to that abhorred race.

Excellent hunters, intrepid horsemen, cruel and piti- less warriors, the Apaches and Comanches are terrible neighbours for the inhabitants of New Mexico. Every year, at the same period, these ferocious warriors rush by thousands from their deserts, cross the rivers by fording or swimming, and invade the Mexican frontiers at several points, burning and plundering all they come across, carrying off women and children into slavery, and spreading desolation and terror for more than twenty leagues into a civilised territory.

At the period of the Spanish rule it was not so. Numerous missions, *presidios*, posts established at regu- lar distances, and bodies of troops scattered along the entire frontier, repulsed the attacks of the Indians, drove them back on their deserts, and kept them within the limits of their hunting-grounds ; but since the proclamation of their independence the Mexicans have had so much to do in cutting each other's throats, and trampling morality under foot by their incessant revolu- tions, that the posts have been called in, the missions plundered, the presidios abandoned, and the frontiers left to guard themselves. The result has been that the Indians gradually drew nearer, and finding no serious resistance before them—for the very simple reason that the Mexican Government forbids, under heavy penalties, any fire-arms being given to the civilised Indians, who alone could fight successfully against the invaders—the savages have nearly reconquered in a few years wl at Spain, in her omnipotence, took ages in wresting from them. The result of this is that the most fertile country in the world remains untilled; not a step can be taken in this hapless country without stumbling on still smoking ruins; and the boldness of the savages has so increased, that they now do not even take the trouble to hide their expeditions, which they make annually at the same period, in the same month, nearly on the same day, and that the month is called by them in derision the "Mexican Moon;" that is to say, the moon during which the Mexicans are plundered.

All the facts we narrate here would be the height of buffoonery were they not also the height of atrocity.

The Black Bear had founded the great confederation to which we have previously alluded, for the purpose of restoring himself in the credit of his fellow-countrymen, whom several unsuccessful expeditions had turned against him. Like all Indian chiefs of any standing, he was ambitious. He had already succeeded in destroying several smaller tribes, and incorporating them with his nation: he now aspired to nothing less than humbling the Comanches, and compelling them to recognise his authority. It was a difficult, if not impossible enterprise; for the Comanche nation is justly recognised as the most warlike and dangerous in the desert. This nation, which proudly calls itself the Queen of the Prairies, can hardly endure the presence of the Apaches on the ground they consider belonging to themselves, and forming their hunting territory. The Comanches have an immense advantage over the other prairie Indians—an advantage which causes their strength, and makes them so terrible to the nations they combat. Owing to the precaution they have taken of never drinking spirits, they have escaped the general degradation and most of the diseases which decimate the other Indians, and have remained vigorous and intelligent.

The Jester, like the Black Bear, had no great faith in the duration of the alliance formed between the two nations : the hatred he bore the Apaches was, indeed, too profound for him to desire it ; but the foundation of the Guetzalli colony by the French, by permanently establishing the white men on a territory they regarded as belonging to themselves, was a too serious menace for the Comanches and other Indios Bravos, and they attempted every possible scheme to get rid of these troublesome neighbours.   Hence they had temporarily hung up their old rancour and private enmities on behalf of the general welfare, but for that only.   It was tacitly agreed between them that, so soon as the strangers were expelled, each nation would be free to act as it pleased.

We have seen in what way the Jester began hostilities.   The Black Bear had a scheme which he had been ripening for a long time, though not possessing the means to put it in execution ; but knowing where to obtain the information he needed, he went to Guaymas. The Tigrero, by proposing to him to enter the colony as a guide, had unsuspectingly supplied him with the pretext he sought.   Thus, during the few hours he spent at the hacienda, he had not lost his time, and with that cunning peculiar to the Indians, discovered all the weak points of the place.

There was another reason to inflame his desire to seize the hacienda.   Like all the red-skins, his dream was to have a white woman in his lodge.   Fatality, by bringing him across Dona Anita, had suddenly re-enkindled the secret hope he entertained, and made him suppose he would at length possess the woman he sought so long without being able to find her. It must not be thought that the Black Bear loved the Spanish maiden : no, he wanted a white squaw, that was all. He was humiliated by the knowledge that the other chiefs of his nation had slaves of that colour, while he alone had none. Had Dona Anita been ugly, he would have tried to carry her off all the same. She was lovely—all the better ; and we may add here that the Apache chief did not consider her beautiful. According to his Indian notions she was passable, that was all ; the only thing he valued in her was her colour.

The Black Bear, standing with his principal warriors on the point of the island, remained silent, with his arms crossed on his chest, his eyes fixed on vacancy, till the moment when the first gleams of the fire kindled by the Jester tinged the horizon with a blood-red hue.

" My brother, the Jester, is an experienced chief," he said, " and a faithful ally. He has well fulfilled the mission intrusted to him. He is now smoking the pale-face dogs. What the Comanches have begun the Apaches will finish."

" The Black Bear is the first warrior of his nation," the Little Panther replied. " Who would dare to contend with him ?"

The Indian Sachem smiled at this flattery.

" If the Comanches are antelopes, the Apaches are otters ; they can, if they please, swim in the water, or march on land. The pale-faces have lived. The Great Spirit is in me ; it is He who dictates to me the words my tongue utters."

The warriors bowed. The Black Bear continued, after a moment's silence :—

" What do the Apache warriors care for the fire tubes of the pale-faces ? Have they not long, barbed arrows

and intrepid hearts ?   My brothers will follow me ; we
will take the scalps of these pale dogs, and fasten them
to our horses' manes, and their wives shall be our
slaves."

Shouts of joy and enthusiasm greeted these words.

"The river is covered with numerous trunks of trees :
my sons are not squaws to fatigue themselves uselessly.
They will place themselves on these dead trees, and
drift with the current down to the great lodge of the
pale-faces.   Let my brothers prepare.   The Black Bear
will set out at the sixth hour, when the blue jay has
sung twice, and the walkon has uttered its shrill cry. I
have spoken.   Two hundred warriors will follow the
Black Bear."

The chiefs bowed respectfully before the sachem,
and left him alone.   He wrapped himself up in his
buffalo robe, sat down by the fire, lit his calumet by
means of a medicine staff adorned with bells and
feathers, and remained silent, with his eyes fixed on
the gradually extending prairie fire.

The island in which the Apache chief had formed his
camp was at no great distance from the French colony.
The project of floating down had no very great danger
for these men, accustomed to every sort of bodily exercise,
and who swam like fish : it possessed the great advantage
of completely concealing the approach of the warriors
hidden by the water and the branches, and who, at the
proper moment, would rush on the colony like a swarm
of famished vultures.

The Black Bear was so convinced of the success of
this stratagem, which only an Indian brain could have
conceived, that he only took with him two hundred
chosen men, thinking it unnecessary to lead more against
enemies taken by surprise, and who, compelled to

defend themselves against the Comanches led by the Jester, would be attacked in the rear and massacred before they had time to look around them.

Night sets in rapidly and suddenly in countries where the twilight does not last longer than a lightning flash. Soon all became darkness, save that, in the distance, a wide strip of coppery red announced the progress of the flames, behind which the Comanches galloped like a pack of hideous wolves over the still glowing earth, trampling under their horses' hoofs the charred wood which was still smouldering.

When the Black Bear considered the moment had arrived he put out his calumet, scattered the fire, and gave a signal perfectly well understood by the Little Panther, who was watching to execute the orders the chief might be pleased to give. Almost immediately the two hundred warriors selected for the expedition made their appearance. They were all picked men, armed with clubs and lances, while their shields hung on their backs. After a moment's silence, employed by the sachem in a species of inspection, he said in a deep voice,—

"We are about to set out; the pale-faces we are destined to fight are not Yoris; they are said to be very brave, but the Apaches are the bravest warriors in the world; no one can contend against them. My sons may be killed, but they will conquer."

"The warriors will suffer themselves to be killed," the Indians replied with one voice.

"Wah!" the Black Bear continued, "my sons have spoken well; the Black Bear has confidence in them. The Wacondah will not abandon them; he loves the red men. And now, my sons, we will collect the dead trees floating on the river, and float down the current

with them.   The cry of the condor will be their signal
to rush on the pale-faces."

The Indians immediately began executing their
chief's orders.   All strove to reach the trunks of trees
or stumps.   In a few moments a considerable quantity
was collected near the point of the island.   The Black
Bear turned a parting glance around, gave the signal
for departure, and was the first to enter the water and
clamber on a tree.   All the rest followed him immediately without the slightest hesitation.

The Apaches behaved so cleverly in bringing the
tree trunks to the island, and had chosen their position
so well, that when they set the trees in motion again
they almost immediately struck the current, and began
to follow the river gently, drifting imperceptibly in the
direction of the colony where they wished to land.

Still this navigation, so essentially eccentric, offered
grave inconveniences and even serious dangers to those
who undertook it.   The Indians, left without paddles
on the trees, were obliged to follow the stream, only
succeeding in holding on by extraordinary efforts.   Like
all wood floating at the mercy of the waves, the trees
continually revolved, compelling those holding on to them
to employ all their strength and skill, lest they might
be submerged at every moment.   There was another
difficulty, too : it was absolutely necessary to keep in the
water, so as to give the trees the proper direction and
make them reach the colony, instead of following the
current in the middle of the stream.   A further incon-
venience, not the least grave of all, was that the trees
on which the Apaches were mounted met others as they
floated along, against which they struck, or their
branches became so interlaced that it was impossible to
part them, and they had to be taken on as well; so

that, at the end of half an hour, an immense raft was formed, which appeared to occupy the entire width of the river.

The Indians are obstinate: when they have undertaken an expedition they never give it up till it is irrevocably proved to them that success is impossible. This happened on the present occasion; several men were drowned, others wounded so severely that they were compelled to regain the bank against their will. The others, however, held on; and, encouraged by their chief, who did not cease addressing them, they continued to descend the river.

Long before, the island from which they set out had disappeared behind them in the windings formed by the irregular course of the river: the point on which the buildings of the colony stood appeared but a short way ahead, when the Black Bear, who was at the head of the party, and whose piercing eye incessantly surveyed the scene around, noticed a canoe a few yards ahead gracefully dancing on the water, and attached to a dead stump.

This canoe at once appeared suspicious to the cautious Indian. It did not seem natural to him that, at such an advanced hour of the night, any boat should be thus tied up in the river; but the Black Bear was a man of prompt decision, whom nothing embarrassed, and who rapidly formed his plans. After carefully examining this mysterious canoe, still stationary before him, he stooped over to the Little Panther, who hung on to the same tree in readiness to execute his orders, and, placing his knife between his teeth, the chief unloosed his hold and dived.

He rose again near the canoe, seized it boldly, pulled it over, and leaped in right on Cuchares' chest, and seized him by the throat. This movement was executed so rapidly that the lepero could not employ his weapons, and found himself completely at the mercy of his enemy before he understood what had occurred.

"Wah!" the Indian exclaimed with surprise on recognising him. "What is my brother-doing here?"

The lepero had also recognised the chief, and, without knowing why, this restored him a slight degree of courage.

"You see," he answered, "I am sleeping."

"Wah! my brother was afraid of the fire, and for that reason took to the river."

"Quite right, chief; you guessed it the first time. I *was* afraid of the fire."

"Good!" the Apache continued, with a mocking smile peculiar to himself. "My brother is not alone. Where is the Great Buffalo?"

"Eh? I do not know the Great Buffalo, chief. I don't even know whom you are talking about."

"All the pale-faces have a forked tongue. Why does not my brother speak the truth?"

"I am quite willing to do so, but I do not understand you."

"The Black Bear is a great Apache warrior; he can speak the language of his nation, but he knows badly that of the Yoris."

"I did not mean that. You express yourself excellently in Castilian, but you are speaking of a person I do not know."

"Wah! is that possible?" the Indian said, with feigned amazement. "Does not my brother know the warrior with whom he was two days ago?"

"Oh! now I understand; you are talking of Don Martial. Yes, certainly I know him."

" Good! " the chief replied ; " I knew that I was not mistaken. Why is my brother not with him at this moment ? "

" Probably because I am here," the lepero said with a grin.

" That is true ; but as I am in a hurry, and my brother does not wish to answer me, I am going to kill him."

Saying this in a tone which admitted of no tergiversation, the Black Bear raised his knife. The lepero understood that, if he did not obey the Indian, he was lost, and his hesitation ceased as if by enchantment.

" What do you want of me ? " he said.

" The truth."

" Question me."

" My brother will answer ? "

" Yes."

" Good ! Where is the Great Buffalo ? "

" There," he said, pointing in the direction of the hacienda.

" How long ? "

" For more than an hour."

" For what reason has he gone there ? "

" You can guess."

" Yes. Are they together ? "

" They ought to be so, as she called him to her."

" Wah ! and when will he return ? "

" I do not know."

" He did not tell my brother ? "

" No."

" Will he come back alone ? "

" I do not know."

The Indian fixed a glance on him, as if trying to read qis very heart. The lepero was calm : he had honestly told all he knew.

" Good! " the chief continued the next moment. "Did
not the Great Buffalo agree on a signal with his friend,
in order to rejoin when he pleased? "

" He did."

" What is that signal? "

At this question a singular idea crossed Cucharès'
brain.   The leperos belong to a strange race, which only
bears a likeness to the Neapolitan lazzaroni. At once
prodigal and avaricious, greedy and disinterested,
extremely rash, and frightful cowards, they are the
strangest medley of all that is good and all that is bad.
In them everything is blunted and imperfect.   They
only act on the impulse of the moment, without reflection or passion.   Eternal mockers, they believe in
nothing, and yet believe in everything.   To sum them
up in a word, their life is a constant antithesis ; and
for a jest which may cost their life they will sacrifice
their most devoted friend, just as they will save him.

Cucharès was a perfect personification of this eccentric
race.   Though the Apache chief's knife was scarce two
inches from his breast, and he knew that his ferocious
enemy would show him no mercy, he suddenly resolved
to play him a trick, no matter the cost.   We will not
add that his friendship for Don Martial unconsciously
pleaded on his behalf, for we repeat that the lepero
feels no friendship for any one, not even himself, and
that his heart only exists in the shape of bowels.

" The chief wishes to know the signal? " he said.

" Yes," the Apache replied.

Cucharès, with the utmost coolness, imitated the cry
of the water-hen.

"Silence! " the Black Bear exclaimed; "it is not that."

" Pardon," the lepero replied with a grin; " perhaps
I gave it badly," and he repeated it.

The Indian, roused by his enemy's impudence, rushed upon him, resolved to finish him with his knife; but, blinded by his fury, he calculated badly, and gave too violent an oscillation to the canoe. The light bark, whose equilibrium was disturbed, turned over, and the two men rolled into the river. Once in the water, the lepero, who swam like an otter, set off in the direction of the hacienda as fast as he could speed. But if he swam well, the Black Bear swam at least equally well. The first movement of surprise overcome, the chief almost immediately discovered his enemy's trail.

Then began between the two men a contest of skill and strength. Perhaps it would have ended to the advantage of the white man, who had a considerable start, had not several warriors, witnesses of what had occurred, swum off too, and cut off the fugitive's retreat. Cucharès saw that flight was impossible; hence, not attempting to continue a hopeless struggle, he proceeded towards a tree, to which he clung, and awaited with magnificent coolness whatever might happen.

The Black Bear soon came up with him. The chief displayed no ill-temper at the trick the lepero had played him.

"Wah!" he merely said, "my brother is a warrior; he has the craft of the opossum."

"Of what use is it to me," Cucharès answered carelessly, "if I cannot succeed in saving my scalp?"

"Perhaps," the Indian said. "Let my brother tell me where the Great Buffalo is."

"I have already told you, chief."

"Yes, my brother told me that his friend was in the great lodge of the pale-faces, but he did not say at what place."

"Hum! and if I tell you shall I be free?"

" Yes, if my brother has not a forked tongue : if he speaks the truth, so soon as we land on the bank, he will be free to go where he pleases."

" A poor favour ! " the lepero muttered, shaking his head.

" Well," the chief continued, " what will my brother do ? "

" My faith ! " Cucharès said, suddenly making up his mind, " I have done for Don Martial all it was humanly possible to do. Now that he is warned, each for himself. I must save my skin. Stay, chief : follow the direction of my finger. You see those mangroves on the projecting point ? "

" I see them."

" Well, behind those mangroves you will find the man you call the Great Buffalo."

" Good ! The Black Bear is a chief; he has only one word ; the pale-face shall be free."

" Thanks."

The conversation was hurriedly broken off, more especially as the Apaches were rapidly approaching the banks. They had let go of most of the trees to which they had hitherto been clinging, and were collected in small groups of ten or twelve on the larger trees.

The hacienda was silent ; not a light burned there ; all was calm ; it looked like a deserted habitation. This profound tranquillity excited the suspicions of the Black Bear ; it seemed to forebode an impending storm. Before risking a landing he wished to assure himself positively of what he had to expect. He uttered the cry of the iguana, and swam towards the bank. The Apaches comprehended their chief's intention, and stopped. At the end of a few moments they saw him crawling along the sand. The Black Bear walked a few paces along ; he saw nothing, heard nothing ; then, completely reassured, he returned to the water's edge, and gave the signal for landing.

The Apaches quitted the trees and began swimming. Cucharès profited by the moment of disorder to disappear, which was an easy matter, as no one was thinking of him. Still the Apaches formed in a single line, and swam vigorously ; in a few minutes they reached the bank, and landed ; then they rushed at full speed towards the hacienda.

" Fire ! " a stentorian voice suddenly commanded. A frightful discharge instantaneously followed. The Apaches responded by howlings of rage, and themselves surprised by the men they had hoped to surprise, rushed upon them, brandishing their weapons.

*　　*　　*　　*　　*　　*

CHAPTER XV.

SET A THIEF TO CATCH A THIEF.

We will now return to the hunters, whom we have too long neglected, for during the events we have been narrating they had not remained entirely inactive.

After the departure of the two Mexicans, Belhumeur and his friends remained silent for an instant. The Canadian played with the charcoal that had fallen from the brazier on to the ground ; in fact, he was lost in thought. Don Louis, with his chin resting on the palm of his hand, was watching with distraught air the sparkles which crackled, glistened, and went out. Eaglehead, alone of the party, wrapped up in his buffalo robe, smoked his calumet with that stoicism and calm appearance which belong exclusively to his race.

"However it may be," the Canadian suddenly said, replying to the ideas which bothered him, and thinking aloud rather than intendiug to renew the conversation, "the conduct of those two men seems to me extraordinary, not to say something else."

"Would you suspect any treachery?" Don Louis asked, looking up.

"In the desert you must always suspect treachery," Belhumeur said peremptorily, "especially from chance companions."

"Still this Tigrero, this Don Martial—that is his name I think—has a very honest eye, my friend, to be a traitor."

"That is true; still you will agree that ever since we first met him his conduct has been remarkably queer."

"I grant it; but you know as well as I how much passion blinds a man. I believe him to be in love."

"So do I. Still notice, pray, that in all this affair which regards him specially, and in which we have only mixed ourselves to do him a service, while neglecting our own occupations, he has always kept in the background, as if afraid to show himself."

At this moment Blas Vasquez, after stationing the peons a short distance off, so as to remain unseen, came up and took his seat by the fire.

"There!" he said, "all is ready: the Apaches can come and attack us whenever they think proper."

"One word, capataz," Belhumeur said.

"Two if you like."

"Do you know the man to whom you delivered a letter just now?"

"Why do you ask?"

"To gain some information about him."

"Personally I know very little of him. All I can

tell you is, that he enjoys an excellent reputation through the whole province, and is generally regarded as a caballero and gallant man."

"That is something," the Canadian muttered, shaking his head ; " but, for all that, I do not know why, but his sudden departure makes me very restless."

" Wah ! " Eagle-head suddenly said, withdrawing from his lips the tube of his calumet, and bending forward, while bidding his comrades to silence. All remained motionless, with their eyes fixed on the Indian.

" What is it ? " Belhumeur at length asked.

"Fire ! " the other replied slowly. " The Apaches are coming : they are burning the prairie before them."

" What? " Belhumeur exclaimed, rising and looking all around. " I see no trace of fire."

" No, not yet ; but the fire is coming—I can smell it.'

" Hum ! if the chief says so, it must be true ; he is too experienced a warrior to be deceived. What is to be done ? "

" We have nothing to fear from fire here," the capataz observed.

" We have not," Don Louis quickly exclaimed ; " but the inhabitants of the hacienda?"

" Not more than we," Belhumeur replied. " See, all the trees have been cut down, and rooted up to too great a distance from the colony for the fire to reach it ; it is only a stratagem employed by the Indians to arrive without being counted."

" Still I am of this caballero's opinion," the capataz said ; " we should do well to warn the hacienda."

"There is something even more urgent to do," Don Louis said, " and that is to send off a clever scout to learn positively with whom we have to deal, who our enemies are, and if they are numerous."

"One does not prevent the other," Belhumeur remarked. "In a case like the present, two precautions are worth more than one. This is my advice. Eagle-head will reconnoitre the foe, while we proceed to the hacienda."

"All of us?" the capataz observed.

"No; your position here is secure, and you will be able, in the event of an attack, to render important service. Don Louis and I will proceed alone to the colony. Remember that you must not show yourselves under any pretext. Whatever may happen, await the order for acting. Is that agreed to?"

"Go, caballeros; I will not betray your confidence."

"Good! Now to work. I have no advice to offer you, chief: you will find us at the hacienda if you learn anything of importance."

Upon this these men, so long accustomed to act without losing precious time in useless words, separated; Don Louis and Belhumeur returning to the main land on the side of the hacienda, while the chief rode off in the opposite direction. Blas Vasquez remained alone with his peons; but as he had been for many years accustomed to Indian warfare, and understood the responsibility he took on himself from this moment, he felt that he must redouble his vigilance. Hence he posted sentinels at every point, recommended them the utmost attention, came back to the brazier, wrapped himself in his fressada, and went quietly to sleep, certain that his men would carefully watch all that took place on the main land.

We will, for a moment, leave Don Louis and his friend, to follow Eagle-head.

The mission the chief had undertaken was anything rather than easy; but the Eagle-head was a man of experience, thoroughly versed in Indian tricks, and endowed with that unalterable phlegm which is a great ingredient of success in certain circumstances of life. After leaving his companions he walked quietly down to the water's edge, and when he reached the spot where he intended to cross the river his plan was all arranged in his head.

The chief, instead of passing to that side of the river by which the enemy would come, preceded by the conflagration, crossed to the other. So soon as he reached the bank he allowed his horse a few moments for breathing; then leaping at a bound on to the panther skin that served as his saddle, he galloped at full speed in the direction of the enemy's camp. This furious race lasted two hours. Night had long ago succeeded the day; the pale gleams of the conflagration served as a beacon to the chief, and showed him in the darkness the road he should follow. At the end of these two hours the chief found himself just opposite the most advanced point of the island, where the Apaches were at this moment engaged in collecting the drift-wood they meant to use in the surprise of the colony. Eagle-head stopped. On his right, far behind him, the conflagration raged in the horizon; around him all was silence and obscurity. For a long time the Indian attentively watched the island: a secret presentiment warned him that there was the danger for him.

Still, after careful reflection, the chief resolved to advance a few paces further, and recross the river at the point opposite this island, which seemed to him more suspicious because it was so tranquil. However, before carrying out this plan, a sudden inspiration flashed across his mind. He dismounted, hid his horse in a thicket, laid aside his rifle and buffalo robe; then, after attempting to pierce the surrounding gloom, he stretched himself on the ground, and crawled to the river's bank. He gently entered the water, and swimming and diving in turn, proceeded to the island, which he presently reached.

But at the instant he landed, and was about to rise, an almost imperceptible sound smote his ear; he fancied he could notice an extraordinary commotion in the water all around him. Eagle-head plunged again, and retired from the bank on which he had been on the point of landing. Suddenly, at the moment he rose to the surface to take in a fresh supply of air, he saw two burning eyes flashing before him; he received a violent blow on the chest, and felt a powerful hand clutch his throat as in a vice. Eagle-head saw that, unless he made a desperate effort, he would be lost, and he attempted it. Seizing in his turn his unknown foe, who held him by the throat, he clung round him with the vigour of despair.

Then a horrible and silent struggle commenced in the river—a sinister struggle, in which each sought to kill his adversary, without thinking to repel his attacks. The water, troubled by the efforts of the two combatants, bubbled as if alligators were engaged. At length a bloody and disfigured body rose inertly to the surface, and floated. A few seconds later, and a head appeared above the water, casting startled glances around.

At the sight of his enemy's corpse the victor indulged in a diabolic smile; he swam up to him, seized him by his war-lock, and swimming with one hand, dragged the body, not to the island, but to the main land.

Eagle-head had conquered the Apache who attacked

him in so unforeseen a manner. The chief reached the bank, but did not leave the corpse, which he dragged along till it was completely out of the water; then he lifted the scalp, placed the hideous trophy in his belt, and remounted his horse.

The Indian had divined the Apaches' tactics; the attack of which he had been so nearly the victim revealed to him the stratagem they designed. It was unnecessary for him to push his investigations on the island further. Still, had he abandoned to the current his enemy's corpse, it would have infallibly floated down among his brothers, and revealed the presence of a spy; so he had been careful to convey it to the bank, where no one, save by some extraordinary accident, could discover it before sunrise.

The few minutes' rest he had granted his horse would have been sufficient to restore all its vigour. The chief might have returned to his friends, for what he had discovered was of immense importance to them; but Belhumeur had specially recommended him to discover the strength and nature of the war detachment which was marching on the colony. Eagle-head was anxious to accomplish his mission; and besides, the struggle he had undergone, and from which he had emerged as victor by a miracle, had produced a certain amount of excitement, urging him to carry out the adventure to the end.

He plucked a few leaves to stop the blood from a slight wound he had received in his left arm, fastened them on with a piece of bark, and rode his horse once more into the river. But this time, as he had nothing to examine, and did not wish to be discovered, he took care to pass at a considerable distance from the island. On the other bank, owing to the care taken by the

Indians to burn everything, the trail was wide and
perfectly visible. In spite of the darkness the chief
found no difficulty in following it.

The fire kindled by the Indians had not caused such
ravages as might be supposed. All that part of the
prairie, with the exception of a few scattered clumps
of poplars at great distances apart, was covered with
long grass, already half burned up by the torrid beams
of a summer sun. This grass had burned rapidly, pro-
ducing what the incendiaries desired—a large quantity
of smoke, but scarcely heating the ground, which had
allowed the red-skins to march rapidly on the colony.

Owing to his headlong speed, and the few hours
those who preceded him had been compelled to lose,
the chief arrived almost simultaneously with them
before the hacienda; that is to say, he came up with
them at the moment when, after making a futile
assault on the isthmus battery, they fled, pursued by a
shower of grape, which decimated their ranks; for,
having burnt everything, they had no trees to shelter
them. Still the majority managed to escape, owing to
the speed of their horses.

Eagle-head found himself unexpectedly in the very
midst of the fugitives. At first each man was too
anxious about his own safety to have time to notice
him, and the chief profited by it to turn aside and step
behind a rock. But then a strange thing happened.
The chief had scarce escaped from the fugitives, and
examined them for a moment, ere a strange smile
played on his lips : he spurred his horse, and bounded
into the very midst of the Indians, uttering twice a
shrill and peculiar cry. At this cry the Indians stopped
in their flight, and rushing from all sides toward the
man who uttered it, they ranged themselves tumultu-

ously round the chief with an expression of superstitious fear, and passive and respectful obedience.

The Eagle-head looked haughtily at the crowd that surrounded him, and was a head taller than any man present.

"Wah!" he at length said in a guttural voice, with an accent of bitter reproach. "Have the Comanches become timid antelopes, that they fly like Apache dogs before the bullets of the pale-faces?"

"Eagle-head! Eagle-head!" the warriors shouted with joy mingled with shame, looking down before the chief's flashing glance.

"Why have my sons left the hunting-grounds of the Del Norte without the order of a sachem? Are they now the *rastreros* (bloodhounds) of the Apaches?"

A suppressed murmur ran through the ranks at this cruel reproach.

"A sachem has spoken," Eagle-head continued sharply. "Is there no one to answer him? Have the Comanches of the Lakes no chiefs left to command them?"

A warrior then broke through the ranks of the Comanches, approached Eagle-head, and bowed his head respectfully down to his horse's neck.

"The Jester is a chief," he said in a gentle and harmonious voice.

Eagle-head's face was unwrinkled—his features instantaneously lost their expression of fury. He turned on the warrior who had addressed him a glance full of tenderness, and, offering him his right hand, palm upwards,—

"Och!" he said, "my heart is joyous at seeing my son, the Jester. The warriors will camp here while the two sachems hold a council."

And making an imperious sign to the chief, he withdrew with him, followed by the eyes of the redskins, who hastened to obey the order he had so peremptorily given. Eagle-head and the Jester had gone so far that their conversation could not be overheard.

"Let us hold a council," the chief said, as he sat down on a stone, and signed to the Jester to take a place by his side. The latter obeyed without reply. There was a long silence, during which the two Indians examined each other attentively, in spite of the indifference they affected. At length Eagle-head spoke in a slow and accentuated voice.

"The Eagle-head is a renowned warrior in his nation," he said; "he is the first sachem of the Comanches of the Lakes; his totem shelters beneath its mighty and protecting shadow the innumerable sons of the great sacred tortoise, *Chemiin-Antou,* whose glistening shell has supported the world since the Wacondah hurled into space the first man and the first woman after their fault. The words which come from the breast of Eagle-head are those of a sagamore; his tongue is not forked—a falsehood never sullied his lips. Eagle-head acted as a father to the Jester; he taught him to tame a horse, pierce with his arrows the rapid antelope, or to stifle in his arms the mighty bear. Eagle-head loves the Jester, who is the son of his third wife's sister. Eagle-head gave a place at the council fire to the Jester; he made a chief of him; and when he went away from the villages of his nation he said to him, ' My son will command my warriors; he will lead them to hunt, to fish, and to war.' Are these words true? Does Eagle-head speak falsely?"

"My father's words are true," the chief answered with a bow : " wisdom speaks through his lips."

" Why, then, has my son allied himself with the
enemies of his nation to fight the friends of his father,
the sachem ? "

The chief let his head fall in confusion.

" Why, without consulting the man who has ever
aided and supported him by his counsel, has he undertaken an unjust war ? "

" An unjust war ? " the chief remarked with a certain
degree of animation.

" Yes, as it is carried on in concert with the enemies
of our nation."

" The Apaches are red-skins."

" The Apaches are cowardly and thievish dogs, whose
deceitful tongues I will pluck out."

" But the pale-faces are the enemies of the Indians."

" Those whom my son attacked last night are not
Yoris : they are the friends of Eagle-head."

" My father will pardon the warrior : he did not
know it."

" If the Jester really was ignorant of it, is he ready
to repair the fault he has committed ? "

" The Jester has three hundred warriors beneath his
totem.   Eagle-head has come : they are his."

" Good ! I see that the Jester is still my well-
beloved son.   With what chief has he made alliance ?
It cannot be with the Black Bear, the implacable
enemy of the Comanches, the man who but four moons
past burned two villages of my nation ? "

" A cloud had passed over the mind of the Jester :
his hatred for the white men blinded him ; wisdom
deserted him ; he has allied himself with the Black
Bear."

" Wah ! Eagle-head did right to return toward the
villages of his fathers. Will my son obey the sachem ? "

" Whatever he orders I will obey."

" Good! Let my son follow me."

The two chiefs rose. Eagle-head proceeded toward the isthmus, waving his buffalo robe in his right hand as a sign of peace. The Jester followed a few paces behind. The Comanches saw with amazement their sachems asking an interview with the Yoris ; but accustomed to obey their chiefs without discussing the orders they were pleased to give, they evinced no anger at this step, whose object, however, they did not understand. The sentries posted behind the isthmus battery easily distinguished in the moon's rays the pacific movements of the Indians, and allowed them to approach as far as the trench.

" A sachem wishes an interview with the chief of the pale-faces," Eagle-head then said.

" Good! " a voice replied in Spanish from the inside. " Wait a moment; I will send to him."

The two Comanche warriors bowed, crossed their hands on their breast, and waited.

Don Louis and Belhumeur had had a long conversation with Don Sylva and the count, in which they revealed to them in what way they had learnt that the Indians meant to attack them ; the name of the man who had informed them so correctly ; and his singular conduct, in that, after having in a measure compelled them to mix themselves up in a dangerous affair which did not at all concern them, he had suddenly abandoned them without any valid reason, under the futile pretext of returning to Guaymas, where he said that important business claimed his presence with the least possible delay.

This news had a lively effect on the two hearers: Don Sylva especially could not repress a movement of

anger on learning that this person was no other than
Don Martial. He guessed at once the Tigrero's object
—that he hoped to carry off Dona Anita during the
confusion. Still Don Sylva would not impart his
suspicions to his future son-in-law, intending to tell him,
were it absolutely necessary, at the last moment, but
resolved to watch his daughter closely, for this sudden departure of Don Martial seemed to him to conceal a snare.

Belhumeur then explained to the count the position
in which he had placed the capataz and his peons, and
the mission Eagle-head had undertaken, the result of
which he would probably soon come to the hacienda
to tell. The count warmly thanked the two men who,
without knowing him, rendered him such eminent
services; he offered them all the refreshments they
might need, and then went to give his lieutenant orders
to warn him so soon as an Indian presented himself for
a parley.

On his side, Don Sylva retired with the ostensible
object of reassuring his daughter, but in reality to
inspect the sentries stationed at the rear of the
hacienda. When the Comanches attacked the isthmus,
the French, put on their guard, received them so warmly
that in the very first attack the Indians recognised the
futility of their attempt, and retired in disorder.

Monsieur de Lhorailles was talking with the two
visitors about the incidents of the fight, and was
astonished at the prolonged absence of Don Sylva,
who had disappeared during the last hour without
leaving a trace, when Lieutenant Leroux entered the
room where the three men were conversing.

" What do you want ? " the count asked him.

" Captain," he answered, " two Indians are waiting
at the trench for permission to enter "

" Two ? " Belhumeur asked.

" Yes, two."

" That is strange," the Canadian continued.

" What shall we do ? " the count said.

" Go and have a look at them."

They proceeded to the battery.

" Well ? " the count said.

" Well, sir, one of these men is certainly Eagle-head; but I do not know the other."

" And your advice is———"

" To let them come in. As this Indian, who is apparently a chief, comes in the company of Eagle-head, he can only be a friend."

" Be it so, then."

The count gave a signal; the drawbridge was lowered, and the two chiefs entered. The Indian sachems saluted all present with that native dignity that distinguishes them, and then Eagle-head, on Belhumeur's invitation, gave an account of his mission. The Frenchmen listened to him with an attention mingled with admiration, not only for the skill he had displayed, but also the courage of which he had given proof.

" And now," the chief continued on ending his report, " the Jester has understood the error into which a blind hatred threw him ; he breaks the alliance he formed with the Apaches, and is resolved to obey in all respects his father Eagle-head, in order to repent his fault. Eagle-head is a sachem—his word is granite. He places three hundred Comanche warriors at the disposition of his brothers the pale-faces."

The count looked hesitatingly at the Canadian : knowing the trickery of the Indians, he felt a repugnance to trust them. Belhumeur shrugged his shoulders imperceptibly.

" The great pale chief thanks my brother Eagle-head: he accepts his offer with joy. His hand will ever be open, and his heart pure, for the Comanches. The war detachment of my brother will be divided into two parts : one, under the command of the Jester, will be concealed on the other side of the river, to cut off the retreat of the Apaches ; the other will enter the hacienda with Eagle-head, in order to support the palefaces. The Yori warriors are hidden in the isle, two bow-shots from the great lodge; they will accompany the Jester."

" Good! " Eagle-head replied; " all shall be done as my brother desires."

The two chiefs took leave and withdrew. Belhumeur then explained to the count the arrangements he had made with the Comanche sachem.

" Hang it ! " De Lhorailles said, " I confess that I have not the slightest confidence in the Indians. You know that treachery is their favourite weapon."

" You do not know the Comanches ; and, above all, you do not know Eagle-head. I take on myself all the responsibility."

" Act, then, as you please. I am too much indebted to you to thwart your projects, especially when you are acting for my good."

Belhumeur went himself to advise the capataz of the change effected in the defensive measures. The Jester and one hundred and fifty warriors, accompanied by the forty peons, at once crossed the river, and ambushed themselves on the opposite bank in a clump of mangroves, ready to appear at the first signal. The Frenchmen, with Eagle-head and a second troop of Indians, were left to defend the isthmus, a point where they were almost certain of not being attacked. All

the other colonists concealed themselves in the dense
thickets that masked the rear of the hacienda, with
strict orders to remain invisible till the word was given
to fire. Then, when all the arrangements were made,
the count and his comrades awaited with a beating heart
the Indians' attack. They had not long to wait; and we
have seen in what fashion the Black Bear was received.

The Apache chief was brave as a lion ; his warriors
were picked men. The collision was terrible ; the red-
skins did not give way an inch. Incessantly repulsed,
incessantly they returned to the charge, fighting hand
to hand with the French, who, in spite of their bravery,
their discipline, and superiority of weapons, could not
rout them. The combat had degenerated into a horrible
carnage, in which the fighters clutched each other,
stabbing and mangling, without loosing hold. Belhumeur saw that he must attempt a decisive blow to
finish with these demons, who seemed invincible and
invulnerable. He stooped down to Louis, who was
fighting by his side, and whispered a few words in his
ear. The Frenchman disembarrassed himself of the foe
with whom he was fighting, and ran off.

A few minutes later the war-cry of the Comanches
was heard, strident and terrible ; and the red-skin
warriors bounded like jaguars on the Apaches, swinging
their clubs and long lances. At first the Black Bear
fancied assistance had arrived for him, and that the
colony was in the power of the allies ; but this hope did
not endure a second. Then demoralisation seized on
the Apaches ; they hesitated, and suddenly turned their
backs, rushing into the river, and leaving on the battle-
field more than two-thirds of their comrades.

The colonists contented themselves with firing a
few rounds of canister at the fugitives, feeling certain

they would not escape the ambuscade prepared for them. In fact, the musket shots of the peons could soon be heard mingled with the war-cry of the Comanches. In this unfortunate expedition the Black Bear lost in an hour the most renowned warriors of his nation. The chief, covered with wounds, and only accompanied by a dozen men, escaped with great difficulty from the carnage. The victory of the French was complete. For a long time the colony, through this glorious achievement, was protected from the attacks of the red-skins.

When the combat was ended, people sought in vain in every direction for Don Sylva and his daughter: both had disappeared, and no one knew how. This mysterious and inexplicable event struck the inhabitants of the colony with consternation, and changed the joy of the triumph into mourning, for the same idea suddenly occurred to all:—

" Don Sylva and his daughter have been carried off by the Black Bear ! "

When the count, after repeated researches, was compelled to allow that the haciendero and his daughter had really disappeared without leaving the slightest trace, he gave way to all the violence of his character, vowed a terrible hatred against the Apaches, and swore to pursue them, without truce or mercy, until he found her whom he considered his wife, and whose loss destroyed at one blow the brilliant future he had dreamed of.

CHAPTER XVI.

THE CASA GRANDE OF MOCTECUZOMA.

AT the remote period when the Aztecs, guided by the finger of God, marched forth, without knowing it, to conquer the plateau of Ahanuac, of which they eventually

P

made the powerful kingdom of Mexico, although their eyes were constantly turned toward this unknown land, the permanent object of their greed, they frequently stopped during their migration, as if fatigue had suddenly overpowered them, and the hope of ever arriving had failed them.

In such cases, instead of simply camping on the spot where this hesitation had affected them, they installed themselves as if they never intended to go further, and built towns. After so many centuries have passed away, when their founders have eternally disappeared from the surface of the globe, the imposing ruins of these cities, scattered over a space of more than a thousand leagues, still excite the admiration of travellers bold enough to confront countless dangers in order to contemplate them.

The most singular of these ruins is indubitably that known by the name of the Casa Grande of Moctecuzoma, which rises about two miles from the muddy banks of the Rio Gila, in an uncultivated and uninhabited plain, on the skirt of the terrible sand desert known as the Del Norte. The site on which this house is built is flat on all sides. The ruins which once formed a city extend for more than three miles in a southern direction: in the other directions all the ground is covered with potsherds of every description. Many of these fragments are painted of various colours—white or blue, red or yellow—which, by the by, is an evident sign not only that this was an important city, but also that it was inhabited by Indians differing from those now prowling about this country, as the latter are completely ignorant of the art of making this pottery.

The house is a perfect square, turned to the four cardinal points All around are walls, indicating an enceinte inclosing not only a house, but other buildings, traces of which are perfectly distinct; for a little to the rear is a building having a floor above, and divided into several parts.   The edifice is built of earth, and, as far as can be seen, with mud walls; it had three stories above the ground, but the internal carpentry has long ago disappeared.   The rooms, five in number on each floor, were only lighted, so far as we can judge from the remains, by the doors, and round holes made in the walls facing to the north and south.   Through these openings the man Amer (*el hombre Amargo*, as the Indians call the Aztec sovereign) looked at the sun, on its rising and setting, to salute it.

A canal, now nearly dry, ran from the river, and served to supply the city with water.

At the present day these ruins are gloomy and desolate: they are slowly crumbling away beneath the incessant efforts of the sun, whose burning rays calcine them, and they serve as a refuge to the hideous vultures and the urubus which have selected it as their domicile. The Indians carefully avoid these sinister stations, from which a superstitious terror, for which they cannot account, keeps them aloof.

Thus the Comanche, Sioux, Apache, or Pawnee warrior, whom the accidents of the chase, or any other fortuitous cause, had brought to the vicinity of this dangerous ruin on the night of the fourth or fifth day of the cherry moon—*champasciasoni*—that is to say, about a month after the events we described in the last chapter —would have fled at the top speed of his horse, a prey to the wildest terror, at the strange spectacle which would have presented itself to his awe-stricken gaze.

The old palace of the Aztec kings threw out its gigantic outline on the azure sky, studded with a brilliant

belt of stars. From all the openings—round or square
—formed by human agency or by time in its dilapidated walls, poured floods of reddish light; while songs,
shouts, and laughter incessantly rose from the ruined
apartments, and troubled in their dens the wild beasts,
surprised by these sounds, which disturbed in so unusual a manner the silence of the desert. In the ruins,
beneath the pallid rays of the moon, might be distinguished the shadows of men and horses grouped round
enormous braseros, while a dozen horsemen, well armed,
and leaning on long spears, stood motionless as bronze
equestrian statues at the entrance of the house.

If within the ruins all was noise and light, outside
all was shadow and silence.

The night slipped away; the moon had already traversed two-thirds of her course; the badly-tended
braseros went out one after the other; the old mansion
alone continued to gleam through the darkness like an
ill-omened lighthouse.

At this moment the sharp and regular sound of a
horse trotting on the sand re-echoed in the distance.
The sentinels stationed at the entrance of the house
with difficulty raised their heads, oppressed by sleep
and the vivid cold of the first morning hours, and
looked in the direction whence the noise of footsteps
was audible.

A horseman appeared at the corner of the road leading to the ruins. The stranger, paying but little heed
to what he saw, continued to advance boldly toward
the house. He passed the ruined wall, and on arriving
within ten paces of the sentries, dismounted, threw the
bridle on his horse's neck, and walked with a firm step
toward the sentries, who awaited him silent and motionless. But when he was but about two swords' lengths

from the party all the lances were suddenly levelled at his breast, and a hoarse voice shouted, "Halt!"

The stranger stopped without a remark.

"Who are you? what do you want?" a horseman asked.

"I am a *costeno*. I have taken a long journey to see your chief, with whom I wish to speak," the stranger said.

By the pale and flickering rays of the moon the sentry tried in vain to distinguish the stranger's features ; but that was impossible, so carefully was he wrapped up in his cloak.

"What is your name?" he asked, in an ill-tempered tone, when he recognised that all his efforts were useless.

"What need of that? Your chief does not know me, and my name will tell him nothing."

"Possibly so, but that concerns yourself. Keep your incognito if you think proper ; still, you must not be angry with me if I do not let you trouble the captain. He is at this moment supping with his officers, and certainly will not put himself out in the middle of the night to speak with a stranger."

The man could not conceal a sharp movement of annoyance.

"Possibly so, I will say in my turn," he remarked an instant later. "Listen. You are an old soldier, I think?"

"I am one still," the trooper said, drawing himself up proudly.

"Although you speak Spanish magnificently, I believe I can recognise the Frenchman in you."

"I have that honour."

The stranger chuckled inwardly. He had caught his man ; he had found out his weak point.

"I am alone," he went on. "You have I know not how many comrades. Allow me to speak with your captain. What do you fear?"

"Nothing; but my orders are strict—I dare not break through them."

"We are in the heart of the desert, more than a hundred leagues from every civilised abode," the stranger said pressingly. "You can understand that very powerful reasons were requisite to make me brave the numberless dangers of the long journey I have made to speak for a few moments with the Count de Lhorailles. Would you shipwreck me in sight of port, when it only requires a little kindness on your part for me to obtain what I want?"

The trooper hesitated; the reasons urged by the stranger had half convinced him. Still, after a f w minutes' reflection, he said with a toss of his head,—

"No, it is impossible; the captain is stern, and I do not care to lose my corporal's stripes. All I can do for you is to allow you to bivouac here with our men in the open air. To-morrow it will be day; the captain will come out; you will speak to him, and arrange matters as you please, for it will not affect me."

"Hem!" the stranger said thoughtfully, "it is a long time to wait."

"Bah!" the soldier said gaily, "a night is soon passed. Besides, it is your own fault; you are so confoundedly mysterious. A man needn't be ashamed of his name."

"But I repeat that your captain never heard mine."

"What matter if he hasn't? A name is always a name."

"Ah!" the stranger suddenly said, "I believe I have found a way to settle everything."

" Let's hear it: if it is good I will avail myself of it."

" 'Tis excellent."

" All the better.   I am listening."

" Go and tell the captain that the man who fired a pistol at him a month back at the Rancho of Guaymas is here, and wishes to speak to him."

" Eh ?"

" Did you not understand me ?"

" Oh, perfectly."

" Well, in that case———"

" Between ourselves, the recommendation seems to me rather scurvy."

" You think so ?"

" Parbleu! he was all but assassinated by you. What! it was you ?"

" Yes, on my faith, I and another."

" I compliment you on it."

" Thanks.   Well, are you not going ?"

" I confess to a certain amount of hesitation."

" You are wrong.   The Count de Lhorailles is a brave man ; no one doubts his courage.   He must have retained our chance meeting in pleasant memory."

" After all, that 's possible ; and besides, you are a stranger.   I cannot bear the thought of refusing you so slight a service.   I will go.   Wait here, and do not be impatient, for I do not promise you success."

" I am certain of it."

The old soldier dismounted with a shrug of his shoulders, and entered the house.   The stranger did not appear to doubt the success of the corporal's embassy ; for, as soon as he had disappeared, he walked up to the door.   In a few moments the corporal returned.

"Well," the stranger asked, "what answer did the captain give you?"

"He began laughing, and ordered me to bring you in."

"You see I was right."

"That's true; but, for all that, an attempted assassination is a droll recommendation."

"A meeting," the stranger remarked.

"I don't know if you call it by that name here; but in France we call it waylaying. Come on."

The stranger made no reply; he merely shrugged his shoulders, and followed the worthy trooper.

In an immense hall, whose dilapidated walls threatened to collapse, and to which the star-spangled sky served as roof, four men of stern features and flashing eyes were seated round a table, served with the most delicate luxury, and the most sensual idea of comfort. They were the count and the officers forming his staff, namely, Lieutenants Diégo Léon and Martin Leroux, and Don Sylva's old capataz, Blas Vasquez.

The count had been encamped with his free company for the last five days in the Casa Grande of Moctecuzoma. After the attack on the colony by the Apaches, the count, in the hope of finding again his betrothed, who had disappeared in so mysterious a way during the action, and most probably had been carried off by the Indians, immediately formed the resolution of executing the orders government had given him long previously, and which he had hitherto delayed obeying, with pretexts more or less plausible; but in reality because he did not care, brave as he was, to have a fight with the red-skins, who were so resolute and difficult to overcome, especially when attacked on their own territory. The count drew one hundred and twenty Frenchmen from the colony, to whom the capataz, who burned to recover and deliver his master and young mistress, added thirty resolute peons, so that the strength of the little troop amounted to one hundred and fifty well-armed and experienced horsemen.

The count had asked the hunters, whose help had already been so precious to him, to accompany him. He would have been happy to have not only companions so intrepid, but also guides so sure as they to lead him on the trail of the Indians, whom he was determined to follow up and exterminate. But Count Louis and his two friends, without giving any further excuse than the necessity of continuing their journey at once, took leave of Lhorailles, peremptorily refusing the brilliant offers he made them.

The count was compelled to put up with the capataz and his peons. Unfortunately these men were *costenos*, or inhabitants of the seaboard, perfectly well acquainted with the coast, but entirely ignorant of all relating to the *tierra à dentro*, or interior countries. It was, therefore, under this inexperienced guidance that the count left Guetzalli and marched into Apacheria.

The expedition began under favourable auspices : twice were the red-skins surprised by the French at an interval of a few days, and mercilessly massacred. The count wished to make no prisoners, in the hope of imprinting terror on the hearts of these barbarous savages. All the Indians who fell alive into the hands of the French were shot, and then hung on trees, head downwards.

Still, after these two encounters, so disastrous for them, the Indians appeared to have taken the hint; and, in spite of all the count's efforts, he found it impossible to catch them again. The summary justice exercised by the count appeared not only to have attained, but even outstripped the object he designed; for the Indians suddenly became invisible. For about three weeks the count sought their trail, but was unable to discover it. At length, on the eve of the day on which we take up our story again, some seven or eight hundred horses, apparently free (for, according to the Indian custom, their riders, lying on their flanks, were nearly invisible), entered the ruins about mid-day, and rushed on the Casa Grande at a frightful pace.

A discharge of musketry frcm behind the hastily-erected barricades hurled disorder in their ranks, though it did not check the impetus of their attack, and they fell like lightning on the French. The Apaches had plucked up a spirit. Half naked, with their heads laden with plumes, their long buffalo robes fluttering in the wind, steering their horses with their knees, the Indian warriors had a warlike aspect capable of inspiring the most resolute men with terror. The French received them boldly, however, although deafened by the horrible yells their enemies uttered, and blinded by the long barbed arrows which rained around them like hail.

But the Apaches, as much as the French, wished for no mere skirmish. By a common accord they rushed on each other in a hand-to-hand fight. In the midst of the Indian warriors, the Black Bear could be easily recognised by his long plume and the eagle feathers planted in his war-tuft. The chief urged his men on to avenge their preceding defeats by seizing the Casa Grande. Then one of those fearful frontier actions began, in which no prisoners are made, and which render any description impossible through the ferocity both parties display, and the cruelties of which they are guilty. The *bolas perdidas*, bayonet, and lance were the only weapons employed. This fight, during which the Indians were incessantly reinforced, lasted more than two hours, and the defenders of the barricades allowed themselves to be killed sooner than yield an inch of ground.

Beginning to hope that the Indians must be wearied by so long a struggle and such an obstinate defence, the French redoubled their efforts, when suddenly the cry of "Treason! treason!" was heard in their rear. The count and the capataz, who fought in the first ranks of the volunteers and peons, turned round. The position was critical. The French were really caught between two fires. The Little Panther, at the head of fifty warriors, had turned the position, and taken the barricades in reverse. The Indians, mad with joy at such perfect success, cut down all they came across, uttering the while yells of triumph.

The count took a long glance at the battle-field, and his determination was at once formed. He said a couple of words to the capataz, who returned to the head of his combatants, warned them what to do, and watched for the favourable moment to carry out his chief's instructions. For his part, the count had lost no time. Seizing a barrel of powder, he put into it a piece of lighted candle, and hurled it into the densest ranks of the Indians, where it burst almost immediately, causing irreparable injury. The terrified Apaches fell into disorder, and fled in every direction to avoid being struck by the fragments of this novel shell. Profiting cleverly by the respite produced by the barrel among the assailants, the adventurers led by the capataz turned and rushed on the Little Panther's band, which was only a few paces off by this time. The spot was not favourable for the Indians, who, collected in a narrow entry, could not manœuvre their horses. The Little Panther and the Apaches rushed forward with yells. The French, as brave and as skilful as their adversaries, boldly awaited with levelled bayonets the shock of the tremendous avalanche, which fell upon them with blinding speed. The red-skins were driven back. The rout commenced, and the Apaches began flying in every direction. The count sent several peons after them, who returned toward nightfall, stating that the Apaches, after re-forming, had entered the desert.

The count, although satisfied with the victory he had gained (for the enemy's loss was tremendous), did not consider it decisive, as the Black Bear had escaped, and he had been unable to recover the persons he had sworn to save. He gave orders to his *cuadrilla* to prepare for a forward march in the desert, and on the next day the French would definitively leave the Casa Grande.

The count fêted with his officers the victory gained on the previous day, and urged them to drink to the success of the expedition they were going to attempt on the morrow. Flushed by the numerous potations he had made, by the repeated toasts he had drunk, as well as by the hope of complete success ere long, the count was in the best possible temper to hear the singular message the old corporal delivered so much against the grain.

"And what sort of fellow is he?" he asked, when the other had performed his task.

"On my word, captain," the corporal answered, "so far as I could see, he is a stout, well-built young fellow, and gifted with a sufficient stock of assurance, not to speak more strongly."

The count reflected for a moment.

" Shall I have him shot?" the soldier asked, taking this silence for a condemnation.

" Plague take it, what a hurry you are in, Boiland ! " the count said, laughing and looking up. " No, no ; this scamp's arrival is a piece of good luck for us. On the contrary, bring him here with the utmost politeness."

The soldier bowed and retired.

" Gentlemen," the count continued, " you remember the trap to which I almost fell a victim : a certain amount of mystery, which I have never been able to fathom, has since surrounded this affair. The man who asks speech of me has come, I feel a presentiment, in order to give me the key to many things which have hitherto been incomprehensible."

" Senor conde," the capataz observed, " pray take care. You do not yet know the character of our people : this man may come to draw you into a snare."

" For what purpose ? "

" *Quien sabe ?* " Blas Vasquez answered, employing that phrase which in Spanish is so meaning, and which it is difficult to translate into our tongue.

" Bah, bah ! " the count said. " Trust in me, Don Blas, to unmask this scamp, if he be a spy, as I do not suppose."

The capataz contented himself with an almost imperceptible shrug of his shoulders. The count was one of those men whose lofty and arrogant mind rendered any discussion impossible. The Europeans, and, before all, the French in America, display towards the natives —white, half-breed, or red-skins—a contempt which breaks out in their language and actions. Persuaded they stand intellectually far above the inhabitants of the country in which they happen to be, they display toward them an insulting pity, and amuse themselves with continually turning them into ridicule, by mocking either their habits or their belief, and in their hearts grant them an amount of instinct not greatly superior to that of the brute.

This opinion is not only unjust, but it is also entirely false. The American Hispanos, it is true, are very far behindhand as regards civilisation, trade, mechanical arts, &c.: progress with them is slow, because perpetually impeded by the superstitions that form the basis of their faith; but we ought not to make these people responsible for a state of things from which they are eager to emerge, and for which the Spaniards are alone culpable, owing to the system of brutalising oppression and crushing abjectness in which they kept them. The grinding tyranny which for several centuries weighed Indians down, by rendering them the utter slaves of haughty and implacable masters, has given them the characteristics of slaves—cunning and cowardice.

With a few very honourable exceptions, the mass of the Indian population especially—for the whites have advanced with giant steps in the path of progress during the past few years—is scampish, cunning, cowardly, and depraved. Thus it ever happens that when an European and a half-breed come into collision, the white man, in spite of the intelligence he boasts, is duped by the Indian. It is so well recognised as an article of faith in Spanish America, that the half-breeds and Indians are poor irrational creatures, gifted at the most with enough intelligence to live from hand to mouth, that the whites proudly call themselves *gente de razon*.

We are bound to add that, after a few years' residence in America, the opinions of the Europeans with regard to the half-breeds are greatly modified, because a little acquaintance with the country enables them to take a more healthy view of the people with whom they are mixed up. But the Count de Lhorailles had not reached that stage : he only saw in the Indian or half-breed a being all but lacking reason, and dealt with him on that erroneous principle. This belief was destined, at a later date, to bear most terrible consequences.

The count had noticed the shrug of the shoulders the capataz gave, and was about to reply to him, when the corporal reappeared, followed by the stranger, on whom all eyes were at once fixed. The stranger bore without flinching the cross-fire of glances, and, while remaining completely wrapped up in the folds of his large cloak, saluted the company with unparalleled ease. The appearance of this man in the banqueting hall infected the guests with a feeling of uneasiness they would have been unable to explain, but which suddenly rendered them dumb.

CHAPTER XVII.

CUCHARÈS.

THE silence began to grow embarrassing to all, and the count speedily noticed this. As a thorough gentleman, accustomed to command immediately the most exceptional and difficult positions, he rose, walked toward the stranger with outstretched hand, and turning to his officers,—

" Gentlemen," he said, with a peculiar inflection of voice, and bowing courteously, " allow me to present to you this *caballero*, whose name I am not yet acquainted with, but who, from what he has himself said, is one of my most intimate enemies."

" Oh, senor condé ! " the unknown said in a stifled voice.

" I am delighted at it," the count said quickly. " Pray do not contradict me, my dear enemy, but be good enough to take a seat by my side."

" I never was your enemy: the proof is that I have ridden two hundred leagues to ask a service of you."

" It is granted ere mentioned; so put off serious matters till to-morrow.   Take a glass of champagne."

The unknown bowed, seized the glass, and said, bowing to the company,—

" Gentlemen, I drink to the fortunate issue of your expedition."

And lifting the glass to his lips, he emptied it at a draught.

" You are a famous companion, sir.   I thank you for your toast; it is of good omen to us."

" Commandant, pray be kind enough," Lieutenant Martin said, " to tell us as speedily as possible your amusing relations with this caballero."

" I would do so with pleasure, senores; but I should first like to ask this caballero, who states he has ridden so far to see me, to break an incognito which has lasted too long already, and to inform us of his name, so that we may know whom we have the honour of greeting."

The stranger began laughing, and, allowing the fold of his cloak, which had hitherto concealed his face, to fall, replied,—

" With the greatest pleasure, caballeros; but I fancy that my name, like my face, will teach you nothing. We only met once, senor conde, and during that interview the night was too dark, and the conversation between yourself and my comrade too animated, for my features to have been deeply imprinted on your memory, even had you seen them."

"It is true, senor," the count replied, after attentively examining his features. "I am free to confess that I do not remember ever having seen you before."

"I was sure of it."

"Then," the count exclaimed hotly, "why do you so obstinately hide your face?"

"Come, sir count, I probably had my reasons for doing so. Who knows if you may not some day have cause to regret making me break an incognito which I probably had reasons for maintaining?"

These words were pronounced in a sarcastic voice, mingled with a menace, which each could read in spite of the stranger's apparent coolness.

"It is of littl consequence, senor," the count said haughtily. "I am one of those men whose sword supports his words; so now have the goodness to give me your name without further excuses or vacillation."

"Which will you have, caballero—my *nom de guerre,* or any other of my aliases?"

"Any one you please," the count said furiously, "so long as you give us one."

The stranger rose, and, turning a haughty glance on all present, said in a firm voice,—

"I told you on entering this room, caballero, that I had ridden two hundred leagues to ask a service of you. I deceived you. I expect nothing of you, neither service nor favour; on the contrary, I wish to be useful to you. I have come for that purpose, and no other. What need of your knowing who I am, or what my name is, as I shall not be your obligeé, but you mine?"

"The greater reason, caballero, for you to unmask. I will respect the quality of guest you claim here, and not make you do by force what I ask of you; but remember this, I am resolved, whatever may happen, to

Q

listen to nothing, and beg you to withdraw immediately, if you refuse any longer to satisfy my wishes."

"You will repent of it, senor conde," the stranger replied, with a sardonic smile. "One word more, and a last one. I consent to make myself known but to you privately, the more so as what I have to tell you must only be heard by yourself."

"By Bacchus!" Lieutenant Martin exclaimed, "this surpasses all belief, and such persistency is extraordinary."

"I know not if I am mistaken," the capataz exclaimed meaningly; "but I am certain I hold a great place in the mystery with which this caballero surrounds himself, and that if he fears anybody here it is I."

"You are quite correct, Senor Don Blas," the stranger said with a bow. "You see that I know you. You know me too, if not by face, fortunately for me at this moment, by name and repute. Well, rightly or wrongly, I am convinced that were I to pronounce that name before you, you would induce your friend not to listen to me."

"And what would happen then?" the capataz interrupted him.

"A great misfortune probably," the stranger said in a firm voice. "You see that I act frankly with you, whatever your opinion may be. I only ask of the count ten minutes' conversation; after that he can do whatever he pleases with the secret I intrust to him, and the news I bring him."

There was a moment's silence. The count examined the stranger's calm face while reflecting profoundly. At length the unknown rose, and, bowing to the count, said,—

"Which am I to do, senor—stay or go?"

The count turned a piercing glance upon him, which

the other endured without betraying the slightest emotion.

"Stay!" he said.

"Good!" the unknown remarked, and seated himself again on the *butacca*.

"Gentlemen," the count continued, addressing his guests, "you have heard: be kind enough to excuse me for a few moments."

The officers rose and withdrew without any reply. The capataz was the last to go, after bending on the unknown one of those glances which ransack the depths of a man's heart. But this glance, like the count's, produced no effect on the stranger's cold, impassive face.

"Now, senor," the count said, addressing his guest so soon as they were alone, "I am awaiting the fulfilment of your promise."

"I am ready to satisfy you."

"What is your name? Who are you?"

"Pardon me, sir," the stranger replied with easy raillery, "if we go on thus it will take a long time, and you will learn nothing, or very little."

The count repressed with difficulty a gesture of impatience.

"Proceed as you think proper," he said.

"Good! in that way we shall soon understand each other."

"I am listening."

"You are strange, senor, in this country. Having arrived only a few months back, you do not yet know the habits and customs of the inhabitants. Relying on the knowledge you attained in your own country, you fancied, on arriving among us, that you could do exactly as you pleased, because your intelligence was so superior to ours, and you have acted accordingly."

" To your story, senor!" the count interrupted him passionately.

" I am coming to it, senor. Owing to powerful protectors, you found yourself at once placed in an exceptional position. You have founded a magnificent colony in the richest province of Mexico, on the desert frontier. You then asked and obtained from government the rank of captain, with the right to raise a free corps composed exclusively of your own countrymen, specially intended to hunt the Apaches, Comanches, &c. That is easy to understand, for we Mexicans are such cowards."

" Senor, senor! I would remind you that all you are now saying is at least useless," the count angrily exclaimed.

" Not so much as you suppose," the other said, still perfectly calm; " but set your mind at ease. I have finished, and now reach the point which specially interests you. I only wished to let you see that if you did not know *me*, I, on the other hand, know more of you than you imagined."

The count struck the table with his fist and stamped his foot as an outlet for his passion.

" I will go on," the unknown continued. " Certainly, on landing in Mexico, however great your ambition might be, you did not expect to gain such a brilliant position in so short a time. Facile fortune is a bad adviser. The too much of yesterday becomes the not enough of to-day. When you saw that you succeeded in everything, you wished to crown your work by a masterstroke, and shelter yourself for ever from the freaks of that fortune which is to-day your slave, but might suddenly turn its back on you to-morrow. I do not blame you. You acted like a clever gambler; and, being afflicted with that vice myself, I can appreciate in others a quality I do not myself possess."

"Oh!" the count said.

"Patience! I am there now. You looked around you, and your eyes were naturally fixed on Don Sylva de Torrès. That caballero combined all the qualities you sought in a father-in-law, for what you wished was to contract a rich marriage. Ah! you no longer interrupt me. It seems that the account I am giving of your own history is becoming interesting. Don Sylva is kind-hearted and credulous; moreover, he has a colossal fortune, even for this country, where fortunes are so large; and Dona Anita is a charming girl. In short, you introduced yourself to Don Sylva. You asked his daughter's hand, which he promised you, and the marriage should have come off a month ago. And now, caballero, be good enough to redouble your attention, for I am entering on the most interesting part of my narrative."

"Continue, senor; you see that I am listening with all necessary patience."

"You shall be rewarded for your complaisance, caballero, be at rest," the unknown said with a tinge of mockery.

"I am anxious to hear the end of your story, senor."

"Here you have it. Unfortunately for your schemes, Dona Anita was not consulted by her father in the choice of a husband: for a long time she had secretly loved a young man who had done her an important service."

"And you know the man's name?"

"Yes, senor."

"Tell it me."

"Not yet. This man returned her love. The two young people met without Don Sylva's knowledge, and swore an eternal love. When Dona Anita was constrained by her father to regard you as her husband she feigned submission, for she did not dare openly to resist her father; but she warned the man she loved, and the couple, after renewing their love vows, thought on a way to break off this fatal marriage."

The count had risen several moments back, and was now pacing the room. At the last words he stopped before the stranger.

"Then," he said in a gloomy voice, "the attempted assassination at the Rancho——"

"Was a means employed by the lover to get rid of you? Yes, senor," the stranger calmly said.

"This man, then, is only a dastardly assassin!" he said contemptuously.

"You are wrong, caballero; he only wished to compel you to retire. The proof is that your life was in his hands, and he did not take it."

"To the point, then!" the count exclaimed. "Assassin or not, you will tell me his name, for you have finished now, I suppose?"

"Not yet. After the meeting at the Rancho you proceeded to your hacienda, accompanied by your future father-in-law and wife. Even then, without leaving you a moment's rest, the hatred of Dona Anita's lover pursued you: the Apaches attacked you."

"Well?"

"Well, need I give you further explanation? Cannot you understand that this man was in league with the red-skins?"

"And Dona Anita knew it?"

"I will not affirm that positively, but it is probable."

"Oh!"

"Was not the game well played?"

The count bit his lips till the blood began to flow.

"And you know who carried Dona Anita off?"

"I do."

"It was not the red-skins?"

"No."

"That man, then?"

"Yes."

"But her father was carried off too?"

"I know it; but it was not at all with his will, I assure you."

"Where is Don Sylva now?"

"Quietly at home at Guaymas."

"Is his daughter with him?"

"No."

"She is with that man, I suppose?"

"You are a perfect sorcerer."

"And you know where they are?"

"I do."

Quick as lightning the count bounded on the stranger, seized him by the collar with his left hand, and, placing a pistol against his breast, shouted in a hoarse voice,—

"Now, villain, you will tell me where they are!"

"Is that the game we are playing?" the stranger said. "Well, as you please, caballero."

Then, throwing back his cloak quickly, he aimed at the count two pistols which he held in either hand. The stranger's movement had been so rapid that the count was unable to prevent it. Besides, a sudden idea occurred to him at the moment. Lowering his pistol, and thrusting it back in his girdle, he muttered,—

"I was mad: pardon that angry movement."

"Most heartily," the unknown replied, laying his pistols on the table within reach.

"Pardon me again. Now that I reflect on what you

have just told me, I see that your object was to be of service to me."

The stranger made a gesture of affirmation.

" But there is one thing I cannot explain."

" What is that ?"

" The manner in which you have told me all these details."

" Oh ! that is simple enough."

" I shall feel obliged by your explanation."

" With pleasure, caballero.   Two men attacked you at the Rancho."

" Yes."

" I am he who pulled you off your horse."

" Oh !" the count said, with a singular intonation in his voice.

" In a word, my name is Cucharès !   I am a lepero. that is to say, I like the sun better than the shade, rest than work, and would sooner stab a man, when properly paid for it, than do a good action which brings in nothing.   You comprehend me ?"

" Perfectly."

" Then we can come to an understanding ?"

" I think so."

" Well, so did I, and that is the reason I have come to you."

" One question more."

" Ask it."

" At this moment you are betraying your friends?"

" I ?   Who ?"

" The persons you have hitherto served."

" A man like myself, caballero, has no friends, only customers."

" Friends or customers, you are betraying them."

" Pooh ! we have settled our accounts.   They owe

me nothing, nor I them. We are quits. Look ye,
caballero : in every business there are two sides, which
a skilful man can work equally well. I have drawn all
I could from the first, so I am going to try the other now."

The count heard the lepero develope this strange
theory with an amazement mingled with terror. A
cynicism so ripe and shameless terrified him, and yet
the count was not excessively thin-skinned.

"We will agree, then, that you have come to do me
a service."

The lepero smiled.

"Let us understand one another," he continued. "I
say so not to startle the consciences of the gentlemen
who were present on my entrance; but, between ourselves, I will be more frank."

"Which means?" -

"That I have come to sell it to you."

"Be it so!"

"I shall want a long price."

"Good!"

"A very long price."

"No matter, if it is worth it."

"Come," the lepero exclaimed joyfully, "you are
just the man I expected to find you. Well, you can
trust in me."

"I must do so, I suppose."

"What would you? It is the way of the world.
To-day my turn, to-morrow yours. Bah! you will
have no cause to regret a few thousand piastres."

"First, then, my rival's name."

"It will cost you fifty ounces, and you cannot think
it dear."

"Here they are," the count said, arranging them on
the table.

The lepero made them disappear in a second in his large pockets.

"The name of your rival, caballero, is Don Martial. He is a Tigrero, and very rich."

"I fancy I have heard Don Sylva mention that name."

"It is probable. Don Sylva cannot endure Don Martial, especially since he saved Dona Anita's life."

"I remember that circumstance too : Don Sylva frequently mentioned it to me. And now, how did Don Martial carry the girl off ?"

"Very easily, the more so as she wished nothing better than to follow him. During your fight with the Apaches he placed Dona Anita in a canoe, into which I had already thrown her father, gagged and tied ; then we went off, all four of us. All through the night we kept to the river, so as to leave no traces of our flight, and by daybreak had covered fifteen leagues. No longer fearing discovery, we landed. Indios Mansos sold us some horses. Don Martial ordered me to take the young girl's father to Guaymas, and I fulfilled this difficult commission with all honour. Don Sylva was unwilling to follow me ; but at last I managed to get him into his own house, where I left him, and went back to Don Martial, who had requested me to bring him certain things, and was awaiting me at a spot agreed on between us."

"Ah !" the count said, "and how did you come to leave him ?"

"Good gracious ! caballero, we separated, as so often happens to the best of friends, in consequence of a misunderstanding."

"Very good ! He turned you off ?"

"Nearly so, I am obliged to confess."

" Have you left him long ? "

The lepero winked his right eye.

" No," he answered.

" Can you lead me to the spot where he now is ? "

" Yes, whenever you please."

" Very good !   Is it far ? "

" No ; but pardon me, caballero, let us settle matters at once.   Are you agreeable ? "

" Let us see."

" How much will you give me to learn at what spot Don Martial and Dona Anita are concealed ? "

" Two hundred ounces."

" Hand them over."

" Here they are."

The count took some handsful of money from an iron box in a corner of the room, and gave them to the lepero.

" There is a pleasure in dealing with you," Cucharès said, as he sent these ounces to join the others with admirable celerity.   " Thus you see I was quite right when I told you that I was going to do you a service."

" It is true, and I thank you.   Where are Don Martial and the Dona ? "

" At the mission of Don Francisco.   But now I must ask permission to leave you."

" Not yet."

" Why not ? "

" For two reasons ; the first, because, in spite of all the confidence I have in you, nothing has yet proved to me that you have told the truth."

" Oh ! " the lepero said with a gesture of denial.

" I know very well I am mistaken ; but what would you have ?   I am naturally suspicious."

" Good !   I will remain.   But now for your second reason."

"This is it.   I have in my turn a service to ask of you."

" To be paid for ?"

" Of course."

" I am listening."

" I will give you one hundred ounces to lead me to my rival."

" Canarios !" the lepero exclaimed.

" One hundred ounces," the count said again.

" I understand you.   One hundred ounces—a fine sum.   But look ye, count: I am a costeno, and a lepero in the bargain.   This desert life does not suit my temperament, and injures my health.   I have taken an oath to have no more of it.   The road from here to the mission is difficult.   We shall have to cross the desert. No, taking all things into consideration, it is impossible."

" That is unlucky," the count coldly replied.

" It is."

" Because," he continued, " I would have given you not one, but two hundred ounces."

" Eh ?" the other said, cocking his ears.

" But as you refuse—you do so, I think ?—I shall be obliged, to my great regret, to have you shot."

" What do you say ?" the lepero exclaimed, with a movement of terror.

" By 'r Lady !" the count said simply, " my dear fellow, you are so clever in business matters that, having found two sides of a question, I am terribly frightened lest you should find a third."

And before Cucharès could prevent him he seized the pistols that lay on the table.   The lepero turned livid.

" Pardon me, pardon me !" he said in an ill-assured voice.   " As you desire it so eagerly, I must please you to the best of my power. I accept the two hundred ounces."

"Very good!" the count exclaimed. "I thought, too, that we should come to an understanding."

He went to fetch the money from the iron chest; but, as he turned his back on the lepero, he could not see the singular smile that curved his lips. Had he done so, he would not have chanted his victory so loudly.

CHAPTER XVIII.

IN WHICH THE STORY GOES BACK.

THE lepero's story, true in its foundation, was utterly false and erroneous in its details. Perhaps, however, he had an interest in deceiving the Count de Lhorailles, which the reader will be able to judge of better after reading the following chapter.

After escaping so miraculously from the hands of the Apaches, into whose power he had fallen, Cucharès dived and sought the centre of the river. On mounting to the surface again to take breath, he looked around him : he was alone. The lepero stifled a cry of joy, and, after a moment's reflection, swam vigorously in the direction of the mangroves, where Don Martial, warned by the signal he had been compelled to give, had doubtlessly been awaiting him some time. With a few strokes he reached the trees, beneath whose shade he disappeared. But another piece of good luck awaited him there : the canoe, abandoned to itself, had floated up against the trunk of a tree, and remained stationary.

Cucharès, leaving the water, soon succeeded in emptying the canoe and making it float again. These boats are so light that they can be easily emptied, for in these regions they are made of birch bark, which the Indians strip from the tree by means of boiling water.

He had scarce landed ere a shadow bent over him and muttered in his ear,—

"You have been a long time."

The lepero gave a start of terror; but he recognised Don Martial. In very few words he explained to him all that had happened.

"It is all the better, as you have come here," the Tigrero said. "Hide yourself in the mangroves, and do not stir under any pretext until I return."

And he rapidly retired. Cucharès obeyed with more zeal because he heard at no great distance from him the sound of the obstinate contest going on at that moment between the French and Apaches. Don Martial, dagger in hand, in readiness for any event, had glided like a phantom up to a clump of floripondius, where Dona Anita awaited him all trembling. Just as he was going to pull back the branches that separated him from the young girl, he stopped with panting breast and frowning brow. She was not alone. Her voice, quivering with emotion or anger, was harsh and imperious. Whom could she be speaking to? Who was the man that had succeeded in discovering her in this retired spot, where she fancied herself so well concealed, and who, it seemed, was trying to force her to follow him? The Tigrero listened. Soon he made a gesture of anger and menace. He had recognised the voice of the man with whom Dona Anita was talking : it was her father.

All was lost!

The haciendero was trying to lead his daughter in the direction of the buildings, while employing the most convincing reasons. He did not appear to suspect the motive which had brought his daughter to that spot.

Dona Anita refused to go away, alleging the danger of being met by an Indian marauder, and thus falling into the danger she so earnestly wished to avoid.

Don Martial struck his brow; a singular smile played on his lips; his eyes flashed fire, and he noiselessly slipped back to the river bank. Still the combat was going on : at times it appeared to draw nearer—oaths and yells could be distinguished ; at others, flashes lit up the scene, and a shower of bullets whizzed through the air with that sharp, hissing sound which terrifies novices in warfare.

" In the name of Heaven, my beloved daughter," Don Sylva urged, " come ! We have not a moment to lose ; in a few seconds our retreat may be perhaps cut off. Come, I implore you !"

" No, my father !" she said, shaking her head. " I am resigned : whatever my happen, I repeat to you, I will not leave this spot."

" It is madness," the haciendero exclaimed in great grief. " You wish to die, then ?"

" What matter to me ?" she said sorrowfully. " Am I not condemned in every way ? Heaven is my witness, father, that I would gladly die to escape the marriage prepared for me."

" My daughter, in the Virgin's name——"

" What do you care, father, whether I fall into the hands of Pagan savages to-day, when to-morrow you would surrender me with your own hands to a man I detest?"

" Speak not to me thus, daughter. Besides, the moment is very badly chosen, it seems to me, for a discussion like this. Come, the shouts are growing more furious ; it will soon be too late."

" Go, if you think proper," she said resolutely. " I shall remain here, whatever may happen."

"As it is so, as you obstinately resist me, I will employ force to compel your obedience."

The girl threw her left arm round the trunk of a cedar tree, and looking with intense resolution at her father, exclaimed,—

"Do so if you dare, O my father! but I warn you that, at the first step you take toward me, that will happen which you want to avoid. I will utter such piercing shrieks that they must reach the ears of the Pagans, who will run up."

Don Sylva stopped in hesitation : he knew his daughter's firm and determined character, and that she would at once put this threat in execution. A few minutes elapsed, during which father and daughter stood face to face, not uttering a word, or making even a gesture.

Suddenly the branches were noisily parted, yielding a passage to two men, or rather two demons, who, rushing with panther bounds on the haciendero, hurled him to the ground. Before Don Sylva was able to recognise the enemies who attacked him so unexpectedly by the pale beams of the stars, he was gagged and bound, while a handkerchief twisted round his head hid from him all external objects, and prevented him seeing what his daughter's fate might be. The latter, at this sudden attack, uttered a cry of terror, at once prudently checked, for she had recognised Don Martial.

"Silence!" the Tigrero hurriedly said in a low voice. "I could manage in no other way. Come, come, your father, you know, is a sacred object to me."

The girl made no reply. At a sign from Don Martial, Cucharès seized Don Sylva, threw him on his shoulders, and went toward the mangroves.

"Where are we going?" Dona Anita asked in a trembling voice.

" To a place where we can be happy together," the Tigrero answered gently, as he lifted her with a passionate movement, and ran off with her to the canoe. Dona Anita made no resistance : she smiled, and threw her arms round her lover's neck, to keep her balance during this steeple-chase, in which Don Martial leaped from branch to branch, holding on by the creepers, and encouraging his lovely burden by signs and looks. Cucharès had placed Don Sylva in the bottom of the canoe, and, paddles in hand, was impatiently awaiting the Tigrero's arrival; for the combat seemed doubled in intensity, although, from the number of musket shots, it was easy to see that victory would remain with the French.

" What shall we do ?" Cucharès asked.

" Get into the middle of the river, and slip down with the current."

" But our horses ! "

" Let us save ourselves first; we will think of the horses afterwards. It is evident that the white men are the victors. So soon as the fight is over, Count de Lhorailles will send everywhere in search of his guests. It is important not to leave any trail, for the French are demons, and would find us again."

" Still, I fancy———" Cucharès timidly observed.

" Be off ! " the Tigrero said in a peremptory tone, kicking the canoe vigorously from the bank.

The first moments of the voyage passed in silence : each reflected on the peculiar position in which he was placed.

Don Martial had assumed a tremendous responsibility by staking, as it were, on one throw the happiness of the girl he loved and his own. Besides, the haciendero lying at the bottom of the canoe gave him

B

great subject for thought.   The position was gr*ve, the solution difficult.

Dona Anita, with drooping head and absent glance, was dreamily letting her dainty hand glide throu h the water over the side of the canoe.

Cucharès, while paddling furiously, was thinking that the life he led was anything rather than agree ble, and that he was far happier at Guaymas, as he lay with his head in the shade, and his feet in the sun, in the church porch, enjoying his siesta, refreshed by the sea breeze, and lulled to sleep by the mysterious murmur of the surf on the shingle.

As for Don Sylva de Torrès, he was not reflecting. A prey to one of those dumb passions which, if they lasted any length of time, must end in insanity, he frantically bit the gag that shut his mouth, and writhed in his bonds, while unable to break them.

The various sounds of the contest gradually died out. For some time longer the travellers remained silent, absorbed not only in their thoughts, but affected by that gentle melancholy produced on all nervous natures by that solemn calmness and striking harmony of the desert, whose sublime and majestic grandeur no human pen is capable of describing.

The stars were beginning to pale in the sky ; an opal line was vaguely drawn on the horizon ; the clumsy alligators were quitting the mud, and going in search of their morning meal ; the owl, perched on the tre was saluting the approaching sunrise ; the coyot glided in startled bands along the shore, utter g their hoarse barks ; the wild beasts were retreating to their hidden dens, heavy with sleep and fatigu ; day was on the point of breaking. Dona Anita leaned coquettishly on Don Martial's shoulder.

"Where are we going?" she asked him in a gentle and resigned voice.

"We are flying," he laconically answered.

"We have been descending the river in this way for more than six hours, borne by the current and helped by your four vigorously-pulled paddles. Are we not out of reach of danger?"

"Yes, long ago. It is not any fear of the French which troubles me now——"

"What then?"

The Tigrero pointed to Don Sylva, who, having exhausted his strength and passion, had at length tacitly recognised his powerlessness, and was sleeping quite exhausted.

"Alas!" she said, "you are right. Things can not go on thus, my friend; the position is intolerable."

"If you will allow me to act as I think proper, before a quarter of an hour your father will thank me."

"Do you not know that I am entirely yours?"

"Thanks!" he said. Turning to Cucharès, he muttered a few words in his ear.

"Ah, ah! that is an idea," the lepero said with a grin. Two minutes later the canoe ran ashore. Don Sylva, delicately borne by two powerful hands, was carried ashore without waking.

"Now it is your turn," Don Martial said to the girl: "for the success of the scheme I have formed you must allow yourself to be fastened to this tree."

"Do so, my friend."

The Tigrero took her in his vigorous arms, bore her ashore, and in a twinkling had fastened her tightly by the waist to the stem of a tree.

"Now," he said hurriedly, "remember this. Your father and yourself were carried off from the hacienda by the Apaches; accident brought us in your way, and——"

"You save us, I suppose?" she said with a smile.

"Quite correct; but utter shrill cries, as if you felt in great alarm. You understand, do you not?"

"Perfectly."

The play was performed in the way arranged. The girl uttered piercing shrieks, to which the two adventurers replied by discharging their rifles and pistols; then they rushed toward the haciendero, whom they hastened to liberate from his bonds, and to whom they restored not only the use of his limbs, but also of his eyes and tongue. Don Sylva half rose, and looked around him: he saw his daughter fastened to a tree, from which two men were hastily freeing her. The haciendero raised his eyes to heaven, and uttered a fervent prayer.

So soon as Dona Anita was free she ran to her father, and cast herself in his arms. As she embraced him she hid her face, which blushed, perhaps, for shame at this unworthy deception, on the old man's breast.

"My poor darling child," he murmured, with tears in his eyes, "it was for you, for you alone, I trembled during the whole of this fearful night."

The girl made no reply, for she felt stung to the heart by this reproach. Don Martial and Cucharès, judging the moment favourable, then approached, holding their smoking rifles in their hands. On recognising them a cloud passed over the haciendero's face—a vague suspicion gnawed at his heart: he bent a searching glance on the two men and on his daughter, and rose with frowning brow and quivering lips, though not uttering a word. Don Martial was embarrassed by this silence, which he had been far from anticipating. After the service he was supposed to have done Don Sylva, the duty of speaking first fell upon him.

" I am happy," he said in an embarrassed voice, " to have arrived here so fortunately, Don Sylva, as I was enabled to save you from the red-skins."

" I thank you, Senor Don Martial," the haciendero answered dryly. " I could expect nothing less from your gallantry. It was written, so it seems, that after saving the daughter, you must also save the father. You are destined, I see it, to be the liberator of my entire family : receive my sincere thanks."

These words were uttered with an accent of raillery that pierced the Tigrero like an arrow : he could not find a word in reply, and bowed awkwardly in order to hide his embarrassment.

" My father," Dona Anita said in a caressing tone, " Don Martial has risked his life for us."

" Have I not thanked him for it ? " he continued. " The affair was a sharp one, as it seems, but the heathens escaped very quickly. Was there no one killed ? "

And saying this, the haciendero affected to look carefully around him. Don Martial drew himself up.

" Senor Don Sylva de Torrès," he said in a firm voice, " as chance has brought us once again face to face, permit me to tell you that few men are so devoted to you as myself."

" You have just proved it, caballero."

" Leave that out of sight," he went on hurriedly. " Now that you are free, and can act as you please, command me. What would you of me ? I am ready to do anything you please, in order to prove to you how happy I should be in doing you a service."

"That is language I can understand, caballero, and to which I will frankly respond. Important reasons compel me to return to the French colony of Guetzalli, whence the heathens carried me off so treacherously."

"When do you wish to start?"

"At once, if that be possible."

"Everything is possible, caballero. Still, I would call your attention to the fact that we are nearly thirty leagues from that hacienda; that the country in which we now are is a desert; that we should have great difficulty in finding horses; and, with the best will in the world, we cannot make the journey on foot."

"Especially my daughter, I presume," the other remarked with a sardonic smile.

"Yes," the Tigrero said, "especially the senorita."

"What else is to be done? for I must return there —with my daughter," he added, purposely laying a stress on the last three words, "and that so soon as possible."

The Tigrero did not utter the exact truth in telling Don Sylva they were thirty leagues from the colony. It was not more than eighteen; but in a country like this, where roads do not exist, fifteen leagues are an almost insurmountable obstacle to a man not thoroughly acquainted with desert life. Don Sylva, though he had never travelled under other than favourable circumstances—that is to say, with all the comfort it is possible to obtain in these remote regions—was aware, theoretically, if not practically, of all the difficulties which would rise before him with each step, and what obstacles would check his movements. His resolution was made almost immediately.

Don Sylva, like a good many of his countrymen, was gifted with rare obstinacy. When he had formed a plan, the greater the obstacles which prevented its accomplishment, the greater his determination to carry it out.

" Listen," he said to Don Martial ; " I wish to be frank with you. I fancy I tell you nothing new in announcing my daughter's marriage with the Count de Lhorailles. That marriage must be performed : I have sworn it, and it shall be, whatever may be said or done to impede it. And now I am about to make trial of the devotion you boast of offering me."

" Speak, senor."

" You will send your companion to the Count de Lhorailles; he will carry him a message to calm his uneasiness, and announce my speedy arrival."

" Good ! "

" Will you do it ? "

. " At once."

" Thanks! Now, as regards yourself personally, I leave you at liberty to follow or leave us at your pleasure ; but, in the first place, we want horses, arms, and, above all, an escort. I do not wish to fall once more into the hands of the heathen. Perhaps I shall not have the good fortune to escape from them so easily as on this occasion."

" Remain here : in two hours I will return with horses. As for an escort, I will try and procure you one, although I do not promise it. As you allow me to do so, I will accompany you till you have rejoined the *conde*. I hope, during the period I may have the felicity of passing near you, to succeed in proving to you that you have judged me wrongfully."

These words were pronounced with such an accent of truth that the haciendero felt moved.

" Whatever may happen," he said, " I thank you : you

will not the less have done me an immense service, for which I shall be ever grateful to you."

Don Sylva tore a leaf from his pocket book, on which he wrote a few lines in pencil, folded it, and handed it to the Tigrero.

"Are you sure of that man?" he asked him.

"As of myself," Don Martial answered evasively. "Be assured that he will see the conde."

The haciendero made a sign of satisfaction as the Tigrero went up to Cucharès.

"Listen," he said aloud as he gave him the paper. "Within two days you must have delivered this to the chief of Guetzalli. You understand me?"

"Yes," the lepero replied.

"Go, and may Heaven protect you from all evil encounters! In a quarter of an hour behind that mound," he hurriedly added in a whisper.

"Agreed," the other said with a bow.

"Take the canoe," the Tigrero continued.

Had the haciendero conceived any doubts, they were dissipated when he saw Cucharès leap into the canoe, seize the paddles, and depart without exchanging a signal with the Tigrero, or even turning his head.

"The first part of your instructions is fulfilled," the Tigrero said, returning to Don Sylva's side. "Now for the second part. Take my pistols and musket. In case of any alarm you can defend yourself. I leave you here. Pray do not move, and within two hours at the latest I will rejoin you."

"Do you know, then, where to find horses?"

"Do you not remember that the desert is my domain?" he replied with a melancholy smile. "I am at home here, as I shall soon prove to you. Farewell for the present."

And he went off in a direction opposed to that taken by the canoe. When he had disappeared from Don Sylva's sight behind a clump of trees and shrubs, the Tigrero turned sharply to the right and ran back. Cucharès, carelessly seated on the ground, was smoking a cigarette while awaiting him.

" No words, but deeds," the Tigrero said. " We have no time to waste."

" I am listening."

" Look at this diamond ; " and he pointed to a ring, through which his neck-handkerchief was drawn.

" It is worth 6000 piastres," Cucharès said, examining it like a connoisseur.

Don Martial handed it to him.

" I give it you," he said.

" What am I to do for it ?"

" First hand me the letter."

" Here it is."

Don Martial took it, and tore it into impalpable fragments.

" Next ? " Cucharès continued.

" Next, I have another diamond like that one at your service.   You know me ?"

" Yes ; I accept."

" On one condition."

" I know it," the other said with a significant sign.

" And you accept ?"

" Of course I do."

" It is a bargain."

" He shall never trouble you again."

" Good !   But you understand that I shall need proofs."

" You shall have them."

" Good-by, then "

The two accomplices separated, well satisfied with each other. A nod was as good as a wink in such a case. We have seen how Cucharès acquitted himself of the mission intrusted to him by Don Sylva. Don Martial, after his short conversation with Cucharès, went to look for horses. Two hours later he had returned. He not only brought excellent horses, but had hired four peons, or men who called themselves so, to act as escort. The haciendero comprehended all the delicacy of Don Martial's conduct; and though the air and garb of his defenders were not completely orthodox, he warmly thanked the Tigrero for the trouble he had taken to supply his wants. Reassured as to his journey, he breakfasted with good appetite on a lump of venison, washed down with *pulque*, which Don Martial had procured. Then, so soon as the meal was over, the little band, well armed, set out resolutely in the direction of Guetzalli, where Don Sylva expected to arrive in three days, if nothing thwarted his calculations.

CHAPTER XIX.

IN THE PRAIRIE.

THE Mexican frontier, up to the old Jesuit missions, now abandoned and falling in ruins, forms the skirt of the great prairie of the Rio Gila or of Apacheria, which extends as far as the mournful desert of the Norte. In this portion of the prairie nature coquettishly expands all that richness of growth and vegetation which may be in vain sought elsewhere.

Guetzalli was built by Count de Lhorailles on the ruins of a once flourishing mission of the reverend

Jesuits, which the decree commanding their expulsion had compelled them to abandon. Without entering into any discussion for or against the Jesuits, we will say, *en passant*, that these clergy rendered immense services in America; that all the missions thus founded in the desert prospered; that the Indians flocked in by thousands to range themselves beneath their paternal laws; and that certain missions, whose names we could quote were it necessary, counted as many as sixty thousand neophytes; that, as a proof of the excellence of their system, when the order was given them to give up their mission to other monks, and withdraw, their proselytes implored them to resist this unjust ostracism, and offered to defend them against everybody.

The Jesuits have the greater claim to this tardy justice we now seek to do them in the fact that, in spite of the many years that have elapsed since their departure, and although all the men they brought into the bosom of the church by incessant labour have returned to a savage life, the remembrance of the good deeds of these pious missionaries still lives in the hearts of the Indians, and forms at night round the camp fires the staple of conversation, so deeply engraved on the minds of these primitive beings is the small amount of kindness shown them.

Don Sylva de Torrès wished to reach the colony of Guetzalli again so soon as possible, and by the most direct route. Unfortunately he was obliged to cross, as the crow flies, a large extent of country through which no road ran. Moreover, owing to his topographical ignorance of the prairie, he was compelled to trust in Don Martial, an excellent guide in every respect, whose sagacity and thorough knowledge of the desert he did not for a moment doubt, but in whom he placed but slight confidence, while unable to explain his motive even to himself.

Still the Tigrero (apparently at least) gave proofs of his entire devotion to the haciendero, leading him by the most beaten tracks, making him avoid difficult passages, and watching with unequalled care and solicitude over the safety of his little band. Each evening at sunset the party encamped on the top of an open hill, whence a large quantity of ground could be surveyed, in order to guard against any surprise. On the evening of the fourth day, after a fatiguing march over an irregular tract, Don Martial reached a hill where he proposed to camp.

The haciendero greeted the offer with the greater pleasure, for, being but little accustomed to this mode of travelling, he felt extremely fatigued. After a frugal meal, composed of maize tortillas, and frijoles powdered with the hottest spices, and washed down with pulque, Don Sylva, without even thinking of smoking a cigarette (his custom always after a meal), wrapped himself in his zarapè, laid down with his feet toward the fire, and fell off almost immediately into a profound sleep.

Don Martial and the young girl remained for some time silently opposite each other, their eyes fixed on the haciendero, and uneasily watching the phases of his sleep. At length, when the Tigrero was persuaded that Don Sylva was really asleep, he bent over her, and muttered in her ear in a gentle voice,—

" Pardon, Dona Anita, pardon ! "

" For what ? " she asked in surprise.

" Because you are suffering through me."

" Egotist ! " she said with an enchanting smile, " it is not through myself too, as I love you ? "

" Oh, thank you!" he exclaimed. " You restore to
my heart that courage which I felt dying out. Alas !
how will all this end?"

" Well, I am convinced," she said quickly. " We must
be patient. My father, believe me, will soon change his
opinion about you."

The Tigrero smiled sorrowfully.

" Still," he said, " I cannot carry you about the
prairie indefinitely."

" That is true," she remarked despondently. " What
is to be done?"

" I do not know. For the last two days we have
only been moving round the colony, from which we are
scarce three leagues distant, and yet I cannot resolve to
enter it."

" Alas !" the girl murmured.

" Ah !" he continued, with a degree of animation in
his glance, "why is this man your father, Dona Anita?"

" Speak not so, my friend," she said hurriedly, laying
her little hand on his mouth as if to prevent him saying
more. " Why despair? God is good; He will not fail
us. We know not what He has in reserve for us : let us
place our trust in Him !"

" Still," he replied, shaking his head, " our position
is not tenable. It is impossible to go on at hap-hazard.
Your father, in spite of his ignorance of the country,
will at length perceive I am deceiving him, and I shall
be hopelessly ruined in his opinion. On the other
hand, by proceeding to the colony, I place you in the
hands once more of the man you are to be forced to
marry. I cannot resolve on doing this odious deed.
Oh ! I would joyfully give ten years of my life to know
how I ought to act."

At this moment, as if Heaven had heard his words,

and hastened to reply immediately, the Tigrero, whose
eyes were mechanically fixed on the prairie, which at
this moment was buried in obscurity, saw a short
distance off, in the midst of the tall grass, a luminous
point arise in the air twice, tracing in its passage
quaint parabolas.   At the same moment Don Martial's
practised ear heard, or fancied it heard, the suppressed
snorting of a horse.

" It is extraordinary," he muttered, as if speaking
to himself. " What can it mean ? Is it a signal?
Still we are alone here.   Through the whole of the
past day I have not caught sight of a single trail; but
that light——"

" What is the matter, my friend ? " Dona Anita
asked anxiously. " You seem restless. Can any danger
menace us ?   Speak !   You know I am brave ; and by
your side, what can I fear ?   Hide nothing from me.
Something extraordinary is taking place, is it not ? "

" Well, yes," he replied, resolutely making up his
mind, " something extraordinary is really happening ;
but calm yourself, I do not believe there is anything for
you to fear."

" But what is it ?   I saw nothing."

" Stay : look there! " he said quickly, and stretched
out his arm.

The girl looked attentively, and saw what the Tigrero
had noticed a few moments previously—a reddish dot
sparkling in the gloom, and describing interlaced lines.

" 'Tis evidently a signal," the Tigrero went on.
" Somebody is concealed there."

" Do you expect any one?" she asked him.

" No ; and yet, I know not why, but I fancy that
signal can only be intended for me."

" Still recollect that we are in the prairie, and

probably, without suspecting it, surrounded by bands of Indian hunters. They may be corresponding with each other by means of that light which we have seen twice gleaming before our eyes."

"No, Dona Anita, you are mistaken. We are not, at any rate for the present, surrounded by any Indians : we are alone, quite alone."

"How can you know that, my friend, since you have not left us for a moment to go and look for trails ?"

"Dona Anita, my well-beloved !" he said in a stern voice, "the prairie is a book on which Heaven's secrets are written in ineffaceable letters, which the man accustomed to desert life can read currently. The wind passing through the branches, the water murmuring on the river sand, the bird flying through the air, the deer or buffalo grazing on the tufted grass, the alligator slothfully wallowing in the mud, are to me certain signs in which I cannot be mistaken. For the last two days we have seen no Indian sign; the buffaloes and other animals we have passed growled calmly and without distrust ; the flight of the birds was regular ; the alligators almost disappeared in the mud which covered them. All these animals scent the approach of man, and specially of the Indian, for a considerable distance, and, so soon as they have done so, disappear at headlong speed, so great is the terror with which the Lord of creation inspires them. I repeat to you, we are alone, quite alone here, and therefore that signal is intended for me. See, there it is again !"

"It is true ; I can see it."

"I must know what the meaning of it is," he said, seizing his rifle.

"Oh, Don Martial, I implore you, take care ! Be prudent. Think of me !" she added in agony.

" Reassure yourself, Dona Anita　I am too old a wood-ranger to let myself be deceived by a clumsy trick. I shall return shortly."

And without listening further to the young girl, who tried to retain him by her entreaties and tears, he proceeded to the slope of the hill, which he descended rapidly, though with the utmost prudence. On arriving in the prairie the Tigrero stopped to look around him. The party were encamped about two arrow-shots from the Gila, nearly opposite a large island, which is in reality only a rock, bearing some resemblance to the human form, and which the Apaches call *the master of the life of man.* In their excursions upon Indian territory the red-skins never fail to stop at this island and deposit their offerings, the ceremony consisting in throwing into the water, with dancing, tobacco, hair, and birds' feathers. This rock, which offers a most striking appearance from the distance, has two excavations in it more than 1200 feet in length, and forty wide, the roof being of an arched form.

The fact which had aroused the Tigrero's curiosity, and caused him to undertake the enterprise of discovering the meaning of the signal, was that it came from the island ; and this he could not at all account for, being aware that the Indians felt for the rock a veneration mingled with a superstitious terror so great, that no Indian warrior, however brave he might be, would have dared to spend the night there. It was the knowledge of this peculiarity which urged him to examine into the mystery.

Tall and tufted grass grew profusely down to the river's edge. Concealed by the thickly-growing mangroves and shrubs, intertwined in inextricable confusion, the Tigrero glided cautiously down to the bank. So soon as he reached it he let himself hang from a branch, and entered the water so quietly that his immersion produced no sound.

Holding his rifle over his head to keep it out of the wet, the Tigrero then swam with one hand in the direction of the island. The distance was short; the Tigrero was a vigorous swimmer, and he soon reached the spot where he wished to land. So soon as he was on the island he crawled through the shrubs, listening to the slightest sound, and trying to pierce the darkness. He saw nothing, heard nothing; then he rose, and walked toward one of the grottos, at the entrance of which he could see a fire blazing from the spot where he stood: near it was seated a man, smoking as quietly as if he had been seated before a pulqueria at Guaymas.

Don Martial, after attentively regarding this man, had difficulty in repressing a shout of joy, and walked toward him without further attempt at concealment. He had recognised his confidant, Cucharès, the lepero. At the sound of his footfall Cucharès turned his head.

" You have come at last !" he exclaimed. " For more than an hour I have been racking my brain in inventing fresh signs, to which you would not deign a reply."

" Ah, my dear fellow," the Tigrero joyfully replied, " could I have suspected it was you I should have been with you long ago; but I so little expected you——"

" You are quite right, and in such a country as this it is better to be too prudent than not sufficiently so."

" Ah, ah ! there is something new ? " the Tigrero said, as he sat down to the fire to dry his clothes.

" Caspita ! if there was not, should I be here ? "

" True : you are a good comrade, and I thank you for coming. You know that I have a faithful memory."

" I know it."

" But come, what have you to tell me ? I am anxious
to hear all the news.   But, before beginning, one
question."

" Well ? "

" Is the news good ? "

" Excellent : you shall judge."

" Caraï ! as it is so, take this ring, which I was not to
have given you till our little affair was settled.   But do
not be frightened : when we balance our account I shall
find something to please you."

, The lepero's eye glistened with joy and avarice ; he
seized the ring, and sent it to join company with the
one he had received a few days previously.

" Thanks ! " he said.   " Heaven keep me ! there is a
pleasure in dealing with you.   You do not huckster, at
any rate."

" Now for the news."

" Here it is, short and good.   El senor conde,
rendered desperate by the disappearance of his betrothed,
whom he supposes to have been carried off by the
Apaches, has quitted the hacienda at the head of his
company, and is now crossing the desert in every direction in pursuit of the Black Bear."

" By all the saints ! that is the best news you could
bring me.   And what do you intend doing ? "

" What ! did we not agree that *el conde*———"

" Of course," the Tigrero quickly interrupted him ;
" but to do that you must find him, and that, I fancy, is
not so easy now."

" On the contrary."

" How so ? "

" Why, Senor Don Martial, do you wish to insult
me by taking me for a *pavo* (goose) ? "

" By no means, gossip : still———"

" Still you believe it. Well, you are mistaken, caballero, and I am not sorry to tell you so. During the few hours I spent at the hacienda I made inquiries, and, as I announced myself the bearer of a most important mission for *el senor conde*, no one made any bones about answering me. It seems that the Apaches, instead of pushing on, were so thoroughly beaten by the French (for whom, by the way, they feel an enormous respect), that they are returning on the desert del Norte, in order to regain their villages. The conde is pursuing them, is he not ? "

" You told me so."

" Well, in all probability he will not dare to enter the desert."

" Naturally," the Tigrero said with a shudder, in spite of his tried courage.

" Well, then, he can only stop at one spot."

" At the Casa Grande ! " Don Martial exclaimed quickly.

" Quite right ! I am certain of finding him there."

" Body of me ! go there, then."

" I shall set out immediately after your departure."

The Tigrero looked at him in surprise.

" You 're a fine fellow, Cucharès, on my soul ! " he said presently. " I am delighted to find that I made no mistake about you."

" What would you ? " the scamp answered modestly, while winking his little grey eye. " The relations into which I entered with you are so agreeable to me, that I can refuse you nothing."

The two men began laughing at this sally, which might have been in better taste.

"Now that all is settled between us," Don Martial went on, " let us part."

" How did you come here ? "

" Can't you see ? By swimming; and you ? "

" On my horse. I would offer to land you again, but we are going in opposite directions."

" For the present, yes."

" Do you intend to cross over there soon, then ? '

" Probably," he said with an equivocal smile.

" In that case we shall soon meet again."

" I hope so."

" Stay, Don Martial. Now that your clothes are dry, I should not like you to wet them again. Let us go and see if there be not a canoe about : you know the Indians leave them everywhere."

The Tigrero entered the grotto, and found there a canoe, with its paddles carefully balanced against the sides : he unscrupulously carried it out on his shoulders.

" By the way," he said, " why the deuce did you give me the meeting here ? "

" Not to be disturbed. Would you have liked any one to overhear our conversation ? "

" I allow that. Good-by, then."

" Good-by."

The men separated—Cucharès to commence a long journey, and Don Martial to return to his camping-ground. But they were mistaken in supposing that no one had overheard their conversation. They had scarce quitted the island in different directions ere, from a thicket of dahlias and floripondins growing at the entrance of the grotto, a hideous head was thrust out cautiously, and looked around ; then, at the end of a moment, the bushes were further parted, and an Apache

Indian, painted and armed for war, appeared. It was the Black Bear.

"Wah!" he muttered, with a menacing gesture, "the pale-faces are dogs. The Apache warriors will follow their trail."

Then, after keeping his eyes fixed for a few instants on the star-spangled sky, he entered the grotto.

In the mean while the Tigrero had regained the encampment. Dona Anita, rendered restless by so long an absence, was awaiting him with the most lively anxiety.

"Well?" she asked, running up so soon as she saw him.

"Good news," he answered.

"Oh, I was so frightened!"

"I thank you. It was as I expected. The signal was intended for me."

"Then?"

"I found a friend, who gave me the means to quit the false position in which we are."

"In what way?"

"Do not trouble yourself about anything, I repeat, but leave me to act."

The girl bowed submissively, and, in spite of the curiosity that devoured her, retired without any further questioning into the *jacal* of branches prepared for her. Don Martial, instead of sleeping, sat down on the ground, folded his arms on his chest, leaned against a tree, and remained thus motionless till daybreak, plunged in deep and melancholy thought. At sunrise the Tigrero shook off the effects of his night-watch and aroused his comrades. Ten minutes after the little party was *en route*.

"Oh, oh!" the haciendero said, "you are very early this morning."

" Did you not notice that we did not even breakfast before starting, as we usually do ?"

" Of course I did."

" Do you know the reason? Because we shall breakfast at Guetzalli, where we shall arrive in two hours at the latest."

" Ah, caramba ! " the haciendero exclaimed, " you delight me with that news."

" I thought I should."

Dona Anita, on hearing him speak thus, had looked sorrowfully at Don Martial; but seeing his face so calm, his smile so frank, she felt suddenly reassured, and suspected that his silence of the previous night intended some pleasant surprise for her.

As Don Martial had stated, two hours later they reached the colony. So soon as they were perceived by the sentinels the isthmus drawbridge was lowered, and they entered the hacienda, where they were received with all possible politeness. Dona Anita, with her eyes constantly fixed on the Tigrero, blushed and turned pale, understanding nothing of his perfect calmness. They dismounted in the second courtyard before the gate of honour.

" Where is the Count de Lhorailles? " the haciendero asked, surprised that his future son-in-law had not merely neglected to come to meet him, but was not here to receive him.

" My master will feel highly annoyed, when he hears of your arrival, at not having been present to welcome you," the steward answered, breaking out into profuse apologies.

" Is he absent, then ? "

" Yes, senor."

" But he will soon return ? "

" I hardly think so. The captain started in pursuit of the savages at the head of his entire company."

This news was a thunderbolt for Don Sylva; but the Tigrero and Dona Anita exchanged a glance of delight.

CHAPTER XX.

BOOT AND SADDLE!

THE great desert del Norte is the American Sahara—more extensive, more to be feared, than the African Sahara; for it contains no laughing oases, sheltered by fine trees, and refreshed by sparkling fountains. Beneath a coppery sky extend immense plains, covered with a dirty-greyish sand; in every direction horizons succeed horizons; sand, ever sand, fine impalpable sand, bearing a closer resemblance with human dust, which the wind carries aloft in long whirlwinds, whose desolating aspect varies incessantly at the will of the tempest, which hollows out valleys and throws up hills each time the fearful *cordonazo* howls across this desolate soil.

Greyish rocks, covered with patches of parched lichen, at times lift up their stunted crests in the midst of this chaos, which has not changed its appearance since the creation. The buffalo, the ashata, the swift-footed antelope, shun this desert, where their feet would only rest on a shifting soil; flocks of blear-eyed and ill-omened vultures alone soar over these regions in search of extremely rare prey, for the desert is so horrible that the Indians themselves enter on it with a tremor, and cross it with express speed when they return to their villages after a foray on the Mexican territory. And yet, however rapid their journey may be, their passage is marked in an indelible manner by

the skeletons of mules and horses which they are compelled to abandon, and whose bones blanch in the
desert, until the hurricane, again unchained, covers all
with a cere-cloth of sand.

Still, as the hand of Deity is everywhere visible, in the
desert more profoundly than elsewhere, there spring up
at long intervals, and half buried in the sand, in the
midst of piled-up rocks, vigorous trees, with enormous
trunks and immense foliage, which seem to offer the
traveller rest beneath their shade. But these trees
grow few and far between on the plain, and two are
rarely found together at the same spot. These trees,
revered by the Indians and wood-rangers, are the imprint of Providence on the desert, the proof of His solicitude and inexhaustible goodness. But we repeat it,
with the exception of these few landmarks, lost like
imperceptible dots in the immensity, there are neither
animals nor vegetables on the Del Norte : sand, and
naught but sand.

The Casa Grande of Moctecuzoma, where the Count
de Lhorailles' free company was encamped, rose, and
probably still rises, at the extreme limit of the prairie,
at not more than two leagues from the skirt of the desert.
The line of demarcation was clearly and coarsely traced
between the two regions : on the one side a luxuriant
vegetation, glowing with vigour and health ; verdant
plains covered with a close, tall grass, in which animals
of every description browsed ; the song of birds, the
hiss of reptiles, the lowing of the buffaloes, in a word,
grand, vigorous, and ever-joyous life, exhaling through
every pore of this blessed landscape.

On the other side, the silence of death ; a grey
horizon ; a sea of sand, whose agitated waves pressed
forward on every side, as if to encroach on the prairie ;

not even the most scanty pasture—nothiug—no roots, no moss, naught but sand !

After his conversation with Cucharès the count recalled his lieutenants, and began drinking and laughing again in their society. They rose from table at an advanced hour to retire to sleep. Cucharès, however, did not sleep : he was too busily engaged in thinking. We know now, or nearly so, with what purpose he joined the count at the Casa Grande.

At sunrise the bugles sounded the *réveillé*. The soldiers rose from the ground on which they had been sleeping, shook off the night's cold, and were busily engaged in dressing their horses and preparations for the morning's meal. The camp soon put on that hurry and reckless animation so characteristic of Frenchmen when out on an expedition.

In the great hall of the Casa Grande the count and his lieutenants, seated on the dried skulls of buffaloes, were holding a council. The discussion was animated.

" In an hour," the count said, " we shall set out. We have twenty mules laden with provisions, ten to carry water, and eight for ammunition. We have, therefore, nothing to fear."

' That is true to a certain point, senor conde," the capataz observed.

" Why so ? "

" We have no guides."

" What use are guides ? " the count said passionately. " I fancy we need only follow the Apache trail."

Blas Vasquez shook his head.

" You do not know the Del Norte, excellency," he said candidly.

" This is the first time accident has brought me this way."

" I pray God it be not the last."

" What do you mean?" the count said with a secret shudder.

" Senor conde, the Del Norte is not a desert, but a gulf of shifting sands ; at the slightest breath of air in these desolate regions the sand rises, whirls, and swallows up men and horses, leaving not a trace ; all disappears for ever, buried beneath a cere-cloth of sand.'

" Oh, oh !" the count said thoughtfully.

" Believe me, senor conde," the capataz continued. " Do not venture with your brave soldiers into this implacable desert : not one of you will leave it again."

" Still the Apaches are men too ; they are not braver or better mounted than we, I may say."

" They are not."

" Well, they cross the Del Norte from north to south, from east to west, and that not once a year or ten times, but continually, whenever the fancy takes them."

" But do you know at what price, senor conde? Have you counted the corpses they leave along the road to mark their passage? And then you cannot compare yourselves with the Pagans : the desert possesses no secrets for them. They know its furthest mysteries."

" Then," the count exclaimed impatiently, " your impression is———"

" That in bringing you here, and attacking you two days ago, the Apaches laid a trap for you. They wish to entice you after them into the desert, certain not merely that you will not catch them, but that you and all your men will leave your bones there."

" Still you will agree with me, my dear Don Blas, that it is very extraordinary there is not among all your peons one capable of guiding us in this desert. Hang it, they are Mexicans ! "

"Yes, excellency, but I have more than once had the honour of observing to you that all these men are costenos, or inhabitants of the seaboard. They never before came so far into the interior."

"What shall we do, then?" the count asked with some hesitation.

"Return to the colony," the capataz replied. "I see no other means."

"Shall we abandon Don Sylva and his daughter?"

Blas Vasquez frowned. He replied in a solemn voice, and with much emotion,—

"Excellency, I was born on the estate of the Torrès family. No one is more devoted, body and soul, than I am to the persons whose names you have pronounced; but no one is bound to attempt impossibilities. It would be tempting God to enter the desert in our present state. We have no right to calculate on a miracle, and that alone could bring us back here safe and sound."

There was a moment's silence. These words produced· on the count's mind an impression which he tried in vain to master. The lepero guessed his hesitation, and approached.

"Why," he said in a crafty voice, "did you not tell me that you needed a guide, senor conde?"

"What good would that do?"

"In fact, that is true: it was not worth the trouble, as I promised to conduct you to Don Sylva. You have doubtlessly forgotten that?"

"You know the road, then?"

"Yes, as well as a man can who has only gone along it twice."

"By heavens!" the count exclaimed, "we can push on now; nothing need keep us longer. Diégo Léon, order ' the boot and saddle ' to be sounded, and if you are a good guide you shall have proofs of my satisfaction."

" Oh, you can trust to me, excellency ! " the lepero answered with a dubious smile. " I certify that you will reach the spot whither I have to guide you."

" I ask no more."

Blas Vasquez, with that instinctive suspicion innate in all honest minds when they come across wicked persons, felt an irresistible repugnance for the lepero. This repugnance had displayed itself from the first moment of Cucharès' appearance in the hall the previous evening. While he was talking to the count he therefore examined him closely. When he had ended, Blas made a sign to the count, who came up to him. The capataz led him to a distant corner of the room, and whispered in his ear,—

" Take care ; that man is deceiving you."

" You know it ? "

" I am certain of it."

" Why so ? "

" Something tells me so."

" Have you any proofs ? "

" None."

" You must be mad, Don Blas ; fear troubles your senses."

" God grant that I am deceived ! "

" Listen ! Nothing forces you to follow us. Remain here till we return : in that way, whatever may happen, you will escape the dangers which in your idea menace us."

The capataz drew himself up to his full height.

" Enough, Don Gaëtano," he said coldly. " In warning you I acted as my conscience commanded. You will not attend to my advice—you need not do so :

I have done my duty as I was bound to do. You wish
to march forward. I will follow you, and hope soon to
prove to you that if I am prudent, I can be as brave
as any man when it is necessary."

"Thanks!" the count answered, affectionately pressing
his hand; "I felt sure that you would not abandon me."

At this moment a great disturbance was heard outside, and Lieutenant Diégo Léon entered precipitately.

"What is the matter, lieutenant?" the count
asked him sternly. "What means this startled face?
Why do you enter in this way?"

"Captain," the lieutenant answered in a panting
voice, "the company has revolted."

"Eh? What is that you say, sir? My troopers have
revolted?"

"Yes, captain."

"Ah!" he said, biting his moustaches, "and why
have they revolted, if you please?"

"Because they do not wish to enter the desert."

"They do not wish!" the count continued, weighing
on every word. "Are you sure of what you say,
lieutenant?"

"I swear it, captain; but listen."

In fact, shouts and oaths, an ever-increasing noise,
which was beginning to assume formidable proportions,
were heard outside.

"Oh, oh! that is becoming serious, I fancy," the
count continued.

"Much more than you suppose, captain. The company, I repeat, is in complete mutiny. The rebels
have loaded their arms : they surround the house,
uttering threats against you. They say they want
to speak to you, and that they are sure of obtaining
what they want, by good will or ill."

"I am curious to see that," the count said, still per-fectly calm, as he walked toward the door.

"Stay, captain," the officers exclaimed, as they rushed before him; "our men are exasperated; some accident may happen to you."

"Nonsense, gentlemen," he replied angrily, repulsing them; "you are mad: they do not know me well enough yet. I intend to show these bandits that I am worthy to command them."

And, without listening to any entreaty, he slowly walked out of the room with a firm and calm step.

What had happened may be told in a few words.

Blas Vasquez' peons, during the few days the company had bivouacked in the ruined city, told the troopers, with sufficient exaggeration, mournful and gloomy stories about the desert, giving details about these accursed regions which would have made the hair stand on the head of the bravest. Unfortunately, as we have said, the company was encamped hardly two leagues from the entrance of the Del Norte: the gloomy horizon of the desert added its frightful reality to the terrible tales told by the peons.

All the count's soldiers were French Dauph'yeers, principally men who had escaped the gallows, brave, but, like all Frenchmen, easy to lead backwards and forwards, and equally resolute for good or bad. Since they had been under the command of the Count de Lhorailles, although he had behaved with considerable bravery in action, they only obeyed him with a certain degree of repugnance. The count had grave faults in their eyes: in the first place, that of being a count; next, they considered him too polite, his voice was too soft, his manner too delicate and effeminate. They could not imagine that this gentleman, so well clothed and well gloved, was capable of leading them to great things. They would have liked as a chief a man of rude voice and rough manner, with whom they could have lived, so to speak, on a footing of equality.

In the morning the rumour had spread that the camp was about to be raised, in order to enter the desert and pursue the Apaches. At once groups were formed—commentaries commenced—the men gradually grew excited. Resistance was soon organised, and when the lieutenant came to give orders to raise the camp he was greeted with laughter, jests, and hisses ; in short, he was compelled to give ground before the mutineers, and return to his captain to make his report.

An officer, under such circumstances, acts very wrongly in losing his coolness, and yielding a step in the presence of revolt. He ought sooner to let himself be killed. In a mutiny one concession compels another ; then this inevitably happens—the rebels count their strength, and at the same time their leaders': they recognise the immense superiority brute strength gives them, and immediately abuse the position which the weakness or sloth of their officers has given them, not to ask a simple modification, but even to claim a radical change.

This happened under the present circumstances. So soon as the lieutenant had retired, his departure was at once regarded in the light of a triumph. The soldiers began haranguing, influenced by those among them whose tongues were most loosely hung. It was no longer a question about not entering the desert, but of appointing other officers, and returning at once to the colony. The entire staff must be changed, and the leaders chosen from those who inspired their comrades with most confidence—that is to say, the most dangerous fellows.

The effervescence had reached the boiling point:
the soldiers brandished their weapons furiously, while
directing the most furious threats at the captain and
his lieutenants. Sudddenly the door opened, and the
count appeared. He was pale, but calm. He took a
quiet look at the mutinous band that howled around
him.

"The captain! Here is the captain!" the troopers
shouted.

"Kill him!" others went on.

"Down with him, down with him!" they howled in
chorus.

All rushed upon him, brandishing weapons and
offering insults. But the count did not give way; on
the contrary, he advanced a step. He held in his
mouth a fine husk cigarette, from which he puffed the
smoke with the utmost serenity.

Nothing imposes on masses like cold and unaffected
courage. There was a pause in the revolt. The
captain and his men examined each other, like two
tigers measuring their strength ere bounding forward.
The count profited by the moment of silence he had
obtained to take the word.

"What do you want?" he asked calmly, while withdrawing his cigarette from his mouth, and following
the light cloud of bluish smoke as it rose in spirals in
the sky.

At this question of their captain's the charm was
broken; the shouts and yells recommenced with even
greater intensity; the rebels were angry with themselves for having allowed their chief's firmness momentarily to overawe them. All spoke at once. They
surrounded the count on all sides, pulling him in
every direction, to force him to listen to them. The

count, pressed and hustled by all these rogues, who had thrown discipline overboard, and were sure of impunity in a country where justice only nominally exists, did not lose his countenance—his coolness remained the same. He allowed these men to yell at their ease for some moments, their eyes bloodshot, and foam on their lips ; and when he considered this had lasted long enough, he said, in a voice as calm and tranquil as on the first occasion,—

"My friends, it is impossible for us to go on talking in this way : I understand nothing of what you say. Choose one of your comrades to make your complaints in your name. If they are just, I will do you justice ; but be calm."

After uttering these words the count leaned his shoulder against the door crossed his arms on his chest, and began smoking again, apparently indifferent to what was going on around him. The calmness and firmness displayed by the count from the beginning of this scene had already borne their fruit : he had regained numerous partisans among his soldiers. These men, though they dared not yet openly avow the sympathy they felt with their chief, warmly supported the proposition he had made them.

"The captain is right," they said. "It is impossible, if we continue to badger him in this way, that he can understand our arguments."

"We must be just too," others took up the ball. "How can you expect the captain to do us justice unless we clearly explain to him what we want ?"

The revolt had made an immense backward step. It no longer spoke of deposing its chiefs ; it limited itself to asking justice of the captain. Hence it still tacitly recognised him.

At length, after numberless discussions among the mutineers, one of their number was selected to take the word in the name of the rest. He was a short, square-shouldered fellow, with a cunning face, and little eyes sparkling with wickedness and spite; a regular scoundrel, in a word, the type of the low-class adventurer, with whom everything is comprised in robbery and assassination. This man, whose *nom de guerre* was Curtius, was a Parisian, and hailed from the Faubourg Saint Marceau. An ex-soldier, an ex-sailor, he had been at every trade, except, perhaps, that of an honest man. Since his arrival in the colony he had been remarkable for his spirit of insubordination, brutality, and, above all, his bounce. He boasted of " owing eight dead ; " that is to say, in the language of the country, having committed eight murders. He inspired his comrades with an instinctive terror. When he was selected to take the word, he rammed his hat down on the side of his head, and addressing his comrades, said,—

"You shall see how I 'll walk into him."

And he advanced, insolently swaying from side to side, toward the captain, who watched his approach with a smile of peculiar meaning. Suddenly a great silence fell on the crowd; hearts beat powerfully, faces grew anxious; each guessed instinctively that something decisive and extraordinary was about to happen.

When Curtius was only two paces from his captain he stopped, and, surveying him insolently, said,—

" Come, captain, the business is this : my com——"

But the count gave him no time to finish. Quickly drawing a pistol from his girdle, he pressed it against his temples and blew out his brains. The bandit rolled in the dust with a fractured skull. The captain returned the pistol to his sash, and coolly raising his head, said in a firm voice,—

"Has any one further observations to make?"

No one stirred; the bandits had suddenly become lambs. They stood silent and penitent before their chief, for they understood him. The count smiled contemptuously.

"Pick up this carrion," he said, spurning the corpse with his foot. "We are Dauph'yeers, and woe to the man who does not carry out the clauses of our agreement. I will kill him like a dog. Let this scoundrel be hanged by the feet, that his unclean carcass may become the prey of the vultures. In ten minutes the boot and saddle will sound: all the worse for the man who is not ready."

After this thundering speech the count re-entered the house with as firm a step as he had left it. The revolt was subdued—the wild beasts had recognised the iron grip beneath the velvet glove; they were tamed for ever, and henceforth would let themselves be killed without uttering a murmur.

"'Tis no matter," the soldiers said to each other, "he is a rude fellow for all that: he hasn't any cold in his eyes."

And then each eagerly made his preparations for departure. Ten minutes later, as the captain had announced, he reappeared: the troop was on horseback, ranged in order of battle, and ready to start. The count smiled, and gave the word to set out.

"Hum!" Cucharès muttered to himself, "what a pity that Don Martial has such fine diamonds! After what I have seen I could have broken my word with pleasure."

Before long the free company, with the captain at its head, disappeared in the Del Norte.

CHAPTER XXI.|

THE CONFESSION.

THE haciendero and his daughter left the colony of Guetzalli under the escort of Don Martial and the four peons he had taken into his service. The little band advanced to the west, in the direction in which the free company had marched in pursuit of the Apaches. Don Sylva was the more anxious to rejoin the French because he knew that their expedition had no other purpose than to deliver him and his daughter from the hands of the red-skins.

The journey was gloomy and silent. As the travellers approached the desert the scenery assumed a sombre grandeur peculiar to primitive countries, which exercised an unconscious influence over the mind, and plunged them into a melancholy which they were powerless to overcome.

No more cabins, no more *jacals*, no more travellers found by the side of the road, and offering an affectionate wish for your safe arrival as you pass, but an accidented soil, impenetrable forests peopled with wild beasts, whose eyes sparkled like live coals amid the wildly-interlaced creepers, shrubs, and tall grass. At times the trail of the Frenchmen might be seen on the soil, trodden by a large number of horses; but suddenly the country changed its character, and every trace disappeared.

Each evening, after the Tigrero had beaten the vicinity to drive back the wild beasts, the camp was formed by the bank of a stream, the fires lighted, and a hut of branches hastily constructed to protect Dona Anita from the night cold; then, after a scanty meal, they wrapped themselves up in their fressadas and zarapès, and slept till daybreak. The only incidents which at times disturbed the monotony of their life were the discovery of an elk or deer, in pursuit of which Don Martial and his peons galloped at full speed, and it often took hours ere the poor brute was headed and killed.

But there were none of those pleasant chats and confidences which make time appear less tedious, and render the fatigues of an interminable road endurable. The travellers maintained a reserve toward each other, which not only kept all intimacy aloof, but also any confidence. They only spoke when circumstances rendered it compulsory, and then only exchanged words that were indispensable. The reason of this was that two of the travellers had a secret unknown to the third, which weighed upon them, and at which they blushed inwardly.

Man, with his necessarily incomplete nature, is neither entirely good nor entirely bad. Most frequently, after committing actions under the iron pressure of passion or personal interest, when his coolness has returned, and he measures the depth of the abyss in which he has precipitated himself, he regrets them, especially if his life, though not exemplary, has at least hitherto been exempt from deeds which are offensive to morality. Such was at this moment the situation of Don Martial and Dona Anita. Both had been led by their mutual love to commit a fault they bitterly repented ; for we will state here, to prevent our readers forming an erroneous estimate of their character, that their hearts were honest, and when, in a moment of madness, they arranged and carried out their flight, they were far from foreseeing the fatal consequences which this hopeless step would entail.

Don Martial, especially after the orders he had given Cucharès, and the haciendero's unshaken determination of rejoining the Count de Lhorailles, clearly comprehended that his position was growing with each moment more difficult, and that he was proceeding along a path that had no outlet. Thus the two lovers, fatally attached by the secret of their flight, still kept hidden from each other the remorse that devoured them; they felt at each step that the ground on which they walked was undermined, and that it might suddenly give way beneath their feet.

In such a situation life became intolerable, as there was no longer a community of thought or feeling between these three persons. A collision between them was imminent, though it happened, perhaps, sooner than they anticipated, through the pressure of the circumstances in which they were entangled. After a journey of about a fortnight, during which no noteworthy incident occurred, Don Martial and his companions, guided partly by the information they had picked up at the hacienda, and partly by the trail left by the persons they were following, at length reached the ruins of the Casa Grande of Moctecuzoma. It was about six in the evening when the little party entered the ruins: the sun, already below the horizon, only illumined the earth with those changing beams which glisten for a long while after the planet-king has disappeared. Marching a short distance from each other, Don Sylva and Don Martial looked searchingly around, advancing cautiously, and with finger on the rifle trigger, through this inextricable maze, so favourable for an Indian ambuscade. They at length reached the Casa Grande, and nothing extraordinary had met their sight. Night had almost set in, and objects began to grow confused in the shadows. Don Martial, who was preparing to dismount, suddenly stopped, uttering a cry of astonishment, almost of terror.

" What is it ? " Don Sylva asked quickly as he walked up to the Tigrero.

" Look ! " the latter said, stretching out his arm in the direction of a clump of stunted trees which stood a short distance from the entrance. The human voice exerts a strange faculty over animals—that of inspiring them with insurmountable fear and respect. To the few words exchanged by the two men hoarse and confused cries responded, and seven or eight savage vultures rose from the centre of the clump, and began flying heavily over the travellers' heads, forming wide circles in the air, and continuing their infernal music.

" I can see nothing," Don Sylva went on ; " it is as black as in an oven."

" That is true : still, if you look more carefully at the object I point out, you will easily recognise it."

Without any reply the haciendero pushed on his horse.

" A man hung by the feet ! " he uttered, stopping his horse with a gesture of horror and disgust. " What can have happened here ? "

" Who can say ? It is not a savage—his colour and dress do not allow the least doubt on that point : still he has his scalp, so the Apaches did not kill him. What is the meaning of it?"

" A mutiny perhaps," the haciendero hazarded.

Don Martial became pensive ; his eyebrows contracted. " It is not possible," he said to himself ; but a moment after added, " Let us enter the house ; we must not leave Dona Anita any longer alone. Our absence must surprise her, and might alarm her if prolonged. When the encampment is arranged I will go and look, and T shall be very unlucky if I do not discover the clue to this ill-omened mystery."

The two men retired and rejoined Dona Anita, who was awaiting them a few paces off, under the guard of the peons. When the travellers had dismounted and crossed the threshold of the casa, Don Martial lighted several torches of *ocote* wood to find their way in the darkness, and guided his companions to the large hall to which we have already introduced our readers. It was not the first time Don Martial had visited the ruins: frequently, during his long hunting expeditions in the western prairies, they had offered him a refuge. Thus he knew their most hidden nooks.

It was he, too, who had urged his companions to proceed to the Casa Grande, for he was convinced that the count could only find there a safe and sure bivouac for his troop. The hall, in which a table still stood, presented unmistakable signs of the recent passage of several persons, and a tolerably prolonged stay they had made at the spot.

"You see," he said to the haciendero, "that I was not mistaken; the persons we seek stopped here."

"It is true. Do you think that they have long left it?"

"I cannot tell you yet; but while supper is being prepared, and you are making yourselves comfortable, I will take a look round outside. On my return I trust to be more fortunate, and be able to satisfy your curiosity."

And placing the torch he held in his hand in an iron bracket fastened to the wall, the Tigrero quitted the house. Dona Anita fell pensively back on to a species of clumsy sofa, accidentally left by the side of the table. Aided by the peons, the haciendero began making preparations for the night. The horses were unsaddled, driven into a species of inclosure, and had an ample stock of alfalfa placed before them. The trunks were unloaded, the bales carried into the hall, where they were piled up, after one had been opened to take out the requisite provisions ; and then an enormous brazier was kindled, over which a quarter of deer-meat was hung.

When these various preparations were ended the haciendero sat down on a buffalo's skull, lighted a husk cigarette, and began smoking, while every now and then turning a sad glance on his daughter, who was still plunged in melancholy thought. Don Martial's absence was rather long, for it lasted nearly two hours At the end of that time his horse's hoofs could be heard echoing on the stone flooring of the ruins, and he re-appeared.

" Well ? " Don Sylva asked him.

" Let us sup first," the Tigrero answered, pointing to the girl in a way her father comprehended.

The meal was short, as might be expected from persons pre-occupied and wearied with a long day's march. Indeed, with the exception of the roast venison, it only consisted of *caine*, maize tortillas, and *frijoles con aji*. Dona Anita ate a few spoonsful of tamarind preserve ; then, after bowing to her friends, she rose and walked into a small room adjoining the hall, where a bed had been made up for her with her father's wraps, and the entrance to which was closed by hanging up, in place of the absent door, a horse blanket attached to nails driven in the wall.

" You fellows," the Tigrero said, addressing the peons, " had better keep good watch, if you wish to save your scalps. I warn you that we are in an enemy's country,

and if you go to sleep you will probably pay dearly
for it."

The peons assured the Tigrero that they would redouble their vigilance, and went out to execute the
orders they had received. The two men remained
seated opposite each other.

"Well," Don Sylva began, again asking his companion the question he had already begun, "have you
learned anything?"

"All that it was possible to learn, Don Sylva," the
Tigrero sharply replied. "Were it otherwise I should
be a scurvy hunter, and the jaguars and tigers would
have had the best of me long ago."

"Is the information you have obtained favourable?"

"That depends on your future plans. The French have
been here, and bivouacked for several days. During their
stay in the ruins they were vigorously attacked by the
Apaches, whom, however, they succeeded in repulsing.
Now it is probable, though I cannot assert it, that the
troopers revolted for some cause of which I am ignorant,
and that the poor wretch we saw hanging to the tree
like rotten fruit paid for the rest, as generally happens."

"I thank you for your information, which proves to
me that we were not mistaken, but followed the right
trail. Now, can you complete your information by
telling me if the French have long left the ruins, and
in what direction they have marched?"

"Those questions are very easy to answer. The free
company left their bivouac yesterday, a few moments
after sunrise, and entered the desert."

"The desert!" the haciendero exclaimed, letting his
arms sink in despondency.

There was a silence of some moments, during which
both men reflected. At length Don Sylva took the word.

" It is impossible," he said.

" Still, it is so."

" But it is an extraordinary act of imprudence, almost of madness."

" I do not deny it."

" Oh, the unhappy men ! "

" They are lost ! "

" The fact is, that if they escape, Heaven will perform a miracle in their favour."

" I think with you; but it is now an accomplished fact, which no recriminations of ours can alter ; so, Don Sylva, I believe that the wisest thing is to trouble ourselves no more about them, but let them get out of it as they best can."

" Is that your notion ? "

" It is," the Tigrero replied carelessly. " I propose to remain here two or three days, and see if anything turns up. After that time, if we have seen or heard nothing, we will remount, and return to Guetzalli by the road we came, without stopping to look back, that we may arrive more speedily, and the sooner quit these horrible regions."

The haciendero shook his head like a man who has just formed an irrevocable determination.

" Then you will go alone, Don Martial," he said dryly.

" What ! " the latter exclaimed, looking him firmly in the face. " What is your meaning ? "

" I mean that I shall not turn back on the path I have hitherto followed ; in a word, that I will not fly."

Don Martial was confounded by this answer.

" What do you intend doing, then ? "

" Can you not guess that ? Why did we come to this place? For what purpose have we been travelling so long?"

" Excuse me, Don Sylva, but the question is now

changed. You will do me the justice to allow that I
have followed you without any observations—that I have
been a faithful guide to you during this journey."

" I do so indeed. Now explain to me your notion."

" It is this, Don Sylva. So long as we only wandered
about the prairies, at the risk of being devoured by wild
beasts, I bowed my head, without attempting to oppose
your designs, for I tacitly recognised that you were
acting as you were bound to do. Even now, were you
and I alone, I would bow without a murmur before the
firm determination that animates you. But reflect that
you have your daughter with you—that you condemn
her to undergo nameless tortures in this fearful desert,
where you force her to follow you, and which will probably swallow up both."

Don Sylva made no reply, so the Tigrero continued,—

" Our party is weak. We have provisions for only a
few days ; and you know, once in the Del Norte, we find
no more water or game. If, during our excursion, we
are assailed by a *temporal*, we are lost—lost, without
resources, without hope !"

" All that you tell me is correct, I am well aware ;
still, I cannot follow your advice. Listen to me in
your turn, Don Martial. The Count de Lhorailles is
my friend ; he will soon be my son-in-law. I do not
say this to vex you, but only that you may thoroughly
understand my position with regard to him. It was
for my sake, to save me from those whom he supposed
to have carried me off, that, without calculation, and
solely urged by his noble heart, he entered the desert.
Can I allow him to perish without trying to bring him
succour ? Is he not a stranger to Mexico—our guest,
in a word ? It is my duty to save him, and I will
attempt it, whatever may happen."

"Since matters are so, Don Sylva, I will no longer try to combat a resolution so firmly made. I will not tell you that the man to whom you give your daughter is an adventurer, driven from his country through his ill-conduct, and who, in the marriage he seeks to contract, sees only one thing—the immense fortune you possess. All these things, and many others, I could supply you with proofs of; but you would not believe me, for you would only read rivalry in my conduct; so let us say no more on that head. You wish to enter the desert: I will follow you. Whatever may happen, you will find me at your side ready to defend and aid you. But as the hour for frank explanations has arrived, I do not wish any cloud to remain between us—that you should thoroughly know the man with whom you are going to attempt the desperate stroke you meditate, so that you may have a full and entire confidence in him."

The haciendero gazed at him with surprise. At this moment the curtain of Dona Anita's room was raised; the young girl came out, walked slowly down the hall, knelt before her father, and turning to the Tigrero,—

"Now speak, Don Martial," she said. "Perhaps my father will pardon me on seeing me thus implore his forgiveness."

"Pardon you!" the haciendero said, his eyes wandering from his daughter to the man who was standing before him with blushing brow and downcast eyes. "What is the meaning of this? What fault have you committed?"

"A fault for which I am alone culpable, Don Sylva, and for which I alone must suffer the punishment. I deceived you disgracefully: it was I who carried off your daughter."

"What!" the haciendero shouted with an outburst of fury. "I was your plaything, your dupe, then?"

"Passion does not reason. I will only say one word in my defence: I love your daughter! Alas! Don Sylva, I now perceive how culpable I have been. Reflection, though tardy, has at length arrived, and, like Dona Anita, who is weeping at your feet, I humble myself before you, and say, ' Pardon me! ' "

"Pardon, father!" the poor girl said in a weak voice.

The haciendero made a gesture.

"Oh!" the Tigrero said quickly, "be generous, Don Sylva. Do not spurn us. Our repentance is true and sincere. I am eager to repair the evil I have done. I was mad then: passion blinded me. Do not overwhelm me."

"Father," Dona Anita continued in a tearful voice, "I love him. Still, when we left the colony, we might have fled, and abandoned you; but we did not do it. The idea never once occurred to us. We were ashamed of our fault. You see us both here ready to obey you, and perform without a murmur the orders it may please you to give us. Be not inflexible, O my father, but pardon us!"

The haciendero drew himself up.

"You see," he said severely, "I can no longer hesitate. I must save the Count de Lhorailles at all hazards, else I should be your accomplice."

The Tigrero walked in great agitation up and down the hall: his eyebrows were contracted—his face deadly pale.

"Yes," he said in a broken voice, "yes, he must be saved. No matter what becomes of me after. No cowardly weakness! I have committed a fault, and will undergo all the consequences."

"Aid me frankly and loyally in my search, and I will pardon you," Don Sylva said gravely. "My honour is compromised by your fault. I place it in your hands."

"Thanks, Don Sylva; you will have no cause to repent," the Tigrero nobly replied.

The haciendero gently raised his daughter, drew her to his bosom, and embraced her several times.

"My poor child!" he said to her, "I forgive you. Alas! who knows whether in a few days I shall not have, in my turn, to ask your forgiveness for all the sufferings I have inflicted on you? Go and rest; the night is drawing on—you must have need of repose."

"Oh, how kind you are, and how I love you, father!" she cried from her heart. "Fear nothing. Whatever sufferings the future may have in store for me, I will endure them without a murmur. Now I am happy, for you have pardoned me."

Don Martial's eye followed the maiden.

"When do you intend starting?" he said, stifling a sigh.

"To-morrow, if possible."

"Be it so. Let us trust in Heaven."

After conversing for some short time longer, and making their final arrangements, Don Sylva wrapped himself up in his coverings, and soon fell asleep. As for the Tigrero, he left the house to see that the peons were carefully watching over their common safety.

"Provided that Cucharès has not fulfilled my orders!" he muttered.

CHAPTER XXII.

THE MAN HUNT.

On the next morning at daybreak the little band quitted the Casa Grande, and two hours later entered the Del Norte. At the sight of the desert the maiden felt her heart contract ; a secret presentiment seemed to warn her that the future would be fatal. She turned back, cast a melancholy glance on the gloomy forests which chequered the horizon behind her, and could not repress a sigh.

The temperature was sultry, the sky blue, not a breath of wind was stirring : on the sand might still be seen the deep footsteps of the count's free troop.

" We are on the right road," the haciendero said ; " their trail is visible."

" Yes," the Tigrero muttered, " and it will remain so till the temporal is unchained."

" Then," Dona Anita remarked, " may Heaven come to our aid ! "

" Amen ! " all the travellers exclaimed, crossing themselves, instinctively responding to the secret voice which each of us has in the depths of our heart, and which foreboded to their misfortune.

Several hours passed away : the weather remained fine. At times the travellers saw, at a great distance above their heads, innumerable swarms of birds proceeding toward the hot regions, or *las tierras calientes*, as they are called in that country, and hastening to cross the desert. But everywhere and ever nothing was visible save a grey and melancholy sand, or gloomy rocks wildly piled on each other like the ruins of an unknown and antediluvian world, found at times in remote solitudes.

The caravan, when night set in, camped under the shelter of a block of granite, lighting a poor fire, hardly sufficient to protect them from the icy cold which, in these regions, weighs upon nature at night. Don Martial rode incessantly on the sides of the small band, watching over their safety with filial solicitude, never remaining a moment at rest, in spite of the urging of Don Sylva and the entreaties of the maiden.

"No!" he constantly answered; "on my vigilance your safety depends. Let me act as I think proper. I should never pardon myself if I allowed you to be surprised."

Gradually the traces left by the troops became less visible, and at length disappeared entirely. One evening, at the moment the travellers were forming their camp at the foot of an immense rock, which formed a species of roof over their heads, the haciendero pointed out to Don Martial a thin white vapour, which stood out prominently against the blue sky.

"The sky is losing its brightness," he said; "we shall probably soon have a change of weather. God grant that a hurricane does not menace us!"

The Tigrero shook his head.

"No," he said, "you are mistaken. Your eyes are not so accustomed as mine to consult the sky. That is not a cloud."

"What is it, then?"

"The smoke of a *bois de vache* fire kindled by travellers. We have neighbours."

"Oh!" the haciendero said. "Can we be on the trail of those friends we have lost so long?"

Don Martial remained silent. He minutely examined the smoke, which was soon mingled with the atmosphere. At length he said,—

U

"That smoke bodes us no good. Our friends, as you
call them, are Frenchmen; that is to say, profoundly
ignorant of desert life. Were they near us, it would
be as easy to see them as that rock down there. They
would have lighted not one fire, but twenty braseros,
whose flames, and, above all, dense smoke, would have
immediately revealed their presence to us. They do
not select their wood: whether it be dry or damp
they care little. They are unaware of the importance
in the desert of discovering one's enemy, while not
allowing one's own presence to be suspected."

"You conclude from this?"

"That the fire you discovered has been lit by savages,
or at least by wood-rangers accustomed to the habits of
Indian life. All leads to this supposition. Judge for
yourself—you who, without any great experience,
though having a slight acquaintance with the desert,
took it for a cloud. Any superficial observer would have
committed the same mistake as yourself, so fine and
undulating as it is, and its colour harmonises so well
with all those vapours the sun incessantly draws out of
the earth. The men, whoever they may be, who lit
that fire, have left nothing to chance; they have calculated and foreseen everything, and I am greatly mistaken if they are not enemies."

"At what distance do you suppose them from us?"

"Four leagues at the most. What is that distance
in the desert, when it can be crossed so easily in a
straight line?"

"Then your advice is?" the haciendero asked.

"Weigh well my words, Don Sylva; above all, do
not give them an interpretation differing from mine.
By a prodigy almost unexampled in the Del Norte, we
have now been crossing the desert for nearly three

weeks, and nothing has happened to trouble our security : for a week we have been, moreover, seeking a trail which it is impossible to come on again."

" Quite true."

" I have, therefore, worked out this conclusion, which I believe to be correct, and which you will approve, I am convinced. The French only accidentally formed the resolution of entering the desert : they only did it to pursue the Apaches. Is not that your view ? "

" It is."

" Very good. Consequently, they crossed it in a straight line. The weather which has favoured us favoured them too : their interest, the object they wished to attain, everything, in a word, demanded that they should display the utmost speed in their march. A pursuit, you know as well as I, is a chase in which each tries to arrive first."

" Then you suppose——? " Don Sylva interrupted him.

" I am certain that the French left the desert long ago, and are now coursing over the plains of Apacheria : that fire we noticed is a convincing proof to me."

" How so ? "

" You will soon understand. The Apaches have the greatest interest in driving the French from their hunting-grounds. Desperate at seeing them out of the desert, they have probably lit this fire to deceive them, and compel their return."

The haciendero was thoughtful. The reasons Don Martial offered him seemed correct : he knew not what determination to form.

" Well," he said presently, " and what conclusion do you arrive at from all this ?"

" That we should do wrong," Don Martial said resolutely, "in losing more time here in search of people who are no longer in the desert, and running the risk of being caught by a tempest, which every passing hour renders more imminent in a country like this, which is continually exposed to hurricanes."

"Then you would return?"

"By no means. I would push on, and enter Apacheria as quickly as possible, for I am convinced I should then be speedily on the trail of our friends."

"Yes, that appears to me correct enough; but we are a long way yet from the prairies."

"Not so far as you suppose; but let us break off our conversation at this point. I wish to go out and examine that fire more closely, for it troubles me greatly."

"Be prudent."

"Is not your safety concerned?" the Tigrero said, as he bent a gentle and mournful glance on Dona Anita. He rose, saddled his horse in a second, and started at a gallop.

"Brave heart!" Dona Anita murmured, on seeing him disappear in the mist. The haciendero sighed, but made no further reply, and his head fell pensively on his chest.

Don Martial pressed on rapidly by the flickering light of the moon, which spread its sickly and fantastic rays over the desolate scene. At times he perceived heavy rocks, dumb and gloomy sentinels, whose gigantic shadows striped the grey sand for a long distance; or else enormous ahuehuelts, whose branches were laden with that thick moss called Spaniard's beard, which fell in long festoons, and was agitated by the slightest breath of wind.

After nearly an hour and a half's march the Tigrero

stopped his horse, dismounted, and looked attentively around him. He soon found what he sought. A short distance from him the wind and rain had hollowed a rather deep ravine; he drew his horse into it, fastened it to an enormous stone, bound up its nostrils to prevent it neighing, and went off, after throwing his rifle over his shoulder.

From the spot where he was this moment standing the fire was visible, and the red flash it traced in the air stood out clearly in the darkness. Round the fire several shadows were reclining, which the Tigrero recognised at the first glance as Indians. The Mexican had not deceived himself; his experience had not failed him. They were certainly red-skins encamped there in the desert at a short distance from his party. But who were they? Were they friends or enemies? He must assure himself about that fact.

This was not an easy matter on this flat and barren soil, where it was almost impossible to advance without being noticed; for the Indians are like wild beasts, possessing the privilege of seeing in the night. In the gloom their pupils expand like those of tigers, and they distinguish their enemies as easily in the deepest shadow as in the most dazzling sunshine.

Still Don Martial did not recoil from his task. Not far from the red-skins' bivouac was an enormous block of granite, at the foot of which three or four ahuehuelts had sprung up, and in the course of time so entangled their branches in one another that they formed, at a certain distance up the rock, a thorough thicket. The Tigrero lay down on the ground, and gently, inch by inch, employing his knees and elbows, he glided in the direction of the rock, skilfully taking advantage of the shadow thrown by the rock itself. It took the Tigrero nearly half an hour to cross the forty yards that still separated him from the rock. At length he reached it : he then stopped to draw breath, and uttered a sigh of satisfaction.

The rest was nothing : he no longer feared being seen, owing to the curtain of branches that hid him from the sight of the Indians, but only being heard. After resting a few seconds he began climbing again, raising himself gradually on the abrupt side of the rock. At length he found himself level with the branches, into which he glided and disappeared. From the hiding-place he had so fortunately reached he could not only survey the Indian camp, but perfectly hear their con-versation. We need scarcely say that Don Martial understood and spoke perfectly all the dialects of the Indian tribes that traverse the vast solitudes of Mexico.

These Indians Don Martial at once recognised to be Apaches. His forebodings, then were realised. Round a *bois de vache* fire, which produced a large flame, while only allowing a slight thread of smoke to escape, several chiefs were gravely crouching on their heels, and smoking their calumets while warming themselves, for the cold was sharp. Don Martial distinguished in the midst of them the Black Bear. The sachem's face was gloomy ; he seemed in a terrible passion ; he frequently raised his head anxiously, and fixing his piercing glance on the space, interrogated the darkness. A noise of horse-hoofs was heard, and a mounted Indian entered the lighted part of the camp. After dismounting, the Indian approached the fire, crouched near his comrades, lighted his calumet, and began smoking with a perfectly calm face, although the dust that covered him, and his panting chest, showed that he must have made a long and painful journey.

On his arrival the Black Bear gazed fixedly at him,

and then went on smoking without saying a word; for
Indian etiquette prescribes that the sachem should not
interrogate another chief before the latter has shaken
into the fire the ashes of his calumet. The Black
Bear's impatience was evidently shared by the other
Indians; still, all remained grave and silent. At length
the new comer drew a final puff of smoke, which he
sent forth through his mouth and nostrils, and returned
his calumet to his girdle. The Black Bear turned to him.

"The Little Panther has been long," he said.

As this was not a question the Indian limited himself
to replying with a bow.

"The vultures are soaring in large flocks over the
desert," the chief presently continued; "the coyotes are
sharpening their bent claws; the Apaches scent a smell
of blood, which makes their hearts bound with joy in
their breasts. Has my son seen nothing?"

"The Little Panther is a renowned warrior of his
tribe. At the first leaves he will be a chief. He has
fulfilled the mission his father intrusted to him."

"Wah! what are the Long-knives doing?"

"The Long-knives are dogs that howl without knowing how to bite: an Apache warrior terrifies them."

The chiefs smiled with pride at this boast, which they
simply regarded as seriously meant.

"The Little Panther has seen their camp," the Indian
continued; "he has counted them. They cry like women,
and lament like weak children. Two of them will not
take their accustomed place this night at the council
fire of their brothers."

And with a gesture marked with a certain degree of
nobility, the Indian raised the cotton shirt which fell
from his neck about half way down his thighs, and
displayed two bleeding scalps fastened to his waist-belt.

"Wah ! " the chiefs exclaimed joyfully, "the Little Panther has fought bravely ! "

The Black Bear made the warrior a sign to hand him the scalps. He unfastened them and gave them. The sachem examined them attentively. The Apaches fixed their eyes eagerly on him.

"*Asch'eth* (it is good)," he said presently; "my brother has killed a Long-knife and a Yori."

And he returned the scalps to the warrior.

" Have the pale-faces discovered the trail of the Apaches ? "

" The pale-faces are moles; they are only good in their great stone villages."

" What has my son done ? "

" The Panther executed the orders of the sachem point by point. When the warrior perceived that the pale-faces would not see him, he went towards them mocking them, and led them for three hours after him into the heart of the desert."

" Good! my son has done well. What next ? "

" When the pale-faces had gone far enough the Panther left them, after killing two in memory of his visit, and then proceeded to the camp of the warriors of his nation."

" My son is weary : the hour of rest has arrived for him."

" Not yet," the Indian replied seriously.

" Wah ! let my son explain."

At this remark Don Martial, who was listening attentively to all that was said, felt his heart contract, he knew not why. The Indian continued,—

" There are others beside the Long-knives in the desert ; the Little Panther has discovered another trail."

" Another trail ? "

" Yes. It is not very visible : there are seven horses and three mules in all. I recognised one of the horses."

" Wah! I await what my brother is about to tell me."

" Six Yori warriors, having a woman with them, have entered the desert."

The chief's eyes flashed fire.

" A pale-faced woman ? " he asked.

The Indian bowed in affirmation. The sachem reflected for a moment, and then his face re-assumed that stoical mask which was habitual to it.

" The Black Bear is not mistaken," he said ; " he smelt the scent of blood : his Apache sons will have a splendid chase. To-morrow at the *endi-tah* (sunrise) the warriors will mount. The sachem's lodge is empty. Let us now leave the Big-knives to their fate," he added, raising his eyes to heaven ; " Nyang, the genius of evil, will take on himself to bury them beneath the sand. The Master of Life summons the tempest : our task is fulfilled. Let us follow the track of the Yoris, and return to our hunting-grounds at full speed. The hurricane will soon howl across the desert. My sons can go to sleep : a chief will watch over them. I have spoken."

The warriors bowed silently, rose one after the other, and went to lie down on the sand a short distance off. Within five minutes they were all in a deep sleep. The Black Bear alone watched. With his head in his hands, and his elbows on his knees, he looked fixedly at the sky. At times his face lost its severe expression, and a transient smile played around his lips. What thoughts thus absorbed the sachem ? On what was he meditating ?

Don Martial read his thoughts, and felt a shudder of

terror. He remained for another half-hour motionless
in his hiding-place, lest he might run the risk of discovery. Then he went down again as he had come,
employing even greater precautions; for at this moment,
when a leaden silence brooded over the desert, the
slightest sound would have betrayed his presence to the
Indian chief's subtile ear. He feared discovery now
more than ever, after the revelations he had succeeded
in overhearing. At length he reached again, all safe
and sound, the spot where he had left his horse.

For some time the Tigrero let the bridle hang
loosely on his noble animal's neck, went slowly onwards, revolving in his mind all he had heard, and
searching for the means he should employ to shield his
companions from the frightful danger that menaced
them. His perplexity was extreme : he knew not what
to decide on. He knew Don Sylva too well to suppose
that a personal interest, however powerful it might be,
would induce him to abandon his friends in their present peril. But must Doña Anita be sacrificed to this
delicacy—to this false notion of honour ; above all, for a
man in every respect unworthy of the interest the
haciendero felt for him ?

It was possible to avoid and escape the Apaches by
skill and courage ; but how to escape the tempest
which, in a few hours perhaps, would burst on the
desert, destroy every trace, and render flight impossible?

The girl must be saved at any risk. This thought
incessantly returned to the Tigrero's perplexed mind,
and gnawed at his heart like a searing iron : he felt
himself affected by a cold rage on considering the
material impossibilities that rose so implacably before
him. How to save the girl ? He constantly asked
himself this question, for which he found no answer.

For a long time he went on thus with drooping head, seeking in vain a method which would enable him to act on his own inspiration, and escape from the critical position in which he found himself. At length light dawned on his mind; he raised his head haughtily, cast a glance of defiance toward the enemies who appeared so sure of seizing his companions, and digging the spurs into his horse, started at full speed.

When he reached the camp he found every one asleep save the peon who was mounting guard. The night was well on—it was about one o'clock in the morning; the moon spread around a dazzling light, almost as clear as day. The Apaches would not set out before daybreak, and he had, therefore, about four hours left him for action. He resolved to profit by them. Four hours well employed are enormous in a flight.

The Tigrero began by carefully rubbing down his horse to restore the elasticity to its limbs, for he would need all its speed; then, aided by the peons, he loaded the mules and saddled the horses. This last accomplished, he reflected for a moment, and then wrapped round the horses' hoofs pieces of sheep skin filled with sand. This stratagem, he fancied, would foil the Indians, who, no longer recognising the traces they expected, would fancy themselves on a false trail. For greater security he ordered two or three skins of mezcal to be left on the rock. He knew the Apaches' liking for strong liquors, and calculated on their drunken propensities. This done, he aroused Don Sylva and his daughter.

"To horse! to horse!" he said in a voice that admitted of no reply.

"What's the matter?" the haciendero asked, still half asleep.

" That if we do not start at once we are lost !"

" How—what do you mean ?"

" To. horse ! to horse ! Every moment we waste here brings us nearer to death. Presently I will explain all."

" In Heaven's name tell me what the matter is ! "

" You shall know. Come, come."

Without listening to anything, he compelled the haciendero to mount : Dona Anita had done so already. The Tigrero looked around for the last time, and gave the signal for departure. The party started at their horses' topmost speed.

CHAPTER XXIII.

THE APACHES.

NOTHING is so mournful as a night march through the desert, especially under such circumstances as hurried our party on. Night is the mother of phantoms; in the darkness, the gayest landscapes become sinister— everything assumes a form to startle the traveller. The moon, however brilliant the light it diffuses may be, imparts to objects a fantastic appearance and mournful hues which cause the bravest to tremble.

This sepulchral calmness of the desert—this solitude that surrounds you, torments you from every side, and peoples the scenery with spectres—this obscurity which enfolds you like a leaden shroud—all combine to trouble the brain, and arouse a species of febrile terror, which the vivifying sunbeams are alone powerful enough to dissipate.

In spite of themselves our friends suffered from this feeling. They galloped through the night, not able to explain to themselves their motive for doing so, not knowing whither they were going, perhaps not troubling themselves about it. With heavy heads and weighed-down eyelids, they had only one thought—of sleep. Borne along by their horses at headlong speed, the trees and rocks danced around them. They therefore secured themselves in their saddles, closed their eyes, and yielded to the sleep which overwhelmed them, and which they no longer felt the strength to resist.

Sleep is perhaps the most tyrannical and imperious necessity of man : it makes him despise and forget all else. The man overpowered by sleep will give way to it, no matter where he is, or what danger menaces him. Hunger and thirst may be subdued for a while by strength of will and courage, but sleep cannot. It is impossible to contend against it. It strangles you in its iron claws, and in a few moments hurls you down panting and conquered.

With the exception of Don Martial, whose eye was sharp and mind clear, the other members of the party resembled somnambulists. Hanging to their horses as well as they could, with eyes shut and thoughts wandering, they hurried on unconsciously, a prey to that horrible nightmare which is neither sleeping nor waking, but only the torpor of the senses and the oblivion of the mind.

This lasted the whole night. They had travelled ten leagues, and were utterly exhausted. Still at sunrise, beneath the influence of the warm rays, they gradually shook off their heaviness, opened their eyes, looked curiously around them, and an infinity of questions rose from the heart to the lips, as generally happens in such a case.

The party had reached the banks of the Rio Gila, whose muddy waters form, on this side, the desert frontier. Don Martial, after carefully examining the spot where he was, stopped on the bank. The bags of sand were removed from the horses' feet, and they were supplied with food. As for the men, they must temporarily put up with a mouthful of *refino* to restore their strength.

The appearance of the country had completely changed. On the other bank of the river a thick, strong grass covered the ground, and immense virgin forests grew on the horizon.

"Ouf!" Don Sylva said, rolling on the ground with an expression of great satisfaction, "what a journey! I am worn out. If that were to last but one day, *voto à brios!* I could not stand it any longer. I am neither hungry nor thirsty. I will go to sleep."

While saying this the haciendero had arranged himself in the posture most agreeable for a nap.

"Not yet, Don Sylva," the Tigrero said sharply, and shaking him by the arm. "Do you want to leave your bones here?"

"Go to the deuce! I want to sleep, I tell you."

"Very good," Don Martial made answer coldly; "but if you and Doña Anita fall into the hands of the Apaches you will not make me responsible for it?"

"Eh?" the haciendero said, jumping up, and looking him in the face. "What are you saying about Apaches?"

"I tell you again that the Apaches are in pursuit of us. We are only a few hours ahead of them, and if we do not make haste we are lost."

"*Canarios!* we must fly," Don Sylva exclaimed, now thoroughly awake. "My daughter must not fall into the hands of those demons."

As for Doña Anita, little troubled her at this moment. She was fast asleep.

' Let the horses eat, and then we will start. We have a long way to go, and they must be able to bear us. These few moments of rest will allow Doña Anita to regain her strength."

"Poor child!" the haciendero muttered, "I am the cause of what has happened. My unlucky obstinacy brought us here."

"What use is recrimination, Don Sylva? We are all to blame. Let us forget the past, only to think of the present."

"Yes, you are right. What need discussing things that are done? Now that I am perfectly awake, tell me what you did during the night, and why you forced us to start so suddenly."

"My story will be short, Don Sylva; but you, I believe, will find it very interesting. But you shall judge for yourself. After leaving you last night, as you remember, to find out——"

"Yes, you wished to examine a fire that seemed to you suspicious."

"That was it. Well, I was not mistaken: that fire, as I supposed, was a snare laid by the Apaches. I managed to crawl up to them unnoticed, and hear their conversation. Do you know what they said?"

"By my faith, I have little notion what such idiots as those talk about."

"Not such idiots as you fancy somewhat lightly, Don Sylva. One of their runners was telling the sachem the result of a mission intrusted to him. Among other things he mentioned that he had discovered a pale-face trail, and that among the pale-faces was a woman."

"*Caspita!*" the haciendero exclaimed in terror, "are you quite sure of that, Don Martial?"

" The more so because I heard the chief make this reply. Be attentive, Don Sylva——"

" I am listening, my friend : go on."

" ' At sunrise we will set out in pursuit of the pale-faces. The chief's lodge is empty ; he wants a white woman to occupy it.' "

" Caramba ! "

" Yes. Then, finding I had learnt sufficient of the expedition the red-skins were undertaking, I slipped away and regained our camp so soon as possible. You know the——"

" Yes, I know the rest, Don Martial," the haciendero said almost affectionately ; " and I thank you most sincerely, not only for the intelligence you have displayed on this occasion, but also for the devotion with which you compelled us to follow you, instead of being disgusted by our mad sloth."

" I have done nothing but what I should do, Don Sylva. Have I not sworn to devote my life to you? "

" Yes, my friend, and you keep your vow nobly."

Since the haciendero had known Don Martial this was the first time he spoke openly with him, and gave him the title of friend. The Tigrero was touched by this expression ; and if he had hitherto felt some slight prejudice against Don Sylva, it was suddenly dissipated, and only left in his heart a feeling of profound gratitude.

Dona Anita awoke during this conversation, and it was with an indescribable joy that she heard them talking thus amicably together. When her father told her the cause of the hasty journey she had been compelled to undertake in the middle of the night, she warmly thanked Don Martial, and rewarded him for all his sufferings by one-of those glances, the secret of which only women in love possess, and into which they throw their whole soul. The Tigrero, delighted at seeing his devotion appreciated as it deserved to be, forgot all his fatigues, and had only one desire—that of terminating happily what he had so well begun. So soon as the horses were saddled they mounted again.

" I leave myself in your hands, Don Martial," the haciendero said : " you alone can save us."

" With the help of Heaven I shall succeed," the Tigrero replied passionately.

They entered the river, which was rather wide at this spot. Instead of crossing it at right angles, Don Martial, in order to throw the savages off the scent, followed the course of the river for some distance, and made repeated curves. At length, on reaching a point where the river was inclosed by two calcareous banks, where it was impossible for the horses' hoofs to leave any mark, he landed. The party had left the desert. Before them stretched those immense prairies, whose undulating soil gradually rises to the slopes of the *Sierra Madre* and the *Sierra de los Comanches.* They are no longer sterile and desolate plains, denuded of wood and water, but a luxuriant nature, with an extraordinary productive force—trees, flowers, grass ; countless birds singing joyously beneath the foliage ; animals of every description running, browsing, and sporting in the midst of these natural prairies.

The travellers yielded instinctively to the feeling of comfort produced by the sight of this splendid prairie, when compared with the desolate desert they had just quitted, and in which they had wandered about so long hap-hazard. This contrast was full of charms for them : they felt their courage rekindled, and hope returning to their hearts. About eleven o'clock the horses were so

x

fatigued that the travellers were compelled to encamp, in order to give them a few hours' rest, and thus pass the great heats of the day.   Don Martial chose the top of a wooded hill, whence the prairie could be surveyed, while they remained completely concealed among the trees.

The Tigrero would not permit them, however, to light a fire to cook food, as the smoke would have caused their retreat to be discovered; and in their present position they could not exercise too great prudence, as it was evident that the Apaches would have started in pursuit at sunrise.   Those crafty blood-hounds must be thrown off the scent.   In spite of all the precautions he had taken, the Tigrero could not flatter himself with the hope of having foiled them; for the red-skins are so clever in discovering a trail After eating a few hasty mouthfuls he allowed his companions to enjoy a rest they needed so greatly, and rose to go on the watch.

This man appeared made of iron—fatigue took no hold on him: his will was so firm that he resisted every-thing, and his desire to save the woman he loved en-dowed him with a supernatural strength.   He slowly descended the hill, examining each shrub, only ad-vancing with extreme prudence, and with his ear open to every sound, however slight.   So soon as he reached the plain, certain that his presence would be concealed by the tall grass, in which he entirely disappeared, he hastened at full speed toward a sombre and dense primeval forest, whose trees approached almost close to the hill.   This forest was really what it appeared to be —a virgin forest.   The trees and leaves intertwined formed an inextricable curtain, through which a hatchet would have been required to cut a passage.   Had he been alone, the Tigrero would not have been greatly embarrassed by this apparently insurmountable obstacle. Skilful and powerful as he was, he would have travelled 'twixt earth and sky, by passing from branch to branch, as he had often done before. But what a man so desolate as himself could do was not to be expected from a frail and weak woman.

For an instant the Tigrero felt his heart fail him, and his courage give way. But this despair was only momentary. Don Martial drew himself up proudly, and suddenly regained all his energy. He continued to advance toward the forest, looking round like a wild beast on the watch for prey. Suddenly he uttered a stifled cry of joy. He had found what he had been seeking without any hope of finding it.

Before him, beneath a thick dome of verdure, ran one of those narrow paths formed by wild beasts in going to water, and which it required the Tigrero's practised eye to detect. He resolutely turned aside into this path. Like all those made by wild beasts, it took innumerable turnings, incessantly coming back on itself. After following it for a sufficient length of time, the Tigrero went back, and re-ascended the hill.

His companions, anxious at his lengthened absence, were impatiently expecting him. Each noticed his return with delight. He told them what he had been doing, and the track he had discovered. While Don Martial had been on the search, one of his peons, however, had made, on the side of this very hill, a discovery most valuable at such a moment to our travellers. This man, while wandering about the neighbourhood to kill time, had found the entrance to a cave which he had not dared to explore, not knowing whether he might not suddenly find himself face to face with a wild beast.

Don Martial quivered with joy at this news. He seized an *ocote* torch, and ordered the peon to lead him to the cavern. It was only a few paces distant, and on that side of the hill which faced the river. The entrance was so obstructed by shrubs and parasitic plants, that it was evident no living being had ever penetrated it for many a long year. The Tigrero moved the shrubs with the greatest care, in order not to injure them, and glided into the cavern. The entrance was tolerably lofty, though rather narrow. Before going in Don Martial struck a light and kindled the torch.

This cavern was one of those natural grottos, so many of which are found in these regions. The walls were lofty and dry, the ground covered with fine sand. It evidently received air from imperceptible fissures, as no mephitic exhalation escaped from it, and breathing was quite easy; in a word, although it was rather gloomy, it was habitable. It grew gradually lower to a species of hall, in the centre of which was a gulf, the bottom of which Don Martial could not see, though he held down his torch. He looked round him, saw a lump of rock, probably detached from the roof, and threw it into the abyss.

For a long time he heard the stone dashing against the sides, and then the noise of a body falling into water. Don Martial knew all he wanted to know. He stepped past the gulf, and advanced along a narrow shelving passage. After walking for about ten minutes along it, he saw light a considerable distance ahead. The grotto had two outlets. Don Martial returned at full speed.

"We are saved!" he said to his companions. "Follow me: we have not an instant to lose in reaching the refuge Providence so generously offers us."

They followed him.

"What shall we do, though," Don Sylva asked, "with the horses?"

"Do not trouble yourselves about them; I will conceal them. Place in the grotto our provisions, for it is probable we shall be forced to remain here some time; also keep by you the saddles and bridles, which I do not know what to do with. As for the horses, they are my business."

Each set to work with that feverish ardour produced by the hope of escaping a danger; and at the end of an hour at most, the baggage, provisions, and men had all disappeared in the cavern. Don Martial drew the bushes over the entrance, to hide the traces of his companions' passage, and breathed with that delight caused by the success of a daring project; then he returned to the crest of the hill.

He fastened the horses and mules together with his reata, and descended to the plain: he proceeded toward the forest, and entered the path he had previously discovered. It was very narrow, and the horses could only proceed in single file, and with extreme difficulty. At length he reached a species of clearing, where he abandoned the poor animals, leaving them all the forage, which he had taken care to pack on the mules. Don Martial was well aware that the horses would stray but a short distance from the spot where he left them, and that when they were wanted it would be easy to find them.

These various occupations had consumed a good deal of time, and the day was considerably advanced when the Tigrero finally quitted the forest. The sun, very low on the horizon, appeared like a ball of fire, nearly on a level with the ground. The shadow of the trees was disproportionately elongated. The evening breeze

was beginning to rise.   A few hoarse cries, issuing at
intervals from the depths of the forest, announced the
speedy re-awakening of the wild beasts, those denizens
of the desert which, during the night, are its absolute
kings.

On reaching the crest of the hill, and before entering
the grotto, Don Martial surveyed the horizon by the
last rays of the expiring sun.   Suddenly he turned
pale; a nervous shudder passed through his frame; his
eyes, dilated by terror, were obstinately fixed on the
river; and he muttered in a low voice, and stamping
with fury,—

" Already ?   The demons ! "

What the Tigrero had seen was really startling.   A
band of Indian horsemen was traversing the river at
the precise spot where he and his companions had
crossed it a few hours previously.   Don Martial followed
their movements with growing alarm.   On arriving
at the river bank, without any hesitation or delay,
they took up his trail.   Doubt was no longer possible ;
the Apaches had not been deceived by the hunter's
schemes, but had come in a straight line behind the
party, exercising great diligence.   In less than an hour
they would reach the hill; and then, with that diabolical
science they possessed to discover the best hidden trail,
who knew what would happen ?

The Tigrero felt his heart breaking, and half mad
with grief, rushed into the grotto.   On seeing him
enter thus with livid features, the haciendero and his
daughter hurried to meet him.

" What is the matter ? " they asked.

" We are lost ! " he exclaimed with despair.   " Here
are the Apaches ! "

" The Apaches ! " they muttered with terror.

"O heavens, save me!" Dona Anita said, falling on her knees and fervently clasping her hands.

The Tigrero bent over the fair girl, took her in his arms with a strength rendered tenfold by grief, and turning to the haciendero,—

"Come," he shouted, "follow me. Perhaps one chance of salvation is still left us."

And he hurried toward the extremity of the grotto, all eagerly following him. They hurried on for some time in this way. Dona Anita, almost fainting, leaned her lovely head on the Tigrero's shoulders. He still ran on.

"Come, come," he said, "we shall soon be saved."

His companions uttered a shout of joy: they had perceived a gleam of daylight before them. Suddenly, at the moment Don Martial reached the entrance, and was about to rush forth, a man appeared. It was the Black Bear.

The Tigrero leaped back with the howl of a wild beast.

"Wah!" the Apache said, with a mocking voice, "my brother knows that I love this woman, and to please me hastens to bring her to me."

"You have not got her yet, demon!" Don Martial shouted, boldly placing himself before Dona Anita, with a pistol in each hand. "Come and take her."

Rapidly approaching footsteps were heard in the depths of the cavern. The Mexicans were caught between two fires. The Black Bear, with his eye fixed on the Tigrero, watched his every movement. Suddenly he bounded forward like a tiger cat, uttering his war-yell. The Tigrero fired both pistols at him, and seized him round the waist. The two men rolled on the ground, intertwined like two serpents, while Don Sylva and the peons fought desperately with the other Indians.

CHAPTER XXIV.

THE WOOD-RANGERS.

We will now return to certain persons of this story, whom we have too long forgotten.

Although the French had remained masters of the field, and succeeded in driving back their savage enemies when they attacked the hacienda upon the Rio Gila, they did not hide from themselves the fact that they did not owe this unhoped-for victory solely to their own courage. The final charge made by the Comanches, under the orders of Eagle-head, had alone decided the victory. Hence, when the enemy disappeared, the Count de Lhorailles, with uncommon generosity and frankness, especially in a man of his character, warmly thanked the Comanches, and made the hunters the most magnificent offers. The latter modestly received the count's flattering compliments, and plainly declined all the offers he made them.

As Belhumeur told him, they had no other motive for their conduct than that of helping fellow-countrymen. Now that all was finished, and the French would be long free from any attacks on the part of the savages, they had only one thing more to do—take leave of the count so soon as possible, and continue their journey. The count, however, induced them to spend two more days at the colony.

Dona Anita and her father had disappeared in so mysterious a manner, that the French, but little accus-

tomed to Indian tricks, and completely ignorant of the
manner of discovering or following a trail in the desert,
were incapable of going in search of the two persons who
had been carried off. The count, in his mind, had built
on the experience of Eagle-head and the sagacity of his
warriors to find traces of the haciendero and his
daughter. He explained to the hunters, in the fullest
details, the service he hoped to obtain from them, and
they thought they had no right to refuse it.

The next morning, at daybreak, Eagle-head divided
his detachment into four troops, each commanded by a
renowned warrior, and after giving the men their instructions, he sent them off in four different directions.
The Comanches beat up the country with that cleverness and skill the red-skins possess to so eminent a
degree, but all was useless. The four troops returned
one after the other to the hacienda without making
any discovery. Though they had gone over the ground
for a radius of about twenty leagues round the colony—
though not a tuft of grass or a shrub had escaped their
minute investigations—the trail could not be found.
We know the reason—water alone keeps no trace. Don
Sylva and his daughter had been carried down with the
current of the Rio Gila.

" You see," Belhumeur said to the count, " we have
done what was humanly possible to recover the persons
carried off during the fight : it is evident that the
ravishers embarked them on the river, and carried
them a long distance ere they landed. Who can say
where they are now? The red-skins go fast, especially
when flying; they have an immense advance on us, as
the ill success of our efforts proves : it would be madness to hope to catch them. Allow us, then, to take our
leave : perhaps, during our passage across the prairie,

we may obtain information which may presently prove useful to you."

"I will no longer encroach on your kindness," the count replied courteously. "Go whenever you think proper, caballeros; but accept the expression of my gratitude, and believe that I should be happy to prove it to you otherwise than by sterile words. Besides, I am also going to leave the colony, and we may perhaps meet in the desert."

The next morning the hunters and the Comanches quitted the hacienda, and buried themselves in the prairie. In the evening Eagle-head had the camp formed, and the fires lighted. After supper, when all were about to retire for the night, the sachem sent the *hachesto*, or public crier, to summon the chiefs to the council fire.

"My pale brothers will take a place near the chiefs," Eagle-head said, addressing the Canadian and the Frenchman.

The latter accepted with a nod, and sat down by the brasero among the Comanche chiefs, who were already waiting, silent and reserved, for the communication from their great sachem. When Eagle-head had taken his seat he made a sign to the pipe-bearer. The latter entered the circle, respectfully carrying in his hand the calumet of medicine, whose stem was adorned with feathers and a multitude of bells, while the bowl was hollowed out of a white stone only found in the Rocky Mountains.

The calumet was filled and lighted.

The pipe-bearer, so soon as he entered the circle, turned the bowl of the pipe to the four cardinal points, murmuring in a low voice mysterious words, intended to invoke the good-will of the Wacondah, the Master of Life, and remove from the mind of the chiefs the malignant influence of the first man. Then, still holding the bowl in his hand, he presented the mouthpiece to Eagle-head, saying in a loud and impressive voice,—

"My father is the first sachem of the valorous nation of the Comanches. Wisdom resides in him. Although the snows of age have not yet frozen the thoughts in his brain, like all men, he is subject to error. Let my father reflect ere he speak; for the words which pass his lips must be such as the Comanches can hear."

"My son has spoken well," the sachem replied.

He took the tube, and smoked silently for a few moments; then he removed the stem from his lips, and handed it to his nearest neighbour. The pipe thus passed round the circle, and not a chief uttered a word. When each had smoked, and all the tobacco in the bowl was consumed, the pipe-bearer shook out the ash into his left hand, and threw it into the brazier, exclaiming,—

"The chiefs are assembled here in council. Their words are sacred. Wacondah has heard our prayer. It is granted. Woe to the man who forgets that conscience must be his only guide!"

After uttering these words with great dignity the pipe-bearer left the circle, murmuring in a low, though perfectly distinct voice,—

"Just as the ash I have thrown into the fire has disappeared for ever, so the words of the chiefs must be sacred, and never be repeated outside the sachems' circle. My fathers can speak; the council is opened."

The pipe-bearer departed after this warning. Then Eagle-head rose, and, after surveying all the warriors present, took the word.

"Comanche chiefs and warriors," he said, "many

moons have passed away since I left the villages of my
nation; many moons will again pass ere the all-powerful
Wacondah will permit me to sit at the council fire of
the great Comanche sachems.   The blood has ever
flowed red in my veins, and my heart has never worn a
skin for my brothers.   The words which pass my lips
are spoken by the will of the Great Spirit.   He knows
how I have kept up my love for you.   The Comanche
nation is powerful; it is the Queen of the Prairies.   Its
hunting-grounds cover the whole world.   What need
has it to ally itself with other nations to avenge insults?
Does the unclean coyote retire into the den of the
haughty jaguar?   Does the owl lay its eggs in the
eagle's nest?   Why should the Comanche walk on the
war-path with the Apache dogs?   The Apaches are
cowardly and treacherous women.   I thank my brothers
not only for having broken with them, but also for
having helped me to defeat them.   Now my heart is sad,
a mist covers my mind, because I must separate from
my brothers.   Let them accept my farewell.   Let the
Jester pity me, because I shall walk in the shadow far
from him.   The sunbeams, however burning they may
be, will not warm me.   I have spoken.   Have I spoken
well, powerful men?"

Eagle-head sat down amid a murmur of grief, and
concealed his face behind the skirt of his buffalo robe.
There was a great silence in the assembly: the Jester
seemed to interrogate the other chiefs with a glance.
At length he rose, and took the word in his turn to
reply to the sachem.

"The Jester is young," he said; "his head is good,
though he does not possess the great wisdom of his
father.   Eagle-head is a sachem beloved by the
Wacondah.   Why has the Master of Life brought the

chief back among the warriors of his nation? Is it that he should leave them again almost immediately? No; the Master of Life loves his Comanche sons. He could not have desired that. The warriors need a wise and experienced chief to lead them on the war-path, and instruct them round the council fire. My father's head is grey; he will teach and guide the warriors. The Jester cannot do so; he is still too young, and wants experience. Where my father goes his sons will go; what my father wishes his sons will wish. But never let him speak again about leaving them. Let him disperse the cloud that obscures his mind. His sons implore it by the mouth of the Jester—that child he brought up, whom he loved so much formerly, and of whom he made a man. I have spoken : here is my wampum. Have I spoken well, powerful men?"

After uttering the last words the chief threw a collar of wampum at Eagle-head's feet, and sat down again.

"The great sachem must remain with his sons," all the warriors shouted, as, in their turn, they threw down their wampum collars.

Eagle-head rose with an air of great nobility : he allowed the skirt of his buffalo robe to fall, and addressing the anxious and attentive assembly,—

"I have heard the strain of the walkon, the beloved bird of the Wacondah, echo in my ears," he said : "its harmonious voice penetrated to my heart, and caused it to quiver with joy. My sons are good, and I love them The Jester, and ten warriors to be chosen by himself, will accompany me, and the others will ride to the great villages of my nation to announce to the sachems the return of Eagle-head among his brothers. I have spoken."

The Jester then asked for the great calumet, which was immediately brought him by the pipe-bearer, and the chiefs smoked in turn, without uttering a word. When the last puff of smoke had dispersed, the hachesto, to whom the Jester had said a few words in a low voice, proclaimed the names of the ten warriors selected to accompany the sachem. The chiefs rose, bowed to Eagle-head, and silently mounting their horses, started at a gallop.

For a considerable period the Jester and Eagle-head conversed in a low voice: at the end of the palaver, the Jester and his warriors went off in their turn, Eagle-head, Belhumeur, and Don Louis remaining alone. The Canadian watched the Indians depart, and when they had disappeared he turned to the chief.

"Hum!" he said, "will not the hour soon arrive to speak frankly and terminate our business? Since our departure from home we have troubled ourselves a great deal about others, and forgotten our own affairs: is it not time to think of them?"

"Eagle-head does not forget · he is preparing to satisfy his pale brothers."

Belhumeur burst out laughing.

"Excuse me, chief: for my part, my business is very simple. You asked me to accompany you, and here I am. May I be a dog of an Apache Indian if I know anything more! Louis, it is different, is looking for a well-beloved friend: remember that we have promised to help him to find him."

"Eagle-head," the chief replied, "has shared his heart between his two white brothers; each has half. The road we have to go is long, and must last several moons. We shall cross the great desert. The Jester and his warriors have gone to kill buffaloes for the journey. I will lead my white brothers to a spot which I discovered a few moons ago, and which is only known to myself. The Wacondah, when he created man, gave him strength, courage, and immense hunting-grounds, saying to him, 'Be free and happy.' He gave the pale-faces wisdom and science, by teaching them to know the value of sparkling stones and yellow pebbles. The red-skins and the pale-faces each follow the path the Great Spirit has traced for them. I am leading my brothers to a placer."

"To a placer!" the two men exclaimed in amazement.

"Yes. What would an Indian sachem do with these enormous treasures, which he knows not how to use? Gold is everything with the pale-faces. Let my brothers be happy; Eagle-head will give them more than they can ever take."

"An instant, chief. What the deuce would you have me do with your gold? I am a hunter, whom his horse and rifle suffice. At the period that I crossed the prairie in the company of Loyal-heart, we frequently found rich nuggets beneath our feet, and ever turned from them with contempt."

"What need have we of gold?" Don Louis supported his friend. "Let us forget this placer, however rich it may be. Let us not reveal its existence to any one, for crimes enough are committed daily for gold. Give up this scheme, chief. We thank you for your generous offer, but it is impossible for us to accept it."

"Well spoken," Belhumeur exclaimed joyously. "Deuce take gold, which we can make no use of, and let us live like the free hunters we are! By heavens, chief, I assure you, had you told me at the time the object for which you wished me to follow you, I should have let you start alone."

Eagle-head smiled.

" I expected the answer my brothers have given me," he said. " I am happy to see that I have not been mistaken. Yes, gold is useless to them—they are right; but that is not a motive for despising it. Like all things placed on the earth by the Great Spirit, gold is useful. My brothers will accompany me to the placer, not, as they suppose, to collect nuggets, but merely to know where they are, and go to fetch them when wanted. Misfortune ever arrives unexpectedly: the most favoured by the Great Spirit to-day are often those whom to-morrow he will smite most severely. Well, if the gold of this placer is as nothing for the happiness of my brothers, who insures them that it may not serve some day to save one of their friends from despair ? "

" That is true," said Don Louis, touched by the justice of this reasoning. " What you say is wise, and deserves consideration. We can refuse to enrich ourselves; but we have no right to despise riches, which may possibly, at some future day, serve others."

" If that is really your opinion I adopt it; besides, as we are on the road, it is as well to go to the end. Still, the man who had told me that I should one day turn *gambusino* would have astonished me. In the mean while I will go and try to kill a deer."

On this Belhumeur rose, took his gun, and went off whistling. The Jester was two days absent. About the middle of the third day he reappeared. Six horses lassoed in the prairie were loaded with provisions; six others carried skins filled with water. Eagle-head was satisfied with the way in which the chief had performed his mission; but as the journey they had to make was a long one (for they had to cross the Del Norte desert at its longest part), he ordered that each horseman should carry on his saddle, with his alforjas, two little water-skins.

All these measures having been carefully taken, the horses and their riders rested. Fresh and of good cheer, the next morning, at daybreak, the little troop started in the direction of the desert. We will say nothing of the journey, save that it was successful, and accomplished under the most favourable auspices : no incident occurred to mar its monotonous tranquillity. The Comanches and their friends crossed the desert like a tornado, with that headlong speed of which they alone possess the secret, and which renders them so dangerous when they invade the Mexican frontiers.

On arriving in the prairies of the Sierra de los Comanches, Eagle-head ordered the Jester and his warriors to await him in a camp which he formed on the skirt of a virgin forest, in an immense clearing on the banks of an unknown stream, which, after a course of several leagues, falls into the Rio del Norte, and then departed with his comrades. The sachem foresaw everything. Although he placed entire confidence in the Jester, he did not wish, through prudential motives, to let him know the site of the placer. At a later date he had cause to congratulate himself on this step.

The hunters pushed on straight for the mountains, which rose before them like apparently insurmountable granitic walls ; but the nearer they approached the more the mountains sloped down. They soon entered a narrow gorge, at the entrance of which they were forced to leave their horses. It was probably owing to this apparently futile circumstance that the placer had not yet been discovered by the Indians, for the red-skins never, under any circumstances, dismount. It may

Y

justly be said of them, as of the Gauchos of the Pampas, in the Banda Oriental and Patagonia, that they live on horseback.

By a singular accident during one of his hunts, a deer which Eagle-head had wounded entered this gorge to die. The chief, who had been following the animal for several hours, did not hesitate to go in quest of it. After traversing the whole length of the gorge he reached a valley, a species of funnel formed between two abrupt mountains, which, except on this side, rendered access not only difficult, but impossible. There he found the deer expiring on a sand sprinkled with gold dust, and sown with nuggets, which sparkled like diamonds in the sunshine.

On entering the valley the hunters could not repress a cry of admiration and a shudder of delight. However strong a man may be morally, gold possesses an irresistible attraction, and exerts a powerful fascination over him. Belhumeur was the first to regain his calmness.

"Oh, oh!" he said, wiping the perspiration which poured down his face, "there are fortunes enough hidden in this nook of earth. God grant that they may remain so a long time, for the happiness of mankind!"

"What shall we do?" Louis asked, his chest panting, and his eyes sparkling.

Eagle-head alone regarded these incalculable riches with an indifferent glance.

"Hum!" the Canadian continued, "this is evidently our property, as the chief surrenders it to us."

The sachem made a sign of affirmation.

"Hear what I propose," he continued. "We do not need this gold, which at this moment would be more injurious to us than useful. Still, as no one can foresee

the future, we must assure ourselves of the ownership.
Let us cover this sand with leaves and branches, so that
if accident lead a hunter to the top of one of those
mountains, he may not see the gold glistening; then we
will pile up stones, and close the mouth of the valley;
for what has happened to Eagle-head must not happen
to another.   What is your opinion?"

"To work!" Don Louis exclaimed.   "I am anxious
not to have my eyes dazzled longer by this diabolical
metal, which makes me giddy."

"To work, then!" Belhumeur replied.

The three men cut down branches from the trees,
and formed with them a thick carpet, under which the
auriferous sand and nuggets entirely disappeared.

"Will you not take a specimen of the nuggets?"
Belhumeur said to the count.   "Perhaps it may be
useful to take a few."

"My faith, no!" the latter replied, shrugging his
shoulders; "I do not care for it.   Take some if you
will: for my part, I will not soil my fingers with
them."

The Canadian began laughing, picked up two or
three nuggets as large as walnuts, and placed them in
his bullet pouch.

"Sapristi!" he said, "if I kill sundry Apaches with
these they will have no right to complain, I hope."

They quitted the valley, the entrance to which they
stopped up with masses of rock.   They then regained
their horses, and returned to the camp, after cutting
notches in the trees, so as to be able to recognise the
spot, if, at a later date, circumstances led them to the
placer, which, we are bound to say in their favour, not
one of them desired.

The Jester was awaiting his friends with the intensest

impatience. The prairie was not quiet In the morning the runners had perceived a small band of pale-faces crossing the Del Norte, and proceeding toward a hill, on the top of which they had encamped. At this moment a large Apache war-party had crossed the river at the same spot, apparently following a trail.

"Oh, oh!" Belhumeur said, "it is plain that those dogs are pursuing white people."

"Shall we let them be massacred beneath our eyes?" Louis exclaimed indignantly.

"My faith, no! If it depend on us," the hunter said, "perhaps this good action will obtain our pardon for the feeling of covetousness to which we for a moment yielded. Speak, Eagle-head! what will you do?"

"Save the pale-faces," the chief replied.

The orders were immediately given by the sachem, and executed with that intelligence and promptitude characteristic of picked warriors on the war-trail. The horses were left under the guard of a Comanche, and the detachment, divided into two parties, advanced cautiously into the prairie. With the exception of Eagle-head, the Jester, Louis, and Belhumeur, who had rifles, all the others were armed with lances and bows.

"Diamond cut diamond," the Canadian said in a low voice. "We are going to surprise those who are preparing to surprise others."

At this moment two shots were heard, followed by others, and then the war-cry of the Apaches re-echoed far and wide.

"Oh, oh!" Belhumeur said, rushing forward, "they do not fancy we are so near."

All the others followed him at full speed. In the mean while the combat had assumed horrible proportions in the cavern. Don Sylva and the peons resisted

courageously; but what could they do against the swarm
of enemies that assailed them on every side ?

The Tigrero and the Black Bear, interlaced like two
serpents, were seeking to stab each other. Don Martial,
when he perceived the Indian, leaped back so precipitately that he cleared the passage and reached the hall,
in the centre of which was the abyss to which we before
alluded. It was on the verge of this gulf that the two
men, with flashing eyes, heaving chests, and lips closed
by fury, redoubled their efforts.

Suddenly several shots were heard, and the war-cry
of the Comanches burst forth like thunder. The Black
Bear loosed his hold of Don Martial, leaped on his feet,
and rushed on Dona Anita; but the girl, though suffering
from an indescribable terror, repulsed the savage by a
supernatural effort. The latter, already wounded by the
Tigrero's pistols, tottered backwards to the edge of the
abyss, where he lost his balance. He felt that all was
over. By an instinctive effort he stretched out his arms,
seized Don Martial (who, half stunned by the contest
he had been engaged in, was trying to rise), made him
totter in his turn, and the two fell to the bottom of the
abyss, uttering a horrible cry.

Dona Anita rushed forward: she was lost—when
suddenly she felt herself seized by a vigorous hand,
and rapidly dragged backwards. She fainted.

The Comanches had arrived too late. Of the seven
persons composing the little band, five had been killed
a peon seriously wounded, and Dona Anita alone survived. The young girl had been saved by Belhumeur.
When she opened her eyes again she smiled gently, and
in a childlike voice, melodious as a bird's carol, began
singing a Mexican seguedilla. The hunters recoiled
with a cry of horror. Dona Anita was mad!

CHAPTER XXV.

EL AHUEHUELT.

*   *   *   *   *

THE Count de Lhorailles entered the great Del Norte
desert under the guidance of Cucharès. During the
first day all went on famously; the weather was magnificent—the provisions more than plentiful. With their
innate carelessness, the Frenchmen forgot their past
fears, and laughed at the alarm which the Mexican
peons did not cease manifesting; for, better informed,
they did not conceal the terror which the prolonged
stay of the company in this terrible region caused
them.

The days were spent in the desert in wandering
purposelessly in search of the Apaches, who had at
length become invisible. At times they perceived an
Indian horseman in the distance, apparently mocking
them, who presently came up close to their lines.
Boot and saddle was sounded; everybody mounted, and
pursued this phantom horseman, who, after allowing
them to follow him for a long time, suddenly disappeared like a vision.

This mode of life, however, through its very monotony, began to grow insipid and insupportable. To
see nothing but grey sand, ever sand—not a bird or
a wild beast—tawny, weather-worn rocks—a few lofty
ahuehuelts — a species of cedar, with long bare
branches, covered with a greyish moss hanging in
heavy festoons—had nothing very amusing about it.
The troop began to grow dispirited. The reflection of
the sun on the sand caused ophthalmia; the water,
decomposed by the heat, was no longer drinkable; the
provisions were spoiling; and scurvy had commenced

its ravages among the soldiers. This state of things was growing intolerable : measures must be taken to get out of it as rapidly as possible.

The count formed his officers into a council; and it was composed of Lieutenants Martin Leroux and Diégo Léon, Sergeant Boileau, Blas Vasquez, and Cucharès. These five persons, presided over by the count, took their seats on bales, while a short distance off, the soldiers, reclining on the ground, tried to shelter themselves beneath the shadow of their picketed horses.

It was urgent to assemble the council, for th company was rapidly demoralising ; there was revolt in the air, and complaints had already been openly uttered. The execution at the Casa Grande was completely forgotten ; and, if a remedy were not soon found, no one knew what terrible consequences this general dissatisfaction might not entail.

" Gentlemen," the Count de Lhorailles said, " I have assembled you in order to consult with you on the means to put a stop to the despondency which has fallen on our company during the last few days The circumstances are so serious that I shall feel obliged by your giving me your frank opinion. The general welfare is at stake, and in such a state of things each has the right to express his opinion without fear of wounding the self-love of any one. Speak; I am listening to you. You first, Sergeant Boileau : as the lowest in rank, you must take the word first."

The sergeant was an old African soldier, knowing his duties perfectly — a thorough trooper in the fullest sense of the word; but we must confess that he was nothing of an orator. At this direct challenge from his chief he smiled, blushed like a girl, let his head droop, opened an enormous mouth, and stopped short. The count, perceiving his embarrassment, kindly urged him to speak. At length, after many an effort, the sergeant managed to begin in a hoarse and perfectly indistinct voice.

"Hang it, captain!" he said, "I can understand that the situation is not at all pleasant; but what is to be done? A man is a trooper, or he is not. Hence my opinion is that you ought to act as you think proper; and we are here to obey you in every respect, as is our peremptory duty, without any subsequent or offensive after-thought."

The officers could not refrain from laughing at the worthy sergeant's profession of faith, as he stopped all ashamed.

"It is your turn, capataz," the captain said. "Give us your opinion."

Blas Vasquez fixed his burning eyes on the count.

"Do you really ask it frankly?" he said.

"Certainly I do."

"Then listen," he said in a firm voice, and with an accent bearing conviction. "My opinion is that we are betrayed; that it is impossible for us to leave this desert, where we shall all perish in pursuing invisible enemies, who have caused us to fall into a trap which will hold us all."

These words produced a great impression on the hearers, who understood their perfect truth. The captain shook his head thoughtfully.

"Don Blas," he said, "you bring, then, a heavy accusation against some one. Have you conscientiously weighed the purport of your words?"

"Yes," he replied; "but——"

"Remember that we can admit no vague suppositions. Things have reached such a pitch that, if you wish us to give you the credence you doubtlessly deserve, you must bring your charges precisely, and not shrink from pronouncing any name if it be necessary."

"I shall shrink from nothing, senor conde. I know all the responsibility I take on myself. No consideration, however powerful it may be, will make me conceal what I regard as a sacred duty."

"Speak, then, in Heaven's name; and God grant that your words may not compel me to inflict an exemplary chastisement on one of our comrades!"

The capataz collected himself for a moment. All anxiously awaited his explanation: Cucharès especially was suffering from an emotion which he found great difficulty in concealing. Blas Vasquez at length spoke again, while keeping his eye so fixed on the count that the latter began to understand that he and his men were the victims of some odious treachery.

"Senor conde," Blas said, "we Mexicans have a law from which we never depart—a law which, indeed, is inscribed in the hearts of all honest men. It is this: in the same way that the pilot is responsible for the ship intrusted to him to take into port, the pioneer responds with his person for the safety of the people he undertakes to guide in the desert. In this case no discussion is possible: either the guide is ignorant, or he is not. If he is ignorant, why, against the opinion of everybody, has he forced us to enter the desert, while taking on himself the entire responsibility of our journey? Why, if he be not ignorant, did he not guide us straight across the desert as he agreed to do, instead of leading us at venture in pursuit of an enemy who, he knows as well as I do, is never stationary in the desert, but traverses it at his horse's utmost speed when

forced to enter it? Hence on the guide alone must
weigh the blame of all that has happened, as he was
master of events, and arranged them as he thought
proper."

Cucharès, more and more perturbed, knew not what
countenance to keep, his emotion was visible to all.

" What reply have you to make?" the captain asked
him.

Under circumstances like the present, the man attacked has only two means of defence—to feign indig-
nation or contempt. Cucharès chose the latter. Sum-
moning up all his boldness and impudence, he raised
his voice, shrugged his shoulders disdainfully, and
answered in an ironical tone,—

" I will not do Don Blas the honour of discussing his
remarks : there are certain accusations which an honest
man scorns to repel. It was my duty to act in con-
formity with the orders of the captain, who alone commands here. Since we have been in the desert we have
lost twenty men, killed by the Indians or by disease.
Can I be logically rendered responsible for this misfortune? Do I not run the same risk as all of you of
perishing in the desert? Is it in my power to escape
the fate that threatens you? If the captain had merely
ordered me to cross the desert, we should have done so
long ago : he told me that he wished to catch the
Apaches up, and I was compelled to obey him."

These reasons, specious as they were, were still accepted as good by the officers. Cucharès breathed
again, but he had not yet finished with the capataz.

" Good!" the latter said. " Strictly speaking, you
might be right in your remarks, and I would put faith
in your statements, had I not other and graver charges
to bring against you."

The lepero shrugged his shoulders once more.

" I know, and can supply proof, that, by your remarks and insinuations, you sow discord and rebellion among the peons and troopers. This morning, before the *réveillé*, believing that no one saw you, you rose, and with your dagger pierced ten of the fifteen water-skins still left us. The noise I made in running toward you alone prevented the entire consummation of your crime. At the moment when the captain gave us orders to assemble, I was about to warn him of what you had done. What have you to answer to this? Defend yourself, if it be possible."

All eyes were fixed on the lepero. He was livid. His eyes, suffused with blood, were haggard. Before it was possible to guess his intention, he drew a pistol and fired at the capataz, who fell without uttering a cry; then with a tiger-bound he leaped on his horse, and started at full speed. There was an indescribable tumult. All rushed in pursuit of the lepero.

" Down with the murderer !" the captain shouted, urging his men by voice and gestures to seize the villain.

The Frenchmen, rendered furious by this pursuit, began firing on Cucharès as on a wild beast. For a long time he was seen galloping his horse in every direction, and seeking in vain to quit the circle in which the troopers had inclosed him. At length he tottered in his saddle, tried to hold on by his horse's mane, and rolled in the sand, uttering a parting yell of fury. He was dead !

This event caused extreme excitement among the soldiers: from this moment they felt that they were betrayed, and began to see their position as it really was—that is to say, desperate. In vain did the captain

try to restore them a little courage ; they would listen
to nothing, but yielded to that despair which disor-
ganises and paralyses everything. The count gave the
order for departure, and they set out.

But whither should they go ? in what direction turn ?
No trace was visible. Still they marched on, rather to
change their place than in the hope of emerging from
the sepulchre of sand in which they believed themselves eternally buried. Eight days passed away—eight
centuries—during which the adventurers endured the
most frightful tortures of thirst and hunger. The
troop no longer existed ; there were neither chiefs nor
soldiers ; it was a legion of hideous phantoms, a flock
of wild beasts ready to devour each other on the first
opportunity.

They had been reduced to splitting the ears of the
horses and mules in order to drink the blood.

Wandering now on this side, now on that, deceived
by the mirage, dazzled by the burning sunbeams, they
were a prey to a hideous despair. Some laughed with
a silly air ; and these were the happiest, for they no
longer felt their sufferings : they were mad. Others
brandished their weapons furiously, raising their fists,
with menaces and curses, to heaven, which, like an
immense plate of red-hot iron, seemed the implacable
dome of their sandy tomb. Some, rendered raging by
suffering, blew out their brains, while mocking their
comrades who were too weak-minded to follow their
example.

The French are, perhaps, the bravest nation in
existence ; but, on the other hand, the easiest to
demoralise. If their impulse is irresistible in the
onward march, it is the same when they give way.
Nothing will stop them—neither reasoning nor coercive

measures. Extreme in everything, the Frenchman is
more than a man, or less than a child.

The Count de Lhorailles, gloomy and heart-broken,
surveyed the ruin of all his hopes. Ever the first to
march, the last to rest, not eating a mouthful till he
was certain that all his comrades had their share, he
watched with unexampled tenderness and care over
these poor soldiers, who, strangely enough, in the
misery in which they were plunged, never dreamed of
addressing a reproach to him.

Of Blas Vasquez' peons the majority were dead.
The rest had sought safety in flight; that is, they had
gone a little further on to seek a hidden tomb. All
those who remained faithful to the captain were
Europeans, principally Frenchmen, brave Dauph'yeers,
utterly ignorant of the way to combat and conquer the
implacable enemy against whom they struggled—the
desert ! Of the two hundred and forty-five men of which
the squadron was composed on its entering the Del Norte,
one hundred and thirty-three still survived, if we allow
that these haggard, fleshless spectres were men.

The most atrocious pain which a man can suffer in
the desert is the frightful malady called *calentura* by
the Mexicans. The calentura! that temporary madness, which makes you see, during its intermittent
attacks, the most dainty and delicious dishes, the most
limpid water, the most exquisite wines; which satiates
and enervates you ; and, when it leaves you, renders you
more desponding, more broken, than before, for you
retain the remembrance of all you possessed during
your dream.

One day, at length, the wretched men, crushed by
misery and tortures of every description, refused to go
further, and resolved to die where accident had led them.

They lay down in the torrid sand, beneath the shadow of a few ahuehuelts, with the firm will of remaining motionless until death, which they had summoned so loudly, came at length to deliver them from their woes. The sun set in a mist of purple and gold, to the sound of the curses and imprecations of these wretched men, who, expecting nothing more, hoping nothing more, had only retained the cruel instincts of the wild beast.

Still the night succeeded to day—gradually calmness took the place of disorder. Sleep, that great consoler, weighed down the heavy eyelids of the men, who, if they did not sleep, fell into a state of somnolency, which brought a truce to their fearful tortures, if only for a few moments. Suddenly, in the middle of the night, a formidable sound aroused them—a fiery whirlwind passed over them—the thunder burst forth in terrific peals. The sky was black as ink—not a star, not a moonbeam—nothing but dense gloom, which hid the nearest objects from sight.

The poor fellows rose in great terror; they dragged themselves on as well as they could one after the other, crouching together like a flock of sheep surprised by a storm, wishing, with that inborn egotism of man, to die together.

"A temporal, a temporal!" all shouted with an expression of voice impossible to render.

It was in reality the temporal, that fearful scourge, which was unloosing all its fury, and passing over the desert to subvert its surface. The wind howled with extraordinary force, raising clouds of dust, which whirled round with extreme velocity, and formed enormous spouts, that ran along and suddenly burst with a frightful crash. Men and animals caught in the tornado were whisked away into space like straws.

"Down on the ground!" the count shouted in a tremendous voice; "down on the ground! 'Tis the African simoom! Down, all of you who care for life!"

Strange to say, all these men, weighed down with atrocious sufferings, obeyed their chief's orders like children, so great is the terror death inspires in the darkness. They buried their faces in the sand, in order to avoid the burning blast of air that passed over them. The animals crouched on the ground, with outstretched necks, instinctively followed their example. At intervals, when the wind granted a moment's respite to these unhappy men, whom it took a delight in torturing, cries and groans of agony could be heard, mingled with blasphemies and ardent prayers, that rose from the crowd stretched trembling on the earth. The hurricane raged through the entire night with ever-increasing fury; toward morning it gradually grew calmer; by sunrise it had exhausted all its strength, and rushed toward other regions.

The aspect of the desert was completely changed. Where valleys had been on the previous night were now mountains; the sparse trees, twisted, uprooted, or burned by the hurricane, displayed their blackened and denuded skeletons; no trace of a footpath, no sign of man; all was flat, smooth, and even as a mirror. The French had been reduced to sixty men; the others had been carried off or swallowed up, and there was no hope of discovering the slightest sign of them: the sand was stretched over them like an immense greyish shroud.

The first feeling the survivors experienced was terror; the second, despair; and then the groans and complaints broke out again with renewed strength. The count, gloomy and sad, regarded these poor people with an expression of the tenderest pity. Suddenly he burst out

into a feverish laugh, and going up to his horse, which
had hitherto, by a species of miracle, escaped disaster,
he saddled it, while gently patting it and humming a
wild tune between his teeth.

His companions watched him with a feeling of vague
terror, for which they could not account. Although they
were so miserable, their captain still represented superior intellect and a firm will, those two forces which
have so much power over coarse natures, even when
circumstances have forced them to deny them. In
their wretched condition they collected round their
chief, like children seek shelter on their mother's breast.
He had ever consoled them, giving them an example of
courage and abnegation: thus, when they saw him
acting as he was doing, they had a foreboding of evil.

When his horse was saddled the count leaped lightly
on its back, and for a few minutes he made the animals
curvet, though it had the greatest difficulty in keeping
on its feet.

" Hold, my fine fellows !" he suddenly shouted.
" Come up here ! You had better listen to some good
advice—a parting hint I wish to give you before I go."

The soldiers dragged themselves up as well as they
could, and surrounded him.

The count turned a glance of satisfaction around.

" Existence is a miserable farce, is it not ?" he said,
bursting into a laugh; " and it is often a heavy chain to
drag about. How many times, since we have been
wandering about this desert, have I had the thought
which I now utter openly ! Well, I confess to you, as
long as I had a hope of saving you, I struggled
courageously: that hope I no longer possess. As we
must die of want within a few days—a few hours,
perhaps—I prefer to finish it at once   Believe me,

you had better follow my example. It is soon done, as you shall see."

While uttering the last words he drew a pistol from his waist-belt. At this moment cries were heard.

" What is it? What is the matter?"

" Look, captain! People are coming at last to our help: we are saved!" Sergeant Boileau exclaimed, rising like a spectre by his side, and seizing his arm.

The count freed himself with a smile.

" You are mad, my poor comrade," he said, looking in the direction indicated, where a cloud of dust really rose, and was rapidly approaching: " no one can come to our aid. We have not even," he added, with bitter irony, " the resource of the shipwrecked crew of the *Méduse!* We are condemned to die in this infernal desert! Farewell, all—farewell!"

He raised the pistol.

" Captain," the sergeant cried reproachfully, " take care! You have no right to kill yourself. You are our chief, and must be the last to die: if not, you are a coward!"

The count bounded as though a serpent had stung him, and made a gesture as if to rush on the sergeant. The expression of his face was so savage, his movement so terrible, that the sergeant was terrified, and recoiled. The captain profited by this second of respite, put the muzzle of the pistol to his temple, and pulled the trigger. He fell to the ground, with his skull fractured.

The adventurers had not yet recovered from the stupor this frightful event had thrown them into, when the cloud of dust they had noticed burst violently asunder, and they perceived a troop of mounted Indians, in the midst of whom were a woman and two or three white men, galloping toward them at full speed. Convinced that the Apaches had come up to deal them the final blow, like vultures collecting round a fallen buffalo, they did not even attempt an impossible resistance.

"Oh!" one of the hunters shouted, as he leaped from his horse and rushed toward them, "the poor fellows!"

The new comers were Belhumeur, Louis, and their friends the Comanches. In a few words they were apprised of all that had happened, and the tortures the French had endured.

"Good heavens!" Belhumeur shouted, "if provisions failed, you had water in abundance; then why do you complain of thirst?"

Without saying a word, Eagle-head and the Jester dug up the ground with their knives at the foot of an ahuehuelt. Within ten minutes an abundant stream of limpid water poured along the sand. The Frenchmen rushed in disorder toward it.

"Poor fellows!" Don Louis murmured, "shall we not take them from this spot?"

"Do you think I would let them perish, now I have restored them to hope? Poor girl!" casting a melancholy glance at Dona Anita, who was laughing and cracking her fingers like castanets, "why is it not equally easy to restore her to reason?"

Don Louis sighed, but made no reply.

The French then learned a thing, which would have saved them all, probably, had they known it sooner—that the ahuehuelt, which, in the Comanche Indian dialect, signifies the *Lord of the Waters*, is a tree which grows in arid spots, and its presence ever indicates either a spring flush with the soil or a hidden source; that for this reason the red-skins hold it in veneration; and, as it is principally found in the deserts, they designate it also by the name of the *Great Medicine of Travellers.*

*   *   *   *   *

Two days later the adventurers, guided by the hunters and Comanches, quitted the desert. They speedily reached the Casa Grande of Moctecuzoma, where their saviours, after giving them the provisions they stood in such pressing need of, finally left them, hardly knowing how to escape from their hearty thanks and blessings.

[Those of our readers who have felt an interest in Don Louis will find his history continued in another volume, called " THE GOLD-SEEKERS."]

THE END.

CLARKE'S
STANDARD NOVEL LIBRARY.

---o---

GUSTAVE AIMARD'S
NOVELS AND TALES OF INDIAN LIFE.

An Entirely New Edition, with New Picture
Wrappers, Post 8vo, Price 2s.

---o---

THE TRAPPERS OF ARKANSAS.
THE BORDER RIFLES.
THE FREEBOOTERS.
THE WHITE SCALPER.
THE ADVENTURERS.
PEARL OF THE ANDES.
THE TRAIL HUNTER.
PIRATES OF THE PRAIRIES.
TRAPPER'S DAUGHTER.
TIGER SLAYER.
THE GOLD SEEKERS.
THE INDIAN CHIEF.
THE RED TRACK.
THE PRAIRIE FLOWER.
THE INDIAN SCOUT.
THE LAST OF THE INCAS.
QUEEN OF THE SAVANNAH.
THE BUCCANEER CHIEF.
STRONGHAND, a Tale of the Disinherited.
THE SMUGGLER CHIEF.
THE REBEL CHIEF.
STONEHEART, a Romance.
THE BEE HUNTERS.
THE GUIDE OF THE DESERT.
THE INSURGENT CHIEF.
THE FLYING HORSEMAN.

LONDON:
CHARLES HENRY CLARKE, 13, PATERNOSTER ROW.

FROM THE

Floral World & Garden Guide.

"It is sold by the Company at a remarkably cheap rate, and is unsurpassed for forming an inside lining to summer-houses and grottos; indeed, for this purpose it is impossible to say too much in its praise."

VIRGIN CORK

is easily fastened with nails or wire to framework or boxes, and, if desired, can be varnished with oak varnish. Small pieces to cover crevices, or for little ornaments, can be secured with sticks of gutta-percha, melted in the flame of a candle or gas.

Sold in Bales of 1 cwt., ½ cwt., ¼ cwt.

Orders by Post, with remittance, will be punctually executed, and forwarded by all the Railways, as directed. Every information forwarded on application.

Post-Office Orders may be made payable to Mr. A. H. OLDFIELD.

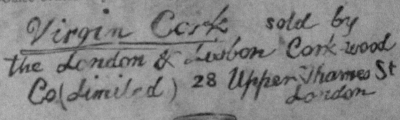

Virgin Cork sold by the London & Lisbon Cork wood Co (Limited) 28 Upper Thames St London

Liverpool Agency—30 Manesty Lane.

Check Out More Titles From HardPress Classics Series In this collection we are offering thousands of classic and hard to find books. This series spans a vast array of subjects – so you are bound to find something of interest to enjoy reading and learning about.

Subjects:
Architecture
Art
Biography & Autobiography
Body, Mind &Spirit
Children & Young Adult
Dramas
Education
Fiction
History
Language Arts & Disciplines
Law
Literary Collections
Music
Poetry
Psychology
Science
…and many more.

Visit us at www.hardpress.net

CPSIA information can be obtained
at www.ICGtesting.com
Printed in the USA
BVHW040954160819
555975BV00042B/1541/P

9 781318 692552